P. A. F

Welfare, Power, and Juvenile Justice

Welfare, Power, and Juvenile Justice

The social control of delinquent youth

Robert Harris and David Webb

Tavistock Publications

First published in 1987 by
Tavistock Publications Ltd
11 New Fetter Lane, London EC4P 4EE

© 1987   Robert Harris and David Webb

Filmset by Mayhew Typesetting, Bristol
Printed in Great Britain at the University Press, Cambridge

All rights reserved. No part of this book may be reprinted or
reproduced or utilized in any form or by any electronic, mechanical, or
other means, now known or hereafter invented, including photocopying
and recording, or in any information storage or retrieval system,
without permission in writing from the publishers.

British Library Cataloguing in Publication Data

Harris, Robert
   Welfare, power, and juvenile justice: the
   social control of delinquent youth. –
   (Social science paperbacks; no. 355)
   1. Juvenile justice, Administration of –
   Great Britain   2. Rehabilitation of
   juvenile delinquents – Great Britain
   I. Title   II. Webb, David, 1946–
   364.6   HV9145.A5

ISBN 0–422–60470–4 Pbk

Contents

Acknowledgements	vii
Prefatory note: The framework of the book	1
1 The development of juvenile justice	7
2 The development of welfare	33
3 The macro level: welfare work and the State	55
4 The mezzo level: conduits of care – welfare organizations and the supervisory State	87
5 The micro level: the experts at work	105
6 Censure and sex: justice and gender	131
7 Towards the future	155
Appendix A: The Criminal Justice Act, 1982	179
Appendix B: Welfare work and the supervision order: a note on research methodology	181
Bibliography	185
Name index	203
Subject index	207

Acknowledgements

Probably more of this book than we are aware is the product of discussions over the years with present and former colleagues and students on the University of Leicester's Masters in Social Work programme. But particular help of different kinds was provided by Claire Wintram, Robert Waters, Noel Timms, Herschel Prins, Christine Hallett, and Gillian Bevis. Citing these friends in reverse alphabetical order is our own modest attempt to override that institutionalized injustice of the alphabet whereby, in the interests of order and classification, B. Zywczyck is doomed to reside permanently on the last page of the final volume of the London Telephone Directory.

Our thanks go to the Home Office for funding the study on which we have drawn, and in particular to Margaret Shaw of the Research and Planning Unit who has been a helpful and amiable colleague. We are grateful to the editors of the *British Journal of Social Work* and *Sociology* for permission to reproduce parts of papers previously published in those journals in Chapters 5 and 6 respectively; part of Chapter 5 was also included in a paper presented to the European Seminar of Schools of Social Work in Angers in 1985.

A particular word of thanks goes to Sheila Wesson, whose speed and accuracy in typing the manuscript involved more effort and skill than anybody could reasonably ask of a secretary, and whose unfailing good humour in doing so demonstrated yet again what an invaluable colleague she is.

To those who have sought us in vain, personally or professionally, during the writing up of this book in the spring of 1986 we send both apologies and thanks for their forbearance. Our families have certainly suffered, not least those members of the first author's household to whom *Welfare, Power, and Juvenile Justice*'s working title was for a while *Not Daddy's Rotten Old Book Again*, and their counterparts in the second author's home, whose phraseology was occasionally even less genteel.

Responsibility for everything in the book is ours alone, and, lest there be any misunderstanding, the theoretical argument is not proved conclusively to be correct by the empirical study reported in the book, though nowhere are the two incompatible.

Belton in Rutland
Tur Langton
May 1986

Prefatory note: the framework of the book

'none of your philanthropic dodges, you know. I don't want to lead a new life, and I don't want to turn over a new leaf, and I don't want a helpin' hand, nor none o' those things. And, what's more, I don't want a situation. I've got all the situation as I need. But I never refuse money, nor beer either. Never did, and I'm forty years old next month. . . . I come across a cove once as told me crime was nothing but a disease and ought to be treated as such. I asked him for a dozen o' port, but he never sent it.'   (A. Bennett 1907:96)

This book is about social control, but social control of a rather particular kind. Its origins lie in a study directed by the authors of the making and management of a hitherto under-researched provision in the juvenile justice system, the supervision order. But the book is no research report; rather it uses the *idea* of supervising young offenders in the community as a springboard for an analysis of the development, purpose, and practice of juvenile justice. In this sense, though we draw repeatedly on the process of one particular justice system, that of England and Wales, our focus of study at a conceptual rather than substantive level reflects issues such as care and control, justice and welfare, power and authority, discretion and accountability which are ubiquitous in juvenile court systems throughout the western world.

The book is structured along two principal dimensions, one temporal and, within that, one conceptual. The *temporal dimension*, crudely expressed, takes us from past through present towards future. In the first two chapters is offered not a potted history so much as a conceptual biography of, respectively, the juvenile justice and the welfare systems of England and Wales. By conceptual biography we mean a thematic presentation of the development of the two systems rather than an historiography. Our intention is to be partial, our fear is of being distortional, though we hope on the whole to have avoided this trap. In Chapter 1 the juvenile justice system is analysed, from its gradual emergence during the Industrial Revolution, first as a function of the intersecting structures and purposes of the adult criminal justice and child care systems, and second as an element in a steady expansion of State control over the working-class young. With these notions as a guide, we then proceed to examine in greater detail the legislation which, though since amended (see Appendix A), still forms the basis of the present system, the Children and Young Persons Act, 1969.

The control of the young, for reasons which will become clear, necessitates their being supervised by extra-judicial professionals at the behest of the court. In England and Wales there are two main agencies employing such supervisory experts, the social services department of the local authority and the probation service. Though these agencies do not have identical functions in the juvenile courts, these functions do converge in the management of supervision orders. These orders, made by courts for periods of between six months and three years, place offenders (and indeed certain categories of non-offender) literally 'under supervision', with instructions to report to the supervisor, receive the supervisor at home, attend school, undertake such other activities as may be decreed, and generally lead an honest and industrious life.

The empirical study we undertook revealed significant differences between the ways the two sets of welfare workers ('welfare workers' is our generic term for the 'social workers' of the social services department and for 'probation officers') undertook their task. Chapter 2, in offering conceptual biographies of these two sets of agents, begins to suggest why historically this might be, in spite of there existing certain commonalities between them, such as training and a 'professional' affiliation to welfare work.

But Chapters 1 and 2 examine the past not as a detailed study in its own right, nor, we hope, as a barely relevant adjunct to the argument, designed to introduce it in some conventional but meaningless way. Rather, by the selection of certain themes and continuities in the lines of juvenile justice and welfare work we hope to excavate some of the present realities which circumscribe the discourse within which both the justice and the welfare systems are located. In similar vein, in our final chapter we project from the logic of that discourse a possible future which, though not a deterministic account of where we are going, decidedly *does* suggest that the notion of community control is by no means unproblematic.

But in addition to a temporal, the book has a *conceptual dimension*. The process and purpose of supervision are analysed at macro, mezzo, and micro levels, each of them characterized by an intersection of the judicial and the administrative.

At a *macro level*, Chapter 3 considers the social and political purposes of supervision. While the experts' own professional literature may seek to persuade us that this purpose is no more than the efficient dissemination of altruism, this simple idea begs too many questions for it to be a sufficient explanation of the existence and proliferation of the experts. Influenced by the work of the French writers Michel Foucault and Jacques Donzelot, we show that the *purpose* of their presence can really be conceived of only as a function of State power and control. To offer this analysis is neither to assume that the exercise of control by the State is intrinsically undesirable (a crude libertarian notion) nor that the altruistic motivation of the reformers and welfare professionals is either naive or hypocritical. The point is simply that such motivations and fine feelings are heavily circumscribed by social function, and in the conflict between the competing ideologies of State bureaucracy and professional autonomy lies the source of some of the frustrations regularly experienced by the workers themselves.

This theme re-emerges in our *mezzo level* analysis of the welfare organizations in Chapter 4. As this analysis and the *micro* analysis of the experts at work in Chapter 5 develop, it will become plain that a chasm exists between the *idea* of the ever-extending net of State control and the *reality* of a form of supervision which is frequently inefficient, lacking in clear objective, casual, and even arbitrary. The sociopolitical purposes of supervision are, as we shall have cause to remark, quite often thwarted by the supervisors themselves.

But our three levels are not intended to imply that the juridicowelfare world of juvenile justice exists as some great machine, some Great Chain of Being in which the directions of the higher participants are transmitted and implemented with, admittedly, varying degrees of competence and efficiency by the inferior actors. Quite the contrary: we shall show that an inherent instability exists at all levels of the system: conflicts, manipulations, re-interpretations designed to subvert the rules by which the game is played yet simultaneously, while subverting the rules, intended also to ensure that the game itself continues. Our systems, and the interplay among them, should be seen not as a machine, but as the *locus* of a struggle to determine both the nature and cure of juvenile deviance. But even the metaphor of the struggle misleads, for there is no struggle between coherent but conflicting ideologies from which will emerge winners and losers. The struggle rather takes place in the sphere of what has been called *the social* (Donzelot 1980, 1984) in which clear roles, duties, and rights are few; everything is almost inextricably intertwined with everything else, with the judges becoming therapists and the therapists judges; nobody's function is precisely circumscribed or monitored, nobody's territory clearly staked out.

Clearly the very knowledge on which the experts base their recommendations and interventions lacks the verifiability and replicability of the laboratory knowledge of the pure and natural sciences. This ambiguity or doubtfulness makes of knowledge a malleable object which further augments the power of those who have it. Hence have knowledge and power in the social world been seen as indistinguishable (Foucault 1977): knowledge is not simply a commodity to be acquired after many years' solitary study, but a vehicle for the imposition of power. Its uncertainty may cause unease among the experts, but – since who can gainsay their opinions – it increases their autonomy while decreasing the likelihood of their acting consistently:

> 'professionals in various state-welfare, health, educational or control systems are not directly nor necessarily acting in the best interests of the state. . . . It is for these two reasons – the particular autonomy of the professional ethic and the contradictory values in professions like social work – that the actual exercise of power at the lower levels of the system is so anarchic and so unpredictable. There is no firm knowledge base, no technology, nor even any agreed criteria of success and failure. In addition, low-level professionals are often poorly supervised, and can easily deviate from organizational norms.' (Cohen 1985: 164–65)

This increase of power among the front-liners has the logical consequence of diminishing the power not only of their managers but also of their 'clients'. The ambiguity of the status of knowledge frees the experts (and a hint of irony can be read into our use of this word) from simple accountability; but in quite the same way it loosens the capacity of the clients to predict to what processes they will be subject. For management, it is difficult to override the professionals; for clients, the linearity of cause and effect is fractured, the capacity for misunderstanding (Mayer and Timms 1970) increased, and the client's power to *know* accordingly diminished.

In welfare work then, certain trump cards lie in the hand of the professional. Such trumps include references to 'professional values', 'confidentiality', 'self-determination', and the like, and particularly to the phenomenon of the 'professional opinion', which, once expressed, is notoriously immune to close examination. But the matter is not a simple one of organizational perverseness – of the subalterns cocking a snook at the officers for the sake of it, and able to be called into line by some new managerial approach or some inspection (though clearly both these strategies have their place). Rather the perversity is inherent in the existence of the organizations and the professionals themselves. Because each of the three levels lacks homogeneity of purpose or value, unambiguous directions cannot easily be passed down the line, and the juvenile justice world is instead characterized by conflicting abstractions – care and control, deterrence and rehabilitation, welfare and justice – which cannot be the basis of a clear instruction to be implemented in a particular case: if simplicity, lucidity, and unambiguity were possible in the supervision of young offenders there would not be any need to have the professionals: lowly paid functionaries would do the job very much better. So it is not quite that the professionals are ducking their duty or self-seekingly expanding their power; rather that their very presence indicates the impossibility of spelling out what precisely that duty and power are. Professionals do not create discretion; rather the inevitability of discretion creates the need for professionals. Since in the vexed world of welfare there is such a cluster of value conflicts combined with an almost complete lack of empirically verified practice procedures, discretion will inevitably be exercised in unpredictable, even capricious ways within the confines available. Indeed, it is sometimes said that such is the plethora of theories available to welfare workers that professional actions can all too easily be determined arbitrarily and explained *post hoc* by reference to almost any convenient theoretical justification for the action selected.

It is a truism to observe that the supervision of offenders can be comprehended only within its own context, but it will be plain already that this particular context is an especially dynamic and erratic one. Conflicts, paradoxes, and instability predominate, and in the vacuum created by these phenomena lies the scope for vast differences to occur in different segments of the system or geographical localities: idiosyncracy, chance, the influence of forceful personality, all bear upon the course of a drama which, though ultimately circumscribed by certain structural realities, is nevertheless volatile and unpredictable. Lower-order participants, though they are playing by rules which they did not invent and of which they may not approve, are anything but powerless, and their power itself breeds unpredictability. So some welfare workers will be veritable Figaros, thwarting their Almavivas at every turn; others, more solid citizens, will doubtless be the unswerving servants of the court. Caught between two masters and two traditions, the experts are in a simultaneously unenviable and influential position: unenviable because of the many uncertainties which arise from these ambiguities; influential because in those very ambiguities lie also conflicts and contradictions which enable them to act with an extraordinary degree of freedom.

The story we are telling is, therefore, of the juvenile justice system today, although it is one which we tell historically and conceptually. Because it is a long tale for a fairly short book, some complexities will probably be glossed over, some controversial assumptions made but not defended. For such we apologize in advance.

Reference will be made from time to time to the empirical study undertaken by the authors, and a brief account of its scope and methodology can be found in Appendix B (though see also Webb and Harris 1984). The study is, however, relevant to a chapter we have yet to mention: Chapter 6, which deals with the supervision of girls. In the course of the study of boys, we generated a subsample of girl offenders on supervision whose criminality, social characteristics, and supervisory experiences could be compared with those of the boys in the main sample (Webb 1984). The chapter draws on the empirical findings, and is here included because it throws particular light on our theme. All supervised offenders experience the potentiality of a censorious monitoring not just of their criminality but of their whole lives – their families, schools, friends, communities, hobbies. And how could it be otherwise when positivist criminology has so signally failed to establish immutable links between any one (or even any cluster) of these factors and criminal behaviour? It is in part this very failure which comes to justify the generalized surveillance of the many rather than the persecutory control of the few: we know so little about crime that in particular instances anything may be relevant.

But girls are subjected to a further form of censure based on gender, for not acting as young ladies should. This is an almost inevitable consequence of the elision in the juvenile sphere of protective and punitive legislation into a whole nexus of State control. But gender censure does mean that girls are a useful case study in what Jacques Donzelot has called 'tutelage' (Donzelot 1980) – that process of moral apprenticeship, of supervised freedom, designed to steer the working-class young into those paths of righteousness defined by their betters in terms of obedient behaviour and regular habits.

This, then, is the framework of the book. It is a conceptual analysis rather than either a research report or a practice handbook. Nevertheless it is hoped that the issues it raises will provide food for thought not only for our fellow students of these matters, but also for those professionally involved in the juvenile justice system. Its implications for them may be indirect, but we believe them to be profound.

1 The development of juvenile justice

'Now, there are but few cases in which the offender is without some extenuating circumstances. . . . In fact, there is no crime in which it is not easy to discover them. It requires but a slight investigation and they swarm on all sides. In short, the only criminals who appear to us to be without excuse, are those for whom we have not taken the trouble to find it.' (Garofalo 1914: xxv)

'Any proposal of change based on the requirement that people would have to get rid of their vices and live up to some fine ideals must be treated with great caution.' (Los 1982: 5)

In this chapter we offer a conceptual biography of the juvenile justice system up to the early 1980s. Our objective in doing so is twofold. First, to demonstrate the immanence of particular themes and issues within the system itself, and second, to provide a necessarily more detailed account of juvenile justice since the early 1960s. Without both these kinds of material, the argument we shall be later developing will have little meaning.

Two themes exemplify the dominant features of juvenile justice, and we trace them historically in the first two sections of this chapter. First we shall demonstrate that from the outset juvenile justice has existed principally as a function of a broad nexus of State control over the deviant which incorporates also – on either side of it, as it were – the adult criminal justice system and the child care system. Secondly we shall analyse juvenile justice of itself as an element in, and a means of, the steady expansion of State control.

If these two themes sound sinister, or even far-fetched, we can reply at this stage by giving a foretaste of our argument that throughout its existence the theory and the practice of juvenile justice have diverged; that the system is riddled with paradox, irony, even contradiction; that matters have consistently failed to turn out as they were intended to do. But nor is that ironic gap between intent and achievement the end of it, for we shall show that the very existence of ambiguity, uncertainty, the non-implementation of what should be done, create a vacuum to be filled in ways which are often capricious, and which can serve to reinforce the powerlessness of the objects of the system.

The third section of this chapter deals with the unfolding of juvenile

Welfare, power, and juvenile justice

justice since the war. It will be plain by the time this section is reached that the developments of the 1960s, hailed by many as revolutionary, in fact draw their meaning and logic from the events of an earlier period. But the attempts by the 1960s reformers to blur the boundaries of delinquency and need had the inevitable consequence of more State control. To assume that such a blurring would diminish the control of the delinquent would be an idealist fiction: rather it brought the needy ever more into the supervisory net, for boundaries, as we shall more than once have cause to remark, do not blur in one direction only.

Viewed thus, the surprising results of liberalizing legislation – more not less incarceration, more not less power for the experts – become perfectly comprehensible, and in fact parallel much earlier developments in juvenile justice. For juvenile justice is *not* a self-contained world, or a world where particular answers can be generated to specific problems. Indeed we make the assumption throughout this book that courts, police, and experts of various kinds are busy themselves attempting to apply technical solutions to a problem of youthful deviance which it is quite beyond their power to remedy. This being so, when the powers which accrue to those people are loosely framed, and when knowledge about the *causes* of crime is so opaque, the potential for a wide-ranging, generalized intervention in the life of the delinquent is considerable: if anything in a particular case might be 'the main problem' then anything – family influences, friends, leisure activities – must be meet for professional consideration and intervention.

It follows from this that the welfare professionals must be central figures in the process. We periodically refer to them as 'experts' because expertise is both their function and their legitimation, though any claim they may make to arcane knowledge about the causes and cures of crime is largely bogus. They serve, though, necessary functions, and as the book moves on we shall be discussing what they are. At this stage we say simply that they present a particular paradox of control, for while clearly and obviously extending the court's powers beyond its direct jurisdiction, they simultaneously transform the ideology which they are conveying into something which more closely resembles their own set of assumptions. The paradox of power being conveyed and transformed simultaneously is one to which we shall return.

Astride two horses: child care and criminal justice

> 'To say that the child was a free agent would be saying simply what was untrue – he is quite the child of circumstances, just as much as the unconscious seedling which cannot help shooting up when the sun's rays are concentrated upon it.' (Day 1858: 36)

The juvenile justice system exists as a function of the child care and criminal justice systems on either side of it, a meeting-place of two otherwise separate worlds. Yet before the system itself was instituted – albeit very patchily – by the Children Act, 1908, no such administrative separation existed between the adult and juvenile criminal justice systems, in spite of a process of sporadic unyoking which dates back to the early nineteenth century. The 1908 Act is a watershed in any analysis of the system, therefore, in that it marks the administrative solution to successive Victorian attempts to reduce contamination and ensure the improved socialization of the young. But in solving one problem the 1908 Act starkly highlighted another, for in giving to juvenile courts both criminal jurisdiction over the offender and civil jurisdiction over the needy, it raised yet more questions about the relationship between crime and deprivation. Such questions were not, of course, created by the Act, but in blurring the administrative boundary between them, in decreeing that the tribunals which dealt with children who were threats dealt also with those who were victims (Eekelaar, Dingwall, and Murray 1982), it made the juvenile court itself a *locus* for conflict and confusion, a vehicle for the simultaneous welfarization of delinquency and the juridicization of need. This strategy has presented a central contradiction: blur the boundaries and one stigmatizes and destigmatizes by the selfsame process; create new boundaries and one apportions blame differentially. Place marginal offenders in accommodation for non-offenders and one transforms it into accommodation for offenders with all its inhabitants sharing the stigma which follows; classify one's accommodation and one heavily stigmatizes those offenders who already carry the greatest degree of opprobrium, thereby presumably rendering less likely their ultimate reformation.

Historically the criminal code has almost always penetrated the lives of the poor. Concern at the growth of vagrancy in the reign of Henry VIII led to a statute of 1531 which permitted the whipping and mutilation (by cutting off the ear) of vagabonds (Sellin 1976); a further (but abortive) statute of 1547, in the reign of Edward VI, legislated for their enslavement ('if they could be brought to be made profitable, and do service, it were much to be desired'); and the Vagrancy Act, 1597, permitted the banishment of 'such rogues as shall be thought fit not to be delivered' (Rusche and Kirchheimer 1939: 59). Milton refers to:

> 'the action of the Justices who ordered two wanderers, aged respectively four and two . . . to be whipped and expelled from the parish.'
> (F. Milton 1959: 111)

The houses of correction (Bridewell, given to the city of London by King Edward VI in 1553 [Salgado 1977] was opened in 1556) and the workhouses, the empowerment of the justices under the Poor Law of 1598 to commit the idle to the house of correction (Bruce 1961), the punitive implementation of the laws which obliged men to work (Melossi and Pavarini 1981), and the eighteenth-century experiments with houses of industry (Ignatieff 1978), all stand testimony to the central disciplinary intent of the criminal code and its relationship to the economic needs of the day (Rusche and Kirchheimer 1939).

The early nineteenth century saw the beginnings of a *de facto* separation of provisions for child criminals. Their execution, though not unknown (Hibbert 1963), was very rare, and much less common than is widely believed (Knell 1965), though whipping, transportation, and imprisonment continued. The view that a relationship of a kind existed between crime and poverty was perfectly familiar by now, and the aim of reclamation of the young a widespread one. Such beliefs underpinned the anti-gin campaigns of the mid-eighteenth century and surfaced periodically thereafter. Hence the words of a witness to the Select Committee on Police, 1817:

> 'It is very easy to blame these poor children, and to ascribe their misconduct to an innate propensity to vice; but I much question whether any human being, circumstanced as many of them are, can reasonably be expected to act otherwise. . . . Much may be done with these boys by kindness; there is scarcely one who will not be powerfully affected by it, but they are so accustomed to be considered as destitute of all moral feeling, that when they receive assurances of kindness, they can hardly believe them to be sincere.'
> (cited in Tobias 1972: 94–5)

And in a nineteenth-century study:

> 'Although pauperism and crime too often act simultaneously as cause and effect, sufficient evidence has been adduced to show that poverty, in numberless instances, leads to the perpetration of offences, which, under different and more favourable circumstances, would not be committed.' (Day 1858: 30)

Early attempts in the nineteenth century to address the particular problems presented by juvenile criminals by creating *ad hoc* separations between adult and juvenile provisions were not conspicuously successful. The institution of the *Euryalus* prison hulk for boys simply created a floating gaol even more verminous and vice-ridden than its adult counterparts; the attempt in the Parkhurst Act, 1837, to create a training prison for pre-transportees aged 9 to 19 failed: a welter of public attacks (orchestrated by Mary Carpenter) on its brutality and corruption culminated in the ending of the Parkhurst Experiment in 1863 (Carlebach 1970; Playfair 1971) and the conversion of Parkhurst itself into a convict prison for the physically or mentally infirm (Nevill 1903: 59). The Larceny Act, 1847, which empowered justices to deal summarily with certain young thieves to avoid their having to be committed to adult prisons while awaiting trial at Quarter Sessions, foundered on the obvious problem that many of these thieves were committed to those same prisons on sentence; and the power of justices from 1866 (Parsloe 1978) to remand children to the workhouse rather than the prison really removed them from the frying pan into the fire. Prison conditions were often preferable to those which appertained in many workhouses, where young criminals were subjected to the same contamination as in the prisons. Workhouse instructors appointed by the Guardians were, to put it at its kindest, of variable character, and the populace of the two institutions in many cases interchangeable:

> 'The pernicious and vicious effects of workhouse association and training upon juvenile paupers cannot well be overrated. If it were intended to make pauperism ineradicable and crime more rampant, no better method could be devised than that now in operation in the 624 unions in England and Wales.'
>
> (Day 1858: 218)

A more decisive development was the statutory recognition of reformatory and industrial schools in 1854 and 1857 respectively, for the children of the 'dangerous' and 'perishing' classes (Carpenter 1851: 2). These institutions constituted a major extension of control over the young, while simultaneously offering the apparent possibility of mass reformation and the near elimination of juvenile crime. The Gladstone Report of 1895 marked a further step towards the development of separate provisions for the young. This report led to the introduction of the probation and Borstal systems (Probation of Offenders Act, 1907; Prevention of Crime Act, 1908) and indirectly to the Children Act, 1908. Indeed Herbert Gladstone, Chairman of the Committee, was, as Home Secretary in Asquith's 1906–14 administration, to oversee the introduction of the new reforms. The Gladstone Report, in spite of certain confusions (Thomas 1972) committed itself to the flexible treatment of young offenders, recommending in particular that offenders under 23 should be able to be committed to a penal reformatory for between one and three years, with the possibility of early discharge on licence. The conversion of the convict prison at Borstal, Kent, into such an institution actualized this recommendation. Certainly the turn of the century marked a significant shift in penal attitudes (Garland 1985), and there was widespread opposition emerging to the practice of imposing short prison sentences (as opposed to longer-term training) on children whose offences were 'nothing worse than boisterous conduct or childish mischief' (Nevill 1903: 295). Indeed it was in 1899 that the Reformatory Schools Amendment Act ended the practice of committing young offenders to a minimum of fourteen days' hard labour prior to a spell in reformatory school.

So by the first decade of this century the juvenile court had emerged as a vehicle by which the related problems of decontaminating and resocializing the young were to be solved, and the phase of *administrative separation* was hence complete. But it left untouched a series of questions about the nature of juvenile crime and the appropriate form of treatment for it, in relation to which today's policies are hardly any clearer than they were then. Then as now it was generally held that the young should be deemed responsible for their actions – but not quite; then as now that the framework for dealing with the young should be bounded by the contradiction that whereas the delinquent young were typically no more deprived than working-class non-delinquents (and so should be punished), they *were* noticeably less sleek than the children of those who sat in judgement over them (and accordingly should not be punished too much). Then as now there was some faith in the idea of reformation by kindness, offering trusting relationships, even love; but such an approach has always sat uneasily with the punishment which one wished simultaneously to mete out.

These contradictions are endemic in almost any system of juvenile justice in which neither unbridled classicism nor unbridled European positivism holds sway to permit of, respectively, retributive punishment or clinical treatment. The neo-classical compromise inevitably, in the name of 'balance' and 'common sense', contains conflicting ideas, and the conflicts cannot be resolved within the structure of the juvenile court itself. Judgements as to the balance between punishment and treatment, care and control, inevitably become the province of reliable citizens who know the individual offenders: who have visited the home, met the parents, talked to the friends, formed their impressions of the offender's character and responsibility. In short, it is experts who are necessary, to assess, classify, advise, and above all to individualize. But it is also imperative that those experts retain a continuing relationship with, and indebtedness to, the court, that they transmit to the offenders that which the court wishes to be transmitted. Hence it is that the twentieth century has become the century of the experts, and experts who will both care *and* control, though not necessarily simultaneously: their job, in the words of the Probation of Offenders Act, 1907, is not only to advise, but also to assist and befriend.

The expansion of state control

> 'It is by making the system appear less harsh, that people are encouraged to use it more often. Far from each benevolent intermediate option slowing down the career of delinquency, it facilitates, promotes and accelerates it by making each consecutive decision easier to take.' (Cohen 1985: 98)

Humanizing the juvenile justice system and blurring the boundaries between the delinquent and non-delinquent young have had as their corollary the expansion of State control over both. In this section we demonstrate the process of this expansion in relation first to reformatory and industrial schools, and then approved schools.

The attractiveness of the idea of reformation in Victorian England lay in good part in its dual promise of creating social stability, and hence protecting life and property, and of fulfilling the Christian imperative to save the sinner. Quite clearly the industrial discipline demanded by both the factory system and the domestic employers of girls in service was precisely what was inculcated in the delinquent or rootless young by the reformatory and industrial schools in the latter half of the nineteenth century. Yet at the same time the schools themselves were rooted in the Christian faith, and sought to offer love and trust. It would be too crude to see the latter simply as a smokescreen for the former: both existed, and it was the mix of the two which proved so powerful. Hence Mary Carpenter, luminary of the reformatory school movement:

> 'spoke of the need for enlisting the child's will as indispensable to the work of reformation, and declared that there must be that degree of confidence which would make the children feel that they were workers together with the teachers . . . the child must be restored to the true position of childhood. . . . The discovery of evil

in the life of a child made her love him more desperately.'

(Hoyles 1952: 210)

The rhetoric of love and faith was potent and echoed both inside and outside Parliament during the passage of the Youthful Offenders Act, 1854, and the Industrial Schools Act, 1857. But the expansion of the reformatories was principally aided by the widespread belief that they were responsible for the fall in the crime rate which took place in the 1870s (Tobias 1972). That this belief was almost certainly mistaken (Stedman-Jones 1971) is not, of course, the point, for the prospect of removing large numbers of actual and potential young offenders for long periods of time and with a clear conscience, in the course of which removal they were to be morally and behaviourally sanitized, was always likely to be irresistible:

> 'Reanimate the useful, virtuous interest that has been so weakened by the crime. The feeling of respect for property – for wealth, but also for honour, liberty, life – this the criminal loses when he robs, calumniates, abducts or kills. So he must be taught this feeling once again. And one will begin by teaching it to him for his own benefit.'
>
> (Foucault 1977: 107)

This trade-off between the length of punishment and its unpleasantness meant that the period of hard labour typically undergone by the youthful offender was reduced from a few months to a few weeks but augmented by between two and five years in a reformatory school.

Of course the reality of these schools was far removed from the rhetoric of Mary Carpenter as she spoke glowingly of the achievements of Kingswood in particular. There were serious problems in the recruitment of suitable staff; punishments were severe, the Revd Sidney Turner of Redhill, for example, advocating solitary confinement, bread and water and, *in extremis*, whipping (H. Jones 1962: 231) thereby mirroring certain of the punishments for adult prisoners then extant. And the work, especially for girls, whose time was mainly spent in the oppressive conditions of the laundry-house, or in scrubbing, was as sterile and mundane as the regimes themselves:

> 'The children were dressed in drab uniforms, and the school door and gates were always locked. They were marched about the school in crocodile formation, often with their hands folded behind their backs. . . . The attitude of the schools towards the children in their care became increasingly patronising: they were receiving charity, and should be duly grateful.' (H. Jones 1962: 232)

So rhetoric and reality diverged fairly starkly, and when it is remembered that by the 1860s committal for hard labour followed by a reformatory school sentence had become the standard disposal for a second offence it can be seen how considerable was the control to which young offenders were by now subject.

But industrial schools involved an even greater expansion of control. The 'perishing classes' who were to be committed to industrial schools included many vagrants, who, as we have seen, had traditionally been treated harshly at both a parish and a national level. But by the mid-nineteenth century urbanization had created a new problem of social order in the cities. Samuel Day commented that in the 1840s 21,000 vagrants were committed annually to prison; that Wolverhampton's 200 common lodging houses (themselves notorious dens of iniquity) took some 511,000 people annually; and that in London two-thirds of the criminal population had 'migratory habits' (Day 1858: 76). Mayhew, in his great survey, regarded vagrancy as the nursery of crime (Mayhew 1861 vol. III: 368 *et seq.*); Dr Barnardo estimated that in 1876 some 30,000 children nightly slept in the streets of London (Tobias 1972: 96); and as late as 1890, General Booth, appealing for a new – indeed dramatic – approach to the children of a generation he dubbed lost, observed:

> 'The lawlessness of our lads, the increased licence of our girls, the general shiftlessness from the home-making point of view of the product of our factories and schools are far from reassuring. Our young people have never learned to obey. The fighting gangs of half-grown lads in Lisson Grove, and the scuttlers of Manchester are ugly symptoms of a social condition that will not grow better by being left alone.' (W. Booth 1890: 66)

Accordingly the prospect of removing these children from the streets once again offered an alluring synthesis of altruism and self-protection for the moneyed classes: kindness could nip crime in the bud. An Industrial Schools Act was passed in 1857 and extended both by a second such Act in 1866 and again by the Children Act, 1908, section 58. By this time courts were empowered to commit to industrial schools until their fifteenth birthday children aged 7 to 14 who were vagrant, begging, or destitute because their parents were serving penal servitude, under the care of a parent or guardian who was unfit 'by reason of criminal or drunken habits', frequenting the company of reputed thieves or prostitutes, or residing in premises used for prostitution. Once in the school the children could be kept, boarded out by the managers, or discharged by the justices.

The neat separation of the two kinds of school was, however, untenable. By 1860 for administrative reasons control of industrial schools had passed from the Committee of Education to the Home Secretary (Rose 1967) so placing them on a similar footing to reformatories; additionally industrial schools were also used to hold minor thieves aged under 12 in order to avoid such children being contaminated by older thieves in the reformatories. The significance of this was not lost on a leading juvenile magistrate of the early years of this century:

> 'Industrial schools have accordingly two functions, which theoretically, at least, should be wholly distinct. Their first object is to act as reformatories for the younger and less hardened delinquent children, and their second to provide for those who, through no fault whatever of their own, are found living in undesirable conditions due to the evil propensities of their parents.'
> (Clarke Hall 1926: 152)

Industrial schools were much used: by 1880 they held 15,000 children, almost three times as many as reformatories. But the dual system fell out of favour this century. Criticism from the press and the inspectorate contributed to the populations of both being halved by 1930, and it is clear that for many magistrates probation supervision, particularly following its national availability on the implementation of the Criminal Justice Act, 1925, had become a preferable option. Sir William Clarke Hall, for example, observed that 'no child should be sent to an industrial or reformatory school if there is a reasonable hope of reforming him by other means' (Clarke Hall 1926: 142). The *coup de grace* to the dual system was administered by the Report of the Departmental Committee on the Treatment of Young Offenders (1927), which averred that, there being no distinction between neglected and delinquent children beyond the fact that the former condition led to the latter, there could not exist any justification for dealing separately with them. Hence the Children and Young Persons Act, 1933, abolished reformatory and industrial schools, creating the approved school system in their stead.

The Act laid upon courts the duty to 'have regard for the welfare of the child or young person' (section 44). Offenders and non-offenders alike could be committed to approved schools, normally for up to three years, with discharge on licence always possible. The effect of this was to reduce the maximum time offenders could be held from five years to three, but to increase the powers of the courts over non-offenders, both by increasing the maximum *age* at which they could be committed to 17, and by extending the *categories* of youngster who could be committed. This latter extension was to be in keeping with the 'welfare of the child' criterion and involved first an extension of the definition of 'being in need of care or protection', and second a new criterion of being 'beyond control'. In 'beyond control' cases the action was to be brought by the parent or guardian beyond whose control the youngster was said to be. The parent or guardian concerned could withdraw the action at any time up to the point at which an order was made, but not subsequently. It seems to have been common for second thoughts to have arisen during the hearings and for actions to have been withdrawn *in medias res*. But since by this time the justices had not infrequently heard enough for them to be persuaded that an order *ought* to be made, negotiations as to the ultimate disposal on occasion occurred. These negotiations appear to have taken the form of reassuring the parents that committal to approved school was not in the court's mind, but only the helpful supervision of a probation officer, with the intention of persuading the complainant to proceed with the action. One magistrate makes plain the possible price of this helpfulness:

> 'the court ought to point out that should the behaviour of the child continue to be unsatisfactory the probation officer would have the right to bring the child back to court, and then if the magistrates thought fit they would send him away without asking the parents for their consent.' (Henriques 1950: 69)

To other magistrates, particularly in the early years of the Act, the boot seemed firmly on the other foot: parents who brought 'beyond control' proceedings were, as like as not, shirking their own duties:

> 'It is not unknown for a boy to be brought before the court by bad parents with an application that he be committed to a Home Office school on the grounds that he is beyond control. The real reason is the parents' laziness, or their desire to save expense. No such committal order should ever be made, under any circumstances whatsoever, without the parents being made to contribute some sum, however small, towards the cost of the child's keep. The word soon goes round the neighbourhood that this particular method of balancing a family budget is not feasible.'(L. Page 1936: 192–93)

But to some magistrates the approved school was such an indubitably beneficial institution that to be sent there was almost a privilege, an opportunity to make good some social or educational deficit. A professional assessment of the child's needs, to be made, according to section 35(2) of the 1933 Act, by the local authority's education department or a probation officer, followed by some weeks at a classifying school, far outweighed any considerations of culpability or desert:

> 'Cases are sometimes featured in the Press under glaring headlines, such as "Three Years for Stealing a Dozen Eggs", which convey the impression that children are being committed to schools for trivial thefts. . . . The schools are intended to be places of re-education and not places of punishment. The gravity or triviality of the offence is therefore of secondary importance compared with the question of whether it is possible to give a child the kind of training he needs if he stays at home.' (Elkin 1938: 250–51)

So – improve the facility, make it attractive or useful (for who could sensibly doubt the real benefits for the young in being better educated?), and the justification for its ever more extensive use is there. It is but a short step from these views to the introduction of more compulsory screening of children's social and educational needs in order that the benefits at present restricted to the working classes could be made more universally available: it is after all, in Foucault's phrase, done to people for their own good.

But of course the approved school never was intended as this kind of universal provision; rather it was a means of resolving the age-old conundrum of how appropriately to deal with delinquents: there must be enough kindness to motivate them, to catch their interest, but not enough to reward misbehaviour. Hence, in the words of another magistrate:

> 'An approved school . . . should be dreaded, even if there are in fact few grounds for such fears.' (Henriques 1950: 150)

And it is by kindness more than cruelty that control most quickly spreads, for its use becomes less unacceptable, a kind of firm caring done in the best interests of its objects. To restrict the actions of the well-meaning is the single strategy most likely to slow down the spread of social control, and the strategy which, for all the attacks on welfare which are made from across the political spectrum, is the most difficult to achieve and sustain. The 1933 Act's attempts to blur further the boundary between the deprived and the depraved was a further step in a process which, in spite of occasional set-backs, has progressed steadily from the mid-nineteenth century to the present day.

Since the war

> 'we should not let loose the psychologist and his collaborators except in a case of clear necessity. We confess to a dislike of probing into the lives of individuals by busy-bodies with a concern for other people's welfare. The poor already suffer too much from the inquisitions of so-called social workers.' (Brockway 1928: 47)

'when each offender (when probation is not used) is sentenced to the care of a "treatment authority" for a fully flexible time period and treatment program, the presentence report will have a new meaning and even with its privacy it will no longer be the threatening sort of document that now it sometimes cannot help being.'

(Keve 1960: 15)

At the start of the post-war period the juvenile justice and child care systems were largely intertwined. Such clearly punitive disposals as were still available for young offenders were not greatly used: the fine was not really to come into its own for juveniles until the 1950s, and birching had fallen into disuse in all but a few vigorously enthusiastic courts. But probation, approved schools, and Borstals were all geared to the compulsory reclamation of the offender, and to the extent that treatment was likewise the objective of the courts when dealing with neglected children, the differences between the way they were treated increasingly became academic. What was not always apparent was the way in which, while juvenile justice was becoming part of the child care system, the child care system was concomitantly becoming enmeshed in the State's criminal justice policy.

Following the social disorganization of war, however, among the characteristics of which was an upsurge in juvenile crime, and in the light of the optimistic expectations of the Welfare State, twin processes occurred which served to create a temporary wedge in this relationship. The Report of the Care of Children Committee (1946) was scathing in its condemnation of the Poor Law provisions for neglected children and also argued that approved schools were no place for most non-offenders (for a fuller discussion of the Curtis Report, see Boss 1971). The upshot of this report was the creation of local authority children's departments which were to assume some of the responsibilities both of the education departments and of the now defunct public assistance committees of the Poor Law: they were to become, that is to say, both the care authority, to which fit person orders were to be made, and also responsible for *receiving* into care certain categories of needy and destitute children in respect of whom no court order existed. It was this latter responsibility which had its origins in poor relief. Children's departments were to have resources for residential care, and trained professional staff to place children for fostering or adoption. The Children Act, 1948, therefore created the first professional social work service exclusively for children.

The Criminal Justice Act, 1948, was more ambiguous, and those commentators who have seen it as almost solely punitive have failed to grasp its complexity. It was by no means merely a response to wartime and post-war criminality, and certain of its provisions were less punitive than those proposed in the Criminal Justice Bill, 1938, which had lapsed with the outbreak of war (Elkin 1957). For example, the aborted Bill had contained a proposal that courts should be empowered to order sixty-hour sentences at attendance centres; the Act reduced this to a mere twelve hours. The detention centre had not been envisaged in the 1938 Bill, but the provision passed through the Commons with surprisingly little interest being shown in it in comparison with that which existed in relation to the treatment of young offenders, the possible abolition of capital punishment and the proposed abolition of corporal punishment (Dunlop and McCabe 1965: 2).

Certainly, however, the Attlee administration faced a serious problem with crime. On the one hand it sought to hold on to criminal justice as part of its social reform policies, but on the other those very policies rendered crime less explicable and less justifiable. The proposal to abolish corporal punishment, though of little practical import, the disposal having fallen into almost complete disuse, had symbolic connotations, and was controversial: in this sense, the detention centre's brisk regimes represented a necessary trade-off. But there is evidence of contemporary confusion as to the detention centre's nature and purpose: the Magistrates' Association thought it unnecessary (Dunlop and McCabe 1965: 2) and Morrison and Hughes, the Act's main contemporary commentators, not only list it as a measure of 'Penal Reform', but also offer this confusing observation:

> 'the tendency of the legislature continues to be towards the provision of more and more opportunities for individualisation, and *treatment which even when punitive, aims at being reformative.*'
> (Italics added. Morrison and Hughes 1952: 4)

The legislative split which partially re-emphasized the distinctions between deprived and depraved was, therefore, an ambivalent rather than decisive one and quickly breached. The Children and Young Persons (Amendment) Act, 1952, permitted child care officers to supervise children on approved school licence, and courts to remand offenders under 12 to local authority reception homes. Though this latter power almost precisely mirrored the much earlier provision for child criminals aged under 12 to be held in industrial rather than reformatory schools, and hence could hardly be described as novel, Packman is probably right to say that together the new powers constituted 'two more small breaches in the line which divided the deprived sheep from the delinquent goats' (Packman 1981: 105).

A more significant indication of how intertwined delinquency and child care still were came with the institution of the Committee on Children and Young Persons (the Ingleby Committee) in 1956 to consider the workings both of juvenile courts and of children's departments. The Ingleby Report (1960) reiterated the conventional liberal wisdom that neglect and delinquency were closely associated, and therefore that preventive intervention in the lives of families was justified. By this time, of course, the concerns of progressive Victorians about the delinquency supposedly generated by pauperism and vagrancy had given way, in a more affluent society, to explanations rooted in psychology or psychiatry. The influential study by Healy and Bronner of the Judge Baker Guidance Center, Boston, remained in print throughout the 1950s and claimed that empirically:

> 'Many of the families from which the delinquents came lived in situations that could be considered thoroughly inimical for the upbringing of a child, yet even under these conditions it was clear that the non-delinquents had distinctly more satisfactory human relationships than had the delinquents.'
>
> (Healy and Bronner 1936: 9)

In the United Kingdom the work of John Bowlby (Bowlby 1944, 1951) on maternal deprivation remained influential in the professional literature, as Bowlby himself did in the training of welfare workers; Kate Friedlander's psychoanalytical study of juvenile delinquency (Friedlander 1947) was similarly widely read; and by 1962 a leading American analyst, Peter Blos, was taking for granted the fact that delinquency resulted from some psychic disturbance:

> 'Delinquency by definition refers to a personality disturbance which manifests itself in open conflict with society.'
>
> (Blos 1962: 230)

Of course explanations of this kind departed further and further from the common-sense view so precisely articulated by back-bench Conservative MPs, to the effect that crime was caused by lack of parental discipline, youthful affluence, the abolition of birching and conscription, and the decline of Christianity (see, for example, Cohen 1972). But though views differed, the rise of juvenile crime from 1956 onwards placed delinquency firmly on the agenda of both professionals and politicians, and the issues raised by crime in an ostensibly affluent society were by no means dealt with by the timorous reforms proposed by the Ingleby Report.

There followed the 1960s debate about juvenile justice (Berlins and

Wansell 1974; D.H. Thorpe *et al.* 1980; Adams *et al.* 1981) which, though complex, was predicated upon certain generalized assumptions:

1 That widespread urban poverty, though concealed by the economic growth of the 1960s, remained a reality;
2 That the promise of *embourgeoisement*, the classless State, forecast in the 1950s, had failed to materialize, and that there continued to exist widespread disparity of wealth and income of a kind and degree likely to prove impervious to the social changes heralded in by the Welfare State;
3 That courts of law were not the best places to determine why youngsters – the majority of whom admitted their guilt – got into trouble;
4 That the existing penal arrangements were seriously deficient and could be improved. *First*, the institutions were inappropriate for dealing with problems which were caused by, and soluble only within, the offender's own community: indeed institutions were themselves coming to be believed to have pathological characteristics which made people worse (Barton 1959; Goffman 1961). *Second*, the idea of scientific sentencing – that for each offender there was an identifiable and desirable sentence which could be determined by the court – was incorrect. Sentencers were less well placed than professional experts who could monitor the progress of their charges, to predict their responses to treatment, and rational sentencing should accordingly reflect this. Better for the sentencers to leave things open and hand the decision-making over to the experts. *Third*, however, the basic tool of the experts themselves, the relationship, was coming to be seen as insufficient to effect change. This argument was by no means new (see, for example, Powers and Witmer 1951), it was confirmed as the decade continued (Meyer, Borgatta, and Jones 1965) and subsequently ratified (Martinson 1974). In one famous statement at the end of the decade, Martin Davies pointed to a contradiction at the heart of the idea of cure by relationship:

> 'the casework relationship – which represents the probation officers' main instrument, is itself found to have a statistical association with environmental stress. Thus the vicious circle, in which the client finds himself trapped, embraces not only his own environment and personality, but also appears to involve the caseworker: the social worker is best able to make a good relationship with those who appear to need least help.'
> (Davies 1969: 121)

Certain clear themes emerged from these assumptions, then. One was an increased scepticism about the simple idea that apprehension and punishment were effective deterrents, and in the 1970s the increasing influence of labelling (or social reaction) theory seemed to support this scepticism (see, for example, Taylor, Walton, and Young, 1973; Scull 1977; Plummer 1979; Hepburn 1977; Albrecht and Albrecht 1977). Related to this theoretical concern – that exposure to criminal justice could itself be criminogenic – was the operational suspicion that sentencing was a remote and ineffective process, and courts the wrong place in which to get at the heart of the matter. A Labour Party report, *Crime – A Challenge to Us All*, advocated the setting up of family councils and family courts geared to achieving agreement with offenders and their families as to what should be done in particular cases (Labour Party 1964). The contents of this report were largely translated the following year into a White Paper, *The Child, The Family and the Young Offender* (1965).

Politically these arguments reflected the growing influence of the child care lobby on both senior civil servants and the Labour government of 1964–70. If institutions were not the answer, and 'making relationships' too restricted a mandate for the experts; if inner city deprivation and social injustice remained central problems in social policy; and if the models of integrated child care and delinquency prevention being developed in a small number of local authorities such as Oxfordshire (Packman 1981: 105 *et seq.*) were so impressive then developing the social service infrastructure and handing the problems over to the experts seemed an appropriate governmental response.

Rather similar debates took place in England/Wales and Scotland, but with notably different outcomes. In Scotland the existing juvenile court system was patchy and half-hearted, and following the implementation of the Social Work (Scotland) Act, 1968, was abolished and replaced by a welfare-oriented panel system, designed in part to keep those offenders whom it was possible to divert out of the system in the first place, and to deal on the basis of the child's needs with those brought before it. (For an excellent study of the workings of these panels, see Martin, Fox, and Murray, 1981.) In England and Wales, however, not only was the case for change shoddily argued (the 1965 White Paper was little more than ten pages long in spite of the radical nature of its proposals), but also there was much more concerted opposition to the plan to abolish juvenile courts, not only from the juvenile magistrates themselves, but also from the police, justices' clerks, and the probation service, all of whose interests were affected by the proposals (Bottoms 1974). The White Paper was withdrawn in disarray and replaced by an alternative, compromise formulation in 1968, *Children in Trouble*, which formed the basis of the Children and Young Persons Act, 1969.

The reformist arguments of the 1960s have been analysed, caricatured, and misunderstood. The reformers themselves were by no means homogeneous. They included a lobby of emergent professionals in the child care service whose explanations of delinquency ranged from psychiatrically derived concepts such as ego weakness in adolescence, maternal deprivation, and oedipal failure to notions of urban decay and the pressures of family life which placed them in the tradition of the Victorian social reformers and Fabian socialists. To these reformers, crime was indeed symptomatic of something deeper, and to punish was to deal with the symptom not the cause. The answer was to extend the remit of the experts not only to enable them to remove these youngsters into care when it seemed desirable to do so, always as a necessary step towards 'reintegrating them' as soon as possible. Hence in the absence of the youngster the problems within the family or community which had caused his or her difficulties were to be solved. So even more flexibility was needed, and accordingly the magistrates' power to commit both offenders and non-offenders to approved schools was replaced by care orders which enabled the experts to determine whether or not youngsters subject to them should live at home until their eighteenth birthday.

But there were other reformers too, including a motley band of sociologists of deviance who were concerned to shift the unit of attention from the offender to the social processes through which he or she passed. Some of these theorists were as critical of the experts as they were of police, courts, and prisons. Welfare workers were the insidious arms of State coercion, soft cops, self-interested professionals seeking to control in the name of care and to persuade members of the proletariat to accept injustices, and to take the blame for circumstances of which they were, in fact, the victims. Of course the logic of this position was quite the reverse of that of the child care lobby: it was, wherever possible, to leave well alone. Justice being impossible under capitalism minimal damage was the honourable course of action for the socialist: radical non-intervention became a slogan (Schur 1973) but confusion and contradiction were endemic:

> 'Criminals started looking like very peculiar creatures, indeed. They made rational choices in the morning, drifted into crime at lunchtime, were brutalised by the social structure in the afternoon, and then faded away in the dusk as mere shadows created by the mass media.' (Cohen 1979)

The concerns of both these sets of reformers were addressed by the device of bifurcation used in the Longford Report *Crime – A Challenge to Us All*, (Labour Party 1964). Most juvenile crime, the report argued, was a normal part of growing up and, being almost universal, was best left alone. Some crime, however, was symptomatic of personal distress, and for this a wide range of help should be available. The process of determining into which camp a particular offender fell was, of course, a matter for professional assessment.

It would be a serious error to regard this position as representative of the crudely deterministic 'medical model' of crime caricatured by some subsequent critics (for example, Bean 1976; Morris *et al.* 1980). Indeed not all critics of the chain of events triggered by Longford's committee seem aware that Lord Longford himself has extensively debated issues of freedom and determinism in relation to crime (see, in particular, Longford 1958, 1961) and has propounded a theologically inspired form of neo-classicism:

> 'One cannot fail to recognize the limited sphere within which freedom of choice has frequently operated. But here one is on the verge of a precipice.
>
> It is but a short step from this point of view . . . to the far-reaching and seductive doctrine that all crime is disease. And if and when one reaches the latter point one is abandoning, surely, all belief in the freedom of the will whether in a Christian or secular sense . . . a Christian can have nothing to do with this doctrine that crime, as such, is disease.' (Longford 1961: 47–8)

Longford on the contrary favours the retention of retribution, though not as a central plank of criminal justice (Longford 1961: 57) and proportionality (Longford 1961: 59). He rejects the notion that crime has 'causes' speaking, in conventional criminological wisdom, of causal influences, which 'do not forcibly compel a criminal to commit a crime but make it more or less likely . . . that he will do so' (Longford 1961: 67–8). This soft determinist position is precisely in the mainstream of liberal social theory; it recalls the language of the several Victorian reformers we have already cited; it is a modern form of Hobbesianism and in different forms characterizes the writings of the empiricist philosophers from Hume to Ayer (O'Connor 1972. See also Matza 1964):

> 'If I deliberately perform an act that would ordinarily be accounted free . . . this is no less a free action because it is the outcome of all sorts of psychological influences and physiological mechanisms.' (O'Connor 1972: 73)

So a social or psychological 'explanation' of an action which associates delinquency with maternal deprivation, super-ego deficiency, and the like should, as a clinical judgement, restrict itself to the patient or patients seen, and aver: 'in my view, had it not been for this complaint or syndrome, this patient would not have committed this offence'. When a hundred or a thousand such conditions are verified and associated with delinquency, we have a predisposing factor; but unless we can uncover not a single maternally deprived or psychically deficient non-offender we do not have a cause of crime. It was central both to Longford and to the ensuing White Papers that most crime was normal, 'an incident', in the words of *Children in Trouble*, 'in the pattern of a child's normal development'. But unless it is perversely to be argued that *no* delinquency is a response to what the same White Paper termed 'unsatisfactory family or social circumstances', it would be difficult to justify the equal treatment of equal crimes, or indeed the abandonment of the experts. At the same time, the ideology of crime based on will which, though constrained, is yet free, poses complex problems for the nature and purpose of the experts' own activities.

The reformist position was, however, substantially modified in the years between Longford and the implementation of the Act. The modification reflected the interests of different supporters of the status quo. Just as there was a lack of homogeneity among the reformers, so were there differences of emphasis amongst those who opposed them. The law and order lobby, comprising a number of shires MPs and significant figures in the press, who clearly enjoyed a high degree of public support, hankered after an orderly society which they saw challenged by the relatively affluent and disrespectful youth of the day. For them, as they pressed for the reintroduction of conscription and corporal punishment, the idea of 'treating' juvenile crime became a central symbol of moral decay, a collusion with a kind of society of which they would have none.

But there was also a different strand of political thought amongst the opponents of the reforms. There has always been a good representation of lawyers on the Conservative side in the Commons, to whom the rule of law protects civil liberties, ensures equality of treatment, is democratically accountable, and permits appeals against injustice. Any shift from the due process of law to executive discretion is, therefore, whatever its motives, ultimately against the interests of the individual offender, and to be resisted. But beyond that, a framework of State intervention based on the notion of treatment demeans the humanness of offenders, diminishes their rationality and regards them as things, as objects to be experimented upon rather than choosing human beings. (For a consideration of issues such as this, see Downie and Telfer 1980.)

The reform movement, therefore, was embroiled in a battle which was fought on the fields of ideology and of self-interest. The result was compromise: the second White Paper compromised the first; the legislation compromised the second; and the implemented legislation further compromised the Act in its pristine form.

The Act retained the juvenile courts. It retained the power to fine and discharge; it retained for the time (but with a view to future abolition) the power to commit juveniles to custody; the same applied to attendance centres. Approved school orders were in effect combined with fit person orders to become care orders, and probation orders were abolished for juveniles, to be replaced by supervision orders which had hitherto been available only for non-offenders. Additionally, as recognition of the view that there was too great a gap between institutional provision and simple supervision in the community (both of which, it will be recalled, had fallen somewhat into disrepute), a form of treatment intermediate between the two was permitted as a condition of a supervision order. This involved unspecified activities organized by the supervisors: the role of courts was restricted to ordering the clients to participate in the activities if ordered to do so by their supervisors, not to order that activities should take place (Children and Young Persons Act, 1969, section 12).

Central to the intention of the Act was the raising of the age of criminal responsibility from 10 to 14. Equally it was intended that offenders aged 14 to 16 should be taken to court only when the police, having statutorily consulted the local authority, were satisfied that it was necessary that this should be done. In fact, neither of these provisions (sections 4 and 5 respectively) has been implemented. Between the Second Reading of the Bill (in March 1969) and the implementation of the Act (in 1971) the General Election of 1970 brought to power the Conservative Opposition which had previously fought it clause by clause during its passage through the House. It is necessary to explain in some detail the consequences of this decision because they are relevant to our theme.

Section 4 would have raised the age of criminal responsibility to 14. This in turn would have transferred responsibility for dealing with offenders aged 10 to 13 from the court's criminal to its civil jurisdiction. Section 1 of the Act dealt with juveniles in need of care or control, in respect of whom a care or supervision order could be made by listing certain criteria, one of which had to be proved in order for an order to be made. These criteria included ill-treatment, neglect of health or development, being in moral danger, being beyond control, and not receiving efficient full-time education: criteria in short which signified that the child was a victim of circumstance. But additionally, for an order to be made not only did one of these conditions have to be satisfied, but also it had, and separately, to be proved that the child was in need of care or control which he would be unlikely to receive unless an order was made. Because the need for care or control had to be proved separately the section has come to be known as including a *double proof requirement*. Now by the simple device of adding a new primary criterion to the list of matters to be proved – that 'he is guilty of an offence, excluding homicide' (section 1(2)(f)) the legislation not only transferred child offenders to the civil jurisdiction but also restricted *ipso facto* their being brought to court, by dint of the fact that commission of an offence was no longer enough: the need for care or control had also to be proved. When it was proved, the court was empowered only to make a supervision or care order (except in mental health cases or where it was simply determined to require the parent to enter into a recognizance to exercise control), not to punish. In short, proof would be harder to establish and, once it had been established, the court's powers would be radically circumscribed by the absence of punitive disposals.

But because section 4 was never implemented, and the age of criminal responsibility remained 10, although it was indeed possible for children to be taken to court under section 1, it was also possible for them to be taken to court under the criminal jurisdiction (section 7). But here there was no double proof requirement and no additional circumscription of the court's powers. So to imagine that the police would bring large numbers of child offenders to court under section 1(2)(f), which would make them work much harder for the finding of guilt and would give the court fewer powers of sentence, would be to assume a commitment on the police's part to the spirit of the Act which it would scarcely be realistic to expect.

Section 5 of the Act was similarly unimplemented. This section would have restricted court proceedings against young persons (aged 14 to 16) to cases where, on the basis of statutory consultations, it was deemed 'necessary'. While it is difficult to have very much confidence that such consultations would have impacted substantially on practice, the ostensible intention of the section was to reduce the numbers of older-age offenders brought to court, and to turn them instead over to the informal ministrations of the experts.

To understand the failings of the Act – of which the main one was a vast but quite unintended increase in custodial sentencing reflecting largely increased punitiveness by courts (Department of Health and Social Security 1981), and the second one was the vast disparities *among* the courts as to their sentencing policies — it is necessary to address the issues at three levels, the *technical*, the *micro-political*, and the *structural*.

At a *technical* level, it will be plain that serious problems arose from the non-implementation of section 4. This seems to have happened in two ways. First for three years after the Act there was a steady increase in the making of care orders in respect of children, which began to reduce only from 1975. The large majority of these orders were made within the court's *criminal jurisdiction*: that is to say for the offence alone, and without the further necessity of it being proved that care or control was necessary. It seems almost certain (D.H. Thorpe *et al.* 1980) that a considerable proportion of these could not have been made under a reasonable interpretation of section 1. In short, the continued power of courts to deal with the 10 to 13 age group as criminals led directly to long-term welfare disposals being made. This was an unintended consequence of failure to implement the Act in full. Secondly, the same factor has led to an increased throughput of children in the juvenile court who, *whatever sentence they received*, acquired a criminal record, which in turn made them especially vulnerable to custodial sentences once they became eligible for detention centre (at 14, if boys) and Borstal (at 15). And it is in the custodial sentencing of young persons that such a vast expansion has taken place. So while it is true that certain of the trends discernible in the 1969 Act were also discernible in the 1960s (Thorpe *et al.* 1980), they have accelerated considerably since, and it was only in 1983 that the same safeguard – the care or control test – was extended to orders made under section 7(7) of the 1969 Act (Criminal Justice Act, 1982, section 23) as applied to orders made under section 1(2)(f).

At a *micro-political* level there has in both the juvenile and the adult jurisdictions been a political reluctance to interfere substantially with the powers of courts to impose those sentences which they consider most likely to reflect local concerns. The reasons for this reluctance are varied, but include both a constitutional concern to protect judicial independence from executive control and the political reality of an effective legal lobby within and outside Parliament itself. Further, any such interference, to the extent that it might be deemed a softening of political resolve in the drive against crime, is an electorally risky strategy. Though certain steps have been taken to discourage custodial sentencing, they have principally taken the form of providing alternative sentencing options to custody, and though there is now a set of conditions to be met before a custodial sentence may be imposed on an offender aged below 21 (Criminal Justice Act, 1982, section 1), the drafting problems in making such restrictions effective are considerable, and the interpretation of the relevant sections is typically a matter of case law handed down from the superior courts – the judiciary, that is to say, controlling the judiciary, not, in fact, an entirely straightforward matter (Ashworth 1983). At the time of writing it is impossible to say what impact this will have on custodial sentencing, though one (perhaps slightly premature) book is somewhat gloomy (Burney 1985), a pessimism which we provisionally rather share.

There is a second way in which the reluctance to structure the court's sentencing discretion affects the quality of sentencing (for the distinction between structuring and confining discretion, see Davis 1971). Though in any human system there will inevitably be certain differences among courts, the conflicts in the 1969 Act make it possible for courts to pursue opposite objectives in their sentencing practices and still remain within its letter. Hence research shows different courts perfectly legitimately regarding themselves as caring welfare tribunals and stern courts of law (Anderson 1978). There is nothing structurally necessary about such incompatibilities, and a degree of political will could reduce though certainly not eliminate the problem.

At a *structural* level there exist the problems, embedded in the system itself with its internal paradoxes and contradictions, to which we have already drawn attention. In some form or another they are the inevitable consequences of a neo-classical system which seeks to retain both the ideas of punishment and of welfare; their presence explains the enthusiastic support which exists in some quarters for the 'back to justice' solution (A. Morris *et al.* 1980) and in others for the opposite 'welfare' solution which largely eliminates the idea of punishment (McCabe and Treitel 1983; Jillings 1985). Justice and welfare reflect two co-existing cultural 'traces' in bourgeois socio-legal thought, the one speaking to the idea of rational, calculating action, the other to an interventionist ideology of a superordinate management of malfunctioning, of establishing social engineering to ensure the appropriate preconditions for the efficient extraction of surplus value within a politically and morally integrated social order. There is, in short, a logic to both cultural trajectories; they are co-present – and hence inherently unstable – dominant ideologies.

It is within this sphere of instability that the space emerges which is to be filled by the experts and the sentencers. When a whole style of life is conducive to delinquency, what could be more natural than for a magistrate to inform the working-class youth found in the middle-class suburbs adjacent to his estate that 'It is a very serious thing to go wandering around the streets in Countyside village' (Parker, Casburn, and Turnbull 1981)? The conflicts within the system permit the courts to follow their predilections within very wide confines; for the experts, the individualization of a sentence means investigations, visits, and questions; the acquisition of information and its translation into professional 'knowledge' of an ambiguous kind are processes which both represent and augment the power of the experts.

Structural matters of this kind are almost by definition impervious to technical solutions. But technical solutions are not, nevertheless, to be spurned either as a means of resolving the technical and micropolitical problems or as *containing* the expression of structural conflict. The capacity of legislative or practice changes to create a truce among conflicting ideologies should not be underestimated.

2 The development of welfare

'the busybody, the quack, the pseudo God Almighty . . . is the irreconcileable enemy, the ubiquitous and iniquitous nuisance, and the most difficult to get rid of because he has imposed his moral pretensions on public opinion, and is accepted as just the sort of philanthropist our prisons and criminals should be left to.'
(Shaw 1946: 116)

'No nobler work can be done by any man than that which is afforded by the position of a probation officer, for it is the complete and practical realization of the whole teaching of the Gospels.'
(Clarke Hall 1926: 131)

Welfare work in the juvenile court today is provided by two separate services, the probation service and the local authority social services department. In this chapter we shall be showing that they have proceeded historically along different routes, the one having invariably had an affiliation with the criminal justice system, the other being more associated with the provisions of the Poor Law and the private charities for the needy.

This being so it would be tempting – though a little too simple – to see the two agencies as representing in themselves the epitome of the fusion of the judicial and the assistancial which we discussed in relation to the juvenile justice system in the last chapter. Too simple because within each of those agencies itself exists just such a fusion, albeit one which variably affects their day-to-day working practices. There are, that is to say, areas of overlap between the two services as well as significant differences; later in the book when we come to examine the activities of the probation officers and social workers who represent these agencies, we shall see just how these similarities, which include training and professional identification, and differences, including occupational tradition and working context, play themselves out.

The juvenile court disposal of the care order is exclusively the responsibility of the local authority which, as we have seen, has been the 'care authority' for many years. Care orders represented not only the transfer of power to the local authority from the court which we described in Chapter 1, but also a transfer from the probation service. Under the former approved school system probation officers had come to be the main agents of after-care, and the approved school system was, like the probation service, responsible to the central government department of the Home Office. The intention of the 1969 Act was to effect the transfer of responsibility for most young offenders from central to local government, so that the probation service would become more identified with the adult criminal justice system and social services have predominant responsibility for juvenile delinquents and children dealt with under the court's civil powers.

The supervision order is an altogether different matter. This disposal, which was the subject of the study described in Appendix B, combines the former supervision order which could be made in 'care or protection' and 'beyond control' cases, and the probation order which was made to the probation service only in respect of offenders. Hence it is a particularly interesting case study of a single order being supervised by two distinct welfare agencies with different traditions, and as such represents the point of confluence of two rather distinct lines on the welfare map. We have shown elsewhere (Webb and Harris 1984) that the historical paths which these two agencies have pursued are reflected in decidedly variant practices in, and attitudes towards, the management of the supervision order.

When it is said, therefore, that the 1969 Act represents a shift of responsibility to the experts, it is more precise to say that the main recipients of that responsibility have been social services departments, whose intervention on the scene substantially reduced the juvenile work of the probation service. But the intention that probation's juvenile role should become residual did not materialize. For reasons both of resources and local politics (between the agencies, and between either one agency and the local court) probation continued to play a role in the supervision of young offenders (Bottoms 1974). The Act specified (section 13(2)) that the supervision of children (aged 10 to 13) should normally be by social workers, but that of young persons (14 to 16) was a matter for local negotiations, and more often than not it fell to the probation service to undertake the task in the case of offenders. That 14- to 16-year-old non-offenders were typically supervised by social workers made plain that these allocations were not merely administrative but reflected certain shared assumptions both about the agencies and about delinquency.

In this chapter we etch the biographies of the two agencies in turn, trying to show certain points of unity and of dislocation. In discussing the juvenile court in Chapter 1 we have painted a picture of increasing amorphousness and lack of differentiation. The counterpoint to that is this discussion of the workings of the two distinct agencies to whom the court allocates responsibility for the management of the orders it makes.

The development of probation

Just as we tried to avoid writing a potted history of the juvenile court in Chapter 1, preferring to develop a conceptual biography structured around particular themes, so do we approach the probation service now. We offer a triphasic analysis of the service's development. These phases, *doing good, professional casework*, and *community corrections*, though oversimplified, are heuristically useful and do not seriously mislead. The phases, though, are not qualitative shifts but rather landmarks in an evolutionary process in which successive stages incorporate aspects of their predecessors.

Doing good: the service's origins are charitable and religious, based on voluntary concern and effort, not on expertise. These origins lie at least as much in the United States of America as in Britain. The pioneer conventionally credited with originating the probation system was John Augustus, an affluent Boston shoemaker who, at the age of 55, and as a member of the Washington Total Abstinence Society, began attending local courts in Boston. His strategy was to provide bail for drunkards, help them during their remand period, accompany them back to court for the subsequent hearing, and report on their progress. If all had gone well they would then be dealt with nominally. By 1846–47 Augustus was working full time in the courts, by now as an agent of Boston's Board of State Charities; his shop was run by his son and apprentices:

> 'John Augustus originated in the rudimentary form many of the techniques of probation officers and other social workers today, including preliminary social investigations, tactful interviewing, family casework, foster-home placement, protective work for women and children, detention, and cooperation with schools, employers, institutions and social agencies. As far as he was able he investigated every case before recommending probation.'
>
> (Chute and Bell 1956: 40)

Although Augustus died in 1859, by 1870 the State of Massachusetts required agents of the Board of State Charities to attend hearings where children were charged, with the effect that around one-third of all such children were placed on probation. An adult probation officer was appointed in 1878, and other states, primarily in New England, followed. Though there was a widespread American opposition to the practice (Augustus himself was on occasion physically assaulted by court officials and gaolers) the system spread, at least in the towns, albeit in a piecemeal way (Rothman 1980), and President Coolidge, who, as a former Governor of Massachusetts, was a keen supporter of probation, was to pilot through a federal probation law in 1925. Interestingly, there was strong opposition to this move from congressional representatives from the 'dry' Southern states, who saw probation as a likely let-off for bootleggers during the Prohibition: hence Congressman Thomas L. Blanton of Texas feared that it 'would allow the judges to put all the bootleggers on probation' (cited in Chute and Bell 1956).

The work of the Board of State Charities was reported to the British Home Secretary, Sir William Vernon Harcourt, by members of the Howard Association who had visited the USA (Bochel 1976). Additionally, Mr J. Sturge, MP, a manager of the Stoke Farm School in Worcestershire, gave evidence to the Reformatory and Industrial Schools Commission in 1882 on the practice (Le Mesurier 1935: 23), and a modest and limited First Offenders Act was passed in 1887, which permitted the supervision of minor first offenders by police court missionaries and other voluntary workers.

Police court missionaries of the Church of England Temperance Society had since 1876 been reporting on the social circumstances and characters of adult inebriates in the London police courts. Section 16 of the Summary Jurisdiction Act, 1879 permitted courts to discharge minor offenders conditionally on security being given that they would appear for sentence when called upon. It became the practice for justices to call on missionaries to give advice and help to offenders thus conditionally discharged (Le Mesurier 1935: 23). By such means the missionaries became 'friends in the community', so that the work of these prototypical probation officers effectively extended the activities of the child savers (Platt 1977) to meeting the needs of adult offenders as well.

Nevertheless, when statutory recognition was afforded to the probation service in 1907, child as well as adult offenders were in the government's mind, and the probation service took its place alongside juvenile courts and Borstals as offering a helping hand and a new opportunity to the wayward young. Under Sir William Clarke Hall's influence, Old Street Juvenile Court was binding over more than half the juveniles who appeared before it with probation, and this figure had extended to the country as a whole by 1932 (Le Mesurier 1935: 41). Yet the figure for adult magistrates courts was only 19 per cent, varying between 30 per cent in London and less than 10 per cent elsewhere (Le Mesurier 1935: 46).

The probation service's orientation remained primarily religious until the 1930s, when the gradual development of professionalism began to fuse Christian imperative and scientific method. This date seems to us surprisingly late, for two main reasons. First the role of the State in managing the probation service was by now well established, and the days of the Police Court Mission long since gone. The impact of successive pieces of legislation since the 1907 Act had been to cement the service's role as a secular State institution: its powers had been strengthened by the Criminal Justice Administration Act, 1914, and the Criminal Justice Act, 1925 required all courts to appoint a probation officer. This increasingly organized State involvement was part of a broader strategy aimed at the co-ordination and increasing State control of a range of voluntary agencies in the penal sector – notably in relation to Borstal and discharged prisoners (see, for example, Garland 1985: 210–14). Secondly, the religious commitment does seem to have been longer lasting than in other spheres of welfare. But gradually the redemption of the sinner became a less persuasive occupational motif in an increasingly secular society, and a more rationalist, even scientific culture saw the service looking to a more empirical and less transcendental *raison d'être*. There was, too, a more overtly political climate generally within which welfare work was operating, and in the literature of the time we find increasing references to unemployment and its consequences; though certainly the probation service never sought to politicize its own activities in the way that the British Federation of Social Workers attempted elsewhere in the welfare world (Lees 1971: D. Webb 1981). Indeed as late as the 1950s magistrates sometimes saw the probation task in quite simple terms:

> 'No good probation officer . . . is insensitive to the most vital of all forces towards the reformation of the offender, the force of religion.'
> (Watson 1950: 165)

By this time, however, the processes of professionalization were coming to challenge such notions. In an influential text, Elizabeth Glover saw ethical and professional problems in indoctrination:

> 'Probation officers, representing as they do Authority in the public mind, are the last persons from whom direction or gratuitous suggestion on religious matters should be tolerated.'
> (Glover 1949: 246)

While in the less professionally aspirant sectors of the probation world, the harsher realities of secularization had decisively impinged on the best of intentions; a hostel warden notes:

> 'a rather emotional lay preacher was giving his sermon. He suddenly leaned from his pulpit, threw his arms wide apart, and said, "If this was your last night on earth whom would you wish to come face to face with?" Quite audibly a rather disgruntled boy muttered, "Marilyn Monroe". This was the last evening service we attended.' (Cooks 1958: 105)

Professional casework: the probation service was, therefore, lagging somewhat behind other sectors of the welfare world, where professionalization and the generation of a knowledge base were already proceeding along secular lines. This knowledge base began with the systematic collection of detailed information and the application of rational problem-solving strategies, and developed gradually in the 1930s with the utilization of insights from analytic psychology (Halmos 1965; Yelloly 1980). In the probation service these processes hardly became dominant until after the war, partly because of the enduring nature of the explicit Christianity of the mission and, more prosaically, because the large majority of probation officers at this time had had the benefit of only an elementary school education (McWilliams 1985), and saw their task in more mundane terms.

The core text of rational and empirical enquiry was Mary Richmond's still monumentally impressive *Social Diagnosis* (Richmond 1917). A social worker of that time, in retrospective mood, has remarked:

> '*Social Diagnosis* was our Bible, and we studied it chapter by chapter and then practised it rigidly . . . before more than $5.00 could be spent on a family, we had to visit at least two previous addresses, near-by relatives, the church, the school, and other social agencies, and previous employers.' (Wilson 1972)

Such detailed enquiry, influenced in the USA by the pragmatism of William James, fitted in the United Kingdom into the blue book sociology which bred the great social surveys of Mayhew (1861), C. Booth (1889, 1891), and Rowntree (1901) as well as the work of Sidney and Beatrice Webb. It was in part this rationalism, combined with the brisk economic theories of Helen Bosanquet and Octavia Hill, which had led to the setting up in 1869 of the Charity Organization Society, with its aim of imposing a levy on all existing charities in return for systematizing their random and undesirable practices of alms giving (Rodgers 1968: 43–8). The society opposed all forms of

The development of welfare

State relief apart from the harsh comforts of the Union workhouse (Bruce 1961: 123), and at least during the 1870s it became indeed a scourge of the poor, a means of censuring and monitoring their very lives, of seeking to close such doors as it could which might have enabled them to struggle on without confronting and dealing with those aspects of their own behaviour which the society took to have brought about their misfortunes. Its aim was:

> 'to impose upon the life of the poor a system of sanctions and rewards which would convince them that there could be no escape from life's miseries except by thrift, regularity, and hard work . . . in 1871, the society reported that it had secured the collaboration of plain clothes police officers in tracking down reports of begging. To clear beggars off the streets, the charitable were to give not alms but tickets to report to the local C.O.S. office where relief would be given if investigation proved a case to be satisfactory.'
> (Stedman-Jones 1971: 271–72)

In spite of the fact that the unrest of the 1880s caused the government to undermine the society's rationalism by buying social order at any price (Stedman-Jones 1971: 298), the society continued to garner influential support for its desire to restrict the giving of alms. Arnold Bennett was one such supporter:

> 'The heart gives pennies in the street. The brain runs the Charity Organisation Society. Of course, to give pennies in the street is much less trouble than to run the C.O.S. As a method of producing a quick, inexpensive, and pleasing effect on one's egotism the C.O.S. is simply not in it with this dodge of giving pennies at random, without enquiry. Only – which of the two devices ought to be accused of heartlessness and callousness?'
> (Bennett 1908: 119)

This rationalist tradition seems, however, to have been subordinate to the child-saving tradition in the probation service until the late 1920s. The year 1930 saw the institution of the Home Office's first training course for probation officers, a course which included teaching in the social sciences as well as practical experience such as visits to institutions. From this time on, references in probation-related literature to a 'medical model' of diagnosis and treatment becme more frequent and explicit, and one can come to understand how the transition was effected from the *acquisition* of detailed information (of the kind prescribed by Mary Richmond) to its translation into *therapy* based on psychoanalysis, for clearly the development of a theory by which to make sense of all this information and to justify its collection became necessary. Here in 1931 is Lilian Le Mesurier on the medical model of diagnosis:

> 'If a patient suffering from chest trouble is brought to a physician, the latter does not choose to prescribe without as full a knowledge of his previous health and antecedents as is obtainable. If he discovers that the man has already suffered from pneumonia and pleurisy and that there is grave suspicion of tuberculosis in the family, he will be influenced, and rightly so, to take more precautions and perhaps order different treatment from what might have appeared necessary from a mere superficial examination. The wise judge and the wise physician are alike in this respect . . . It is more knowledge of the background, and therefore of the prospects of a prescription being successfully carried out, which is sometimes needed.'
> (Le Mesurier 1931: 87)

Hence this second phase of probation development saw grafted on to a spiritual belief in people's innate capacity for good a set of theories, assumptions, and procedures by which the 'relationship' could become a professional one, yet still reflect the 'faith' to which Halmos – uninterested as he seems to have been in the probation service – repeatedly refers (Halmos 1965). And this notion – that casework cured – remained for a long time the justification for the steady growth of the service from no more than 300 officers in 1935 to 750 by the end of the war and over 1,600 in 1960. Probation, it was stressed by a justices' clerk just after the war, was more than just keeping a 'contract':

> 'There must from the point of view of the law, be a clear recital of certain fixed duties on each side, but the relationship between the probation officer and the probationer will have little value if it is regarded as a matter of carrying out the terms of a contract for a certain period . . . The essential power of the probation officer is in his personality; if he can inspire devotion in his charge; if the probationer becomes filled with a genuine desire to gain his approval; if the parents accept him unreservedly as a wise friend of the family and profit by his suggestions on the upbringing of their offspring; if the probationer does not look on him as a sort of policeman whose watchfulness it is almost a point of honour to cheat; then the probation officer may hope for a true success . . . the probation officer can only cure delinquency by effecting a change of heart either in the child or the parent.'
> (A.E. Jones 1945: 76–7)

In this second phase, then, religious concern blended into a professionalism which involved both the detailed acquisition of information and an interpretation of that information based on ideas from the social sciences. But one should not be deceived from discussions of the 'medical model' into believing that a hard determinist approach to crime was ever dominant in Britain. The European positivist criminology of Lombroso and Ferri never held sway here, and in much of the literature of the time psychiatry and causal explanation are tentative and set alongside references to building character and to the need for social reform. Hence, Mrs Le Mesurier, whose comparison of a medical and judicial diagnosis has already been cited, comments:

> 'Some people, indeed, have been over-eager to speak of crime as a disease. Though helpful as a metaphor, this is open to serious objection if pressed to undue lengths, and is certainly not endorsed here.'
> (Le Mesurier 1931: 25)

The liberal notion of constrained freedom, of the role of reformers and helpers as opening doors and expanding options for those whose choices are limited is a notion more familiar in Britain, where, in part under the powerful influence of common law, the consideration of *mens rea* is a constant reminder of the boundaries of determinist accounts of delinquency. Everyday notions such as 'responsibility' or 'just deserts', whether they have their philosophical roots in Utilitarianism or Kantian retributivism, remain strong cultural forces, and, of course, felicitously justify simultaneous punishment and treatment in almost all cases. Seldom, within a framework such as this, do culpability and explanation not co-exist in some form, and seldom accordingly does social enquiry fail to find something that can be done as an adjunct to a penal measure (Hardiker and Webb 1979).

The social influences on probation work, which included Christianity, clinical psychology, empiricism, and judicial expectation increasingly conflicted with each other from the 1960s. At this time the traditional assumptions of the service about what was to be done (whether reclamation or reductionism) and how (casework) were looking rather ragged; but at this time too it was assuming a set of new functions which began to edge it towards a new practice paradigm which constitutes our third phase. To oversimplify, the utility of professional casework had run its course. In the 1930s to 1950s it had begun the process of transforming the service from being an adjunct of the Church to being an adjunct of the medical profession, both of them self-limiting roles. In the 1960s, however, the certainty of a set of new functions being given to the service created for it an opportunity to develop a strengthened occupational base, with its particular and distinct role, functions, knowledge, and professional technology.

Community corrections: the 1950s, in spite of an increase in the service's size and work, saw a proportionate decrease in the number of young offenders placed on probation and an increase in the proportions fined (Grunhut 1956: 71). This reflected both the greater affluence of the period – an obvious precondition for the use of fines to control the working classes (Rusche and Kirchheimer 1939: ch. 10) – and the necessity, resulting from the increased number of offenders, for a simple, swift, and economical disposal. But the service developed in other ways. The Streatfeild Report of 1961 gave greater centrality in the court process to probation reports, which were now not simply to assess an offender's suitability for probation but 'the likely effect on the offender's criminal career of probation *or some other specified form of sentence*' (italics added). This policy was further extended in 1974 when a Home Office Circular (194/74) suggested that 'an experienced probation officer' could make recommendations for other than probation disposals – a suggestion, it must be said, which largely had the effect of giving sanction to an existing practice. It was this circular, however, which officially transformed the report into a quasi-sentencing document (Harris 1985) and increased the quasi-judicial functions of the service. In 1965 came responsibility for the after-care of discharged prisoners; in 1966 for prison welfare; in 1967 for statutory licences of young offenders; in 1968 for parole; in 1972 for suspended sentence supervision orders; and, gradually from 1972, for community service orders (Jarvis 1974).

These duties reflected the early stages of a new set of functions which clearly rendered inadequate the idea of 'casework' as the centre of the professional repertoire of the service. The 1970s saw serious overcrowding in British gaols and the idea of decarceration emerging, in Britain and overseas, not only for offenders but also for mental patients and other institutionalized people (Scull 1977). When successive home secretaries portrayed the service as a likely provider of a range of non-custodial penalties, and when Roy Jenkins in particular described it as being at the centre of the government's penal policy, the inevitability of the service's transformation from a caring service for the marginal offender was clear: the moral regeneration of the hapless and helpless would inevitably be less central in professional ideologies than crime prevention strategies and non-custodial containment.

Doubtless the probation service shook its collective head in bemusement, but its managers came to embrace their role with some alacrity, seizing the new resources on offer with vigour:

'In the period 1972–75 the number of whole-time probation officers

The development of welfare

increased by 32 per cent, bringing the total to 4,869.'
(*Report on the Work of the Probation and After-Care Department 1972-75*, para. 50)

This figure in turn represented an increase in manpower of over 300 per cent since 1958, but equally significantly the period saw a huge increase in the appointment of supervisory grades, so that a small service of professionally motivated but appallingly paid staff became a more complex organization offering probation officers for the first time a realistic vertical career structure. The price to be paid for this was, of course, that increasing constraints were imposed on their previous autonomy, an autonomy often exercised idiosyncratically but excused by the confidentiality and uniqueness of the officer-client relationship.

In part such a structure was made necessary by the formation in 1971 of the local authority social services departments (of which more later) which, with their superior career structure, attracted the interest of many probation officers. The probation service had, therefore, to compete, and did so successfully (*Report on the Work of the Probation and After-Care Department 1972-75*, para. 56) principally by instituting salary comparability between probation officers and social workers (*Report on the Butterworth Inquiry into the Work and Pay of Probation Officers and Social Workers*, 1972). But this reactive explanation is only partial. It will be remembered too that most juvenile offenders were, from 1971, to be supervised by social workers, thereby paving the way for the probation service to concentrate its efforts on precisely those more difficult, adult offenders who would seem likely to require some kind of close and controlled supervision. This intention reflected a political disillusionment with both the efficacy and the economics of the institution (Scull 1977). The bureaucratization of the probation service, therefore, not only reflected certain changes which were occurring in the government's penal and criminal justice policies, but was simultaneously essential if those policies were to succeed. This becomes quite clear when we look forward only to 1974, and to what was to become known as the battle of the Younger Report.

This report, properly *Young Adult Offenders: Report of the Advisory Council on the Penal System* (Home Office 1974), was a clear and explicit attempt to blur the boundaries between institutional and community control, and made plain that the probation service was to be the means of achieving this elision. Though the twenty-one members of the Council who took part in the review produced among them no fewer than five notes of dissent and one of reservation, they were agreed on two new disposals being made available for young adult offenders, of which the first, the Custody and Control Order, makes the point perfectly:

> 'The term "custody and control order" emphasises our view that detention in a custodial establishment is to be seen not as an isolated experience . . . but as the beginning of a period of control and supervision, partly in custody and partly in the community.'
> (Home Office 1974: para. 178)

Courts were to set the boundary of the order, but the determination of how much of it should be spent in custody and how much in the community was to be the responsibility of the executive on the advice of, among others, the probation officers who were to supervise the non-custodial elements of the orders. Failure to conform with an officer's instructions could lead to a return to custody. But whereas the custody and control order really tightened up existing probation arrangements exercised, for example, in relation to parolees, the supervision and control order gave probation officers a significant new duty:

> 'In our investigation of methods employed in California we found that a practice has developed whereby a supervising officer occasionally has an offender removed to temporary detention . . . *we recommend that a supervisor . . . should be empowered to apply to a magistrate for a warrant authorising the arrest of the offender . . . for a maximum period of 72 hours.*' (Italics original. Home Office 1974: paras 284–85)

These proposals were defeated, principally as a result of strong representations from probation officers rejecting what they saw as a significant and undesirable shift away from 'care' and in the direction of 'control'. But the battle was only part of a lengthy period of uncertainty within the probation service in the 1970s, a phase of ambivalence which typically accompanies radical change (Marris 1974; but see also Raynor 1985: ch. 1). The new functions of the 1960s had had a cumulative impact on the service to which it had largely failed to adjust; its very existence had been threatened by the formation of social services departments and the suggestion that they should subsume the probation service; its role in the juvenile court had diminished; and the Younger Report was a decisive step in the direction of the community-controlling functions for which it was destined. The literature of the time – about whether 'care' and 'control' were compatible (see for example Harris 1977, 1980) and about new practice paradigms (Bottoms and McWilliams 1979) reflected these uncertainties and ambivalences, which have to a large degree subsequently been resolved in the direction of community corrections, for assuredly the probation service during this phase changed utterly. In this sense the victory of the probation officers against the Younger Report was against the tide, as the probation service adopted a vast range of new strategies to meet varied needs in new ways, a practice of diversification which as one writer from within the probation service memorably put it, was 'a strategy in search of a theory' (Millard 1979). But to other officers, matters were altogether simpler: the niceties of occupational coherence and meaning, whatever professional debates they aroused, meant little to the probation service's paymasters:

> 'Overnight we have accepted a 17.5% salary increase. . . . That's been a great deal about how to buy the probation service off and put us in the law and order league. . . . Suddenly [we've] jumped overnight into whole different political conceptions of where we stand. . . . We're not social workers.'
>
> (Quoted in Fielding 1984: 164–65)

The probation service did not need new orders to make it an agency of increased control, for more subtle forms of incorporation would operate equally effectively. By challenging the service to take increasing 'risks' by supervising more serious offenders, government was able to construct around the idea of *decarceration* an occupational purpose which would replace both Christian salvation and clinical casework. Decarceration necessitated the acquisition of a range of new skills and methods; new facilities would be needed and could in some circumstances be centrally funded. These changes were presented as a professional challenge to probation officers to develop ways of meeting the needs of those 'hard to reach' clients who would otherwise have been incarcerated (see, for example, Bottoms and McWilliams 1979). Accordingly a range of 'alternatives to custody' has been developed (see, for example, Raynor 1985) themselves involving such fine calibrations of control that:

> 'Those apparently absurd administrative and research questions – When is a prison a prison or a community a community? Is the alternative an alternative? Who is half-way in and who is three quarter way out? – beckon to a future when it will be impossible to determine who exactly is enmeshed in the formal control system, and hence subject to its jurisdiction and surveillance, at any one time.'
>
> (Cohen 1985: 62–3)

The generation and dissemination of explicit priorities for the probation service followed fairly naturally (Home Office 1984) with a clear intention being expressed that the service should as a first priority ensure that it dealt with offenders who would otherwise have been incarcerated, and that by contrast the offer of help to discharged prisoners should 'only command the priority which is consistent with the main objective of implementing non-custodial measures for offenders who might otherwise receive custodial sentences' (Home Office 1984: para. VI(c)). In its statement of purpose, the Home Office made perfectly plain that any notion that the probation service might be accountable to its clients was quite recherché:

'The Probation Service . . . is concerned with preparing and giving effect to a planned and co-ordinated response to crime. It must maintain the community's confidence in its work, and contribute to the community's wider confidence that it is receiving proper protection and that the law is enforced.'(Home Office 1984: para. I)

The latter part of the probation service's expansion, then, has been strongly associated with an occupational ideology of decarceration. Indeed, without such an ideology the expansion would not have taken place. Such an ideology might have been considered a triumph for liberal influences on penal policy had it not been the case that it was accompanied by the largest prison-building programme this century, entailing the creation of almost 8,000 new places at a projected cost of £340 million.

'If community programmes were *replacing* institutions, then systems high in community places would show a less than average use of institutions. But if community was *supplementing* institutions, then systems high in community would also have an above-average use of institutions and this is just what seems to be happening.'
(Cohen 1985: 49)

This is, it need hardly be added, a matter to which we shall return later. Historically, however, we can perceive the slow but steady incorporation of the probation service into the mainstream of the State's controlling apparatus, with an extension of its principal concerns from dealing with the consequences of lawbreaking for individuals towards taking a more central position in criminal justice and penal policy. Its management of such ambiguously punitive disposals as community service orders and the day centre provisions allowed for in Schedule 11 of the Criminal Justice Act, 1982, its more general decarcerative responsibilities, its explicitly reparative programmes, and its involvement with localized victim support and crime prevention schemes have been sustained by a happy confluence of professional ideology and the favoured practices of social control.

The emergent integration of decarceration, community involvement, and the interventionism and social engineering of late Victorian paternalism and Fabianism has served to blur not only the institutional with the community-based disposal but also the preventative efforts of the State with those of the voluntary sector. Hence the community accountability emphasized in the Home Office's priorities statement (Home Office 1984) has contributed to the transformation of the probation service into an agency which is coming to direct its concerned endeavours less towards the offender and more towards the actual or potential victim population: this is community control indeed.

Social services departments

In the probation service, then, a policy trajectory emerges, but very gradually, over the century or so of the agency's existence. Social services departments represent a more sudden manifestation of this trend towards the more general surveillance and management of the deviant. These departments, which share with the probation service responsibility for operating supervision orders, are a recent amalgamation of three smaller, more specialist local authority departments offering personal social services to children, to old and handicapped people, to mentally ill people and families in difficulty (Seebohm Report 1968: Appendix F).

In one sense, the creation of these mega-departments constituted, as we shall see, a rationalization of the piecemeal responsibilities of the former departments, and it is certainly clear that the Seebohm Committee was much exercised by the confusion which resulted from uncoordinated visits being made by representatives of the different departments to the same clientele. But however benign and destigmatizing Seebohm's intended comprehensive service may have been designed to be, the location of social services departments within the armoury of local government, their relation to the social policies of central government, and their supervisory and resource allocating powers additional to those previously possessed by the former departments made it inevitable that they would find themselves mapping and acting upon the inadequacies of the poor and the deviant. The location of social services departments therefore meant by definition that the obverse of providing an efficient service for their consumers would be the equally efficient management of those same consumers (Handler 1973; Jordan 1974). In the personal social services, consumers may be either beneficiaries of a service or its targets; more frequently they are both simultaneously.

So a 'family service' with the functions of the social services department has 'problem families' as its inevitable preoccupation, however accepting and non-judgemental its staff may be in their dealings with them. The increasing co-ordination of health, education, child care, and income maintenance policies simultaneously improves the delivery of these services and comes to stem the tide of family and social dislocation by concentrating on:

> 'family behavior not serious enough to require court intervention but below the higher standard of a stable and secure family.'
>
> (Handler 1973: 60)

It is not necessary to ascribe conspiratorial motives to the originators of these departments to analyse as inevitable these twin consequences. Whereas the historical logic of the development of the probation service has been for it to move gradually from being a marginally helpful to a more centrally controlling agency, the very origins of the social services departments have created an infrastructure of power, whatever the motivations of its architects may have been.

This framework is, then, the basis of our understanding of social services departments. But no more than the basis, for the manner in which social services departments actually exercise, or refrain from exercising, their powers is far removed from the efficiency and routinization which one might, from this short introduction, expect. Indeed, it is in part because the origins of these departments cannot be analysed conspiratorially, or the departments themselves as monoliths, that the equivocations which we shall devote a good part of this book to describing have come about. In this brief section we shall etch some aspects of the historical progression of the local authority social services sector, and then introduce in rudimentary form some of the issues which we believe affect the day-to-day practices of service delivery in these departments. Our historical section will be even shorter than the space we devoted to the probation service, for to write the history of social services departments would be, as will become clear later, to write the history of child care, the Poor Law, and the psychiatric and education services, as well as of such charitable provision as existed for particular need groups. This cannot be done, and is best not attempted except to the extent that it is necessary to do so in order to demonstrate that the convergence of a range of conflicting and at times contradictory traditions in the social services department has created serious and hitherto unsolved problems of occupational meaning for the heirs to these disparate traditions, the social workers themselves. We shall try to show that whereas in the probation service the fairly steady evolution we have been describing has created a relatively coherent structure which is able to shape and give meaning to the particular task of supervising young offenders on supervision orders, this is not the case with social services departments, whose employees have had, among other things, to adapt a professional adherence to supporting children in need to an occupational task of supervising children who constitute a threat. The contradictory traditions and functions of social services departments, therefore, ironically undercut the decisiveness of the departments' location as implementers of a wide and impressive range of social policies, and create an equally ironic gap between the power available to the departments and the studied equivocation with which it is exercised.

It will by now be plain that social services departments and the probation service differ significantly in certain aspects of their history, tradition, and function, but also that they have significant meeting-points. Both of them inhabit the same hazy ground between courts and welfare, and their employees have the same training and qualification. The social services tradition is a complex one, an amalgamation of remnants of the Poor Law, health and psychiatric services, education, an American tradition of voluntary casework, child care, and the development of the municipal corporations in the nineteenth century. Since social services departments were themselves formed only in 1971, the integration of these traditions into a coherent professional activity has been only partially achieved; and the problem of creating a particular professional frame of reference for the management of the new supervision orders overlays these more fundamental questions of occupational identity and function.

Though the probation tradition has always been to be associated with the criminal justice and penal systems, the service has never embodied either of those traditions. Indeed for many years much of the probation officer's work was with just the very young offenders who are now supervised by social workers. The child care and criminal justice systems have, as we demonstrated in Chapter 1, had a certain relationship since the formation of reformatory schools in the 1850s. In that both are charged with the socialization of the deviant young (Poster 1978), they form administratively distinct but conceptually and functionally related parts of the State's social control apparatus.

But how did social services departments come into being? To etch an answer to this question it is necessary to recall the situation after the war, when the Children and Criminal Justice Acts, 1948, briefly placed a wedge between the activities of the probation service and the then children's departments of the local authorities. We have seen that for a number of reasons this wedge was temporary; even at the most simple and obvious level of practice the realities of the jobs of the two agencies were such that probation officers and child care officers often found themselves dealing with the same problems and the same families.

But at a level of policy also there was an overlap. Jean Packman's case study of the Oxfordshire Children's Department shows how that department extended its activities beyond its formal remit largely on the basis of the ideologies and the political successes of its senior managers. So Oxfordshire invested considerable resources in developing preventive services for young people, and a part of this prevention involved 'admitting greater numbers of children to care and keeping some of them in care for a considerable time' (Packman 1981: 110). This rather familiar policy was buttressed, as had been the use of reformatory schools a century earlier, by a falling crime rate which was attributed to the Oxfordshire policy. Its effect from our own point of view is to emphasize that the children's departments never carved out a policy area qualitatively different from that of the probation service. Indeed it would have been rather surprising had they been able to do so.

Prior to the setting up of the social services departments in 1971 (Local Authority Social Services Act, 1970) when Oxfordshire's proactive policy was at its peak, the government's attempt to blur still further the boundaries between the child care and criminal justice systems took the form of locating juvenile justice within the new departments, departments which were themselves to be geared to working with families and communities (Hall 1976). The institution of the Seebohm Committee, whose influential report led directly to the 1970 Act was foreshadowed as early as 1960 (Ingleby Report: para. 47), and was recommended in *The Child, the Family and the Young Offender*, which called for an inquiry into how local authority services would have to be changed to translate provisions for delinquents into a family service. The Seebohm Report itself called this recommendation 'the immediate point of origin of the committee' (Seebohm Report 1968: para. 30) and suggested that the recommendation stemmed from 'a concern at the increase in officially recorded delinquency, the need to concentrate resources and a belief that preventative work with families was of cardinal importance in this context'. It was the committee's strong hope that this responsibility would be located entirely in the new departments:

'the social service department, rather than the probation and after-care service, should carry the responsibility for providing a social work service for the courts, for supervising and assisting young people in the community, and for aftercare work with young people who have left the new kinds of residential provision which are proposed. This work would be part of the general responsibilities the department would have for all other children committed to its care and for social work with those in special schools.'

(Seebohm Report 1968: para. 265)

Although precluded from reviewing the probation service, at several points the committee hinted that the service should either be brought into line with, or subsumed by, the new departments (see, for example, paragraphs 256 and 704). In Scotland the probation service had been abolished in the Social Work (Scotland) Act, 1968, and services for all offenders were made the responsibility of the new social work departments. That this did not occur in England and Wales has already been explained, and nor did social services take over sole responsibility for young offenders. Hence it is that offenders supervised by social workers encounter in the waiting room of their local office not parolees, young adults on statutory licence, and serious offenders on community service orders, but the old and infirm, physically and mentally handicapped people, foster parents, and families in difficulty. The organizational context of their supervision, in short, differs markedly from that experienced by their fellow miscreants queuing up in the probation office down the road. This is not accidental; certain differences in practice between probation officers and social workers reflect not chance variations based on personality or idiosyncracy of a kind which, in an imperfect world, we cheerfully tolerate, but a patterned difference about the very nature and purpose of a supervision order. This organizational division is the administrative corollary of the policy ambiguity at the heart of the juvenile justice system: offenders must be punished, and hence cannot be removed entirely from the criminal justice system; but they have also to be reformed, and if the governing ideology of the system is that problems are caused and have their solution in the family and the community, then it is natural that their reformation should be sought through a medium geared to working in those settings. In short the continuation of both probation and social services departments reflects a crude compromise based almost certainly on a lack of political will. Not surprisingly, the younger, more marginal delinquents are generally the responsibility of social workers; the rest are left to the exercise by probation officers of what they regard as their particular skills and experience in the control of offenders.

The experience of social workers in court since 1971 (when the 1969 Act was implemented and also when social services departments were instituted) has not been especially auspicious. The social workers have taken their place close to the centre of the juvenile court stage, only to find that, far from being a liberalizing influence on court practice, they have had to engage with the various conflicting sentencing objectives which courts themselves face daily (Harris 1982, 1985). They have had to address the possibility of punishment and the necessity of control, the integration of justice and welfare systems having logically involved each taking on some attributes of the other.

The early days of social workers' involvement in the juvenile court were rife with complaints by magistrates and clerks to the justices about their ineptitude in court, their unfamiliarity with procedures, and the quality of their reports. Social workers were typically not at all motivated to take their job by the prospect of working with offenders, and the activity itself constituted a very small part of departmental workloads. It is not surprising, therefore, that this aspect of the work generated anxiety and uncertainty (Webb and Harris 1984), emotions heightened by the collapse, during the early days of their activities, of any professional belief in treatment, and a development of the belief that the principles of retributive justice would at the very least be less harmful to young offenders than were the activities of the welfare workers themselves. Our research suggests that on the whole probation officers assimilated their management of supervision orders into their normal practices of office reporting, periodic home visits, and occasional group and other activities. But social workers did not have this organizational routine on which to fall back; nor it seems, did they wish to replicate it. Indeed the very structure of open plan social services offices with a typically chaotic set of arrangements for booking interviewing rooms made such a pattern difficult to follow in many offices, and the lack of a 'report night' arrangement of the kind which existed in probation offices (which meant that the presence of a particular officer would be guaranteed between set hours on a particular day of the week) doubtless acted as a disincentive to the casual client calling in with a problem to discuss.

But the matter was not simply one of practices and routines. Social workers did face a serious problem, for in the very decision to hand to them responsibility for supervising young offenders there lay a particular message that what was wanted was something different from that which probation officers normally did. There was, in short, an assumption among social workers that a new *modus operandi* was necessary, but no real indication from central government or the professional association as to what it should be. So the Department of

Health and Social Security's (DHSS) guide for the regional planning of intermediate treatment (DHSS 1972) was widely, and justifiably, regarded as vacuous: it begins with a Foreword by the secretary of state ('The wider the opportunities and satisfactions which our society offers its members, the more acute are the problems of adjustment which it poses to a minority of young people') (DHSS 1972: 5), and ends with a list of hypothetical youth facilities to which intermediate treatment schemes might be attached, for the guidance of regional planning committees ('Barset Junior Farmers' Club . . . Buttering No 3 Scout Company'). Almost equally unhelpful was the handbook produced by the social workers' own professional association, the British Association of Social Workers (BASW 1978), which described four models of delinquency in as many pages, assured its readers that 'Social work with juvenile offenders presents the practitioner with virtually every moral and personal dilemma currently available to the profession' (BASW 1978: 8), and after sections on groupwork (four pages) and 'the nature of adolescence' (half a page) concluded with a total of twenty-six recommendations to almost everybody except social workers themselves, including the local health authority and the chief executive's department.

So what were social workers to do? In constructing their *modus operandi* they could scarcely ignore the criminal justice context from which the supervision order emerged without alienating courts, police, and public; but if they merely replicated the probation service's practices they would find it difficult to justify their continuing role as supervisors; and if they opted for some *via media*, a convenient compromise, they faced the charge from without of inconsistency and injustice and the sense from within of *Angst*, of a lack of occupational coherence. These are matters to which we return in Chapter 4 when we explore just how the social workers have responded. At present, the sense we wish to convey is of a new organization with former members of a range of different specialist departments, accustomed to calling themselves 'child care officers' or 'welfare officers' or 'mental welfare officers' suddenly being called social workers; with their own occupational meaning, typically still linked to a particular client group whom they 'understood', itself largely fractured. The process of creating social services departments was frequently rife with acrimony and chaos; there was miscommunication between managers and staff; intense rivalry over appointments to key positions; the over-promotion to senior management posts of people without management skills. There were co-ordinated routines to be established, new teams having to gell, new tasks; and the promised resources seemed in practice either not to have arrived or, if they had arrived, to have been used by management for the wrong purpose. (Satyamurti, 1981, gives a vivid account of the formation of a social services department.)

In addition to all this upheaval, the Children and Young Persons Act, 1969, was implemented on the very day these new generic departments came into being and, squeezed in among the emotional and intellectual energy needed just to survive, had to be found the scope to work out what was to be done with the adolescents who had been handed over to be supervised by the new departments, a majority of whose workers had in all probability never set foot inside a magistrates' court.

Of course the competence of social services departments has improved immeasurably since those early days, but still the supervision of delinquents for many social workers sits uneasily with their professional orientations to sick or handicapped people or to young children. So as the probation service in the 1980s has developed an increasing sense of occupational coherence – we shall speak of it in Chapter 4 as organizational resolve – around the idea of decarceration, the social services department has had no such common denominator to give either unity or coherence to its tasks. Instead a range of different strategies has emerged, from the pursuit of specialisms within the department to a more general sense of uncertainty which we *believe* pervades much of their work and are *certain* impacts on their supervision of young offenders.

But in spite of the inter-organizational differences between the two agencies, we have tried to show in these first two chapters that together with aspects of the development of the juvenile justice system itself the two agencies collectively constitute an increasing state sponsorship of 'altruism under social auspices'. We have spoken of the creation of a category of troubled *and* troublesome youngsters which has emerged from this process of blurring the boundaries and from this in turn the increasing tendency to render the *family* as the unit both of the problem and, hence, of the cure. These factors together constitute the substantive preface of our ensuing attempt to proffer a conceptual map which makes sense of this abundance of historical, legal, and administrative data. Hence it is to be the macro, mezzo, and micro levels of analysis of the supervisory process that we now turn.

3 The macro level: welfare work and the State

'There is no need for the state to act as parent and teacher if parent and teacher can be made to act like the state.'
(Cohen 1985: 136)

'. . . who overcomes
By force, hath overcome but half his foe'
(Milton, *Paradise Lost*, 1: ll. 648–49)

Our subject matter is that nexus of State activity which concerns itself with the care of the needy child, the control of the delinquent child, and the management of the adult offender. In treating our area of study historically we can clearly see that the last century has witnessed an inexorable but often invisible increase in the amount of State control exercised over the young. This should not surprise us, for a similar process has occurred throughout much of the industrialized world (Boli-Bennett and Meyer 1978). The blurring of the boundary between the judicial and the social – the welfarization of crime and the juridicization of need – has been both the means and the end of this process.

At the same time that the controlling net has widened, the social conditions which in Victorian England were taken by liberal reformers to have been the cause of much crime have improved immeasurably. While it is perfectly true that social inequality persists on a grand scale, the theory could no longer be seriously propounded that crime results from starvation or vagrancy, or from the social pathology of a brutalized poor, and liberal or radical reformers are accordingly left with more nebulous targets for their attacks (see, for example, Taylor 1981; Lea and Young 1984).

Yet the lay observer who is unwise enough to assume that this combination of State control and social amelioration must have made at least some inroads into the problem of juvenile crime can be quickly and easily disabused. Indeed in its minor manifestations delinquency seems almost a universal pastime among the young (West and Farrington 1973; Belson 1975), and those of us professionally involved with matters of crime and punishment have the regular and dispiriting experience of being decidedly less clear about what can be done to stop it than are our friends and neighbours from other walks of life. Faced with such a depressing thought, it is difficult sometimes to avoid the positivist trap of comparing the huge advances made over the last century in the pure and natural sciences with the rather static quality of our knowledge about crime.

Certainly the naive reformer of today makes remarkably similar assumptions and deploys similar arguments to those of a century ago. Playfair and Sington, for example, entitle the first three chapters of their book 'Why Imprisonment Must Go', 'What Society Should Tolerate', and 'Civilised Prevention of Crime' (Playfair and Sington 1965); and Martin Wright informs us, as though this were new knowledge rather than tired old truths replicated and ignored for so many years, that:

> 'Many aspects of imprisonment are ineffective and inhumane. It isolates people from their families, and deprives them of their jobs. . . . Many are already poor, and prison makes them more so; many have committed only minor crimes.' (Wright 1972: 19)

And so on a thousand times. In the juvenile sphere we see a familiar pattern of administrative response to an intractable problem: an old provision is replaced by a new one, similar in many respects but with increasingly flexible powers and new, psychologically positive, and above all destigmatizing nomenclature. When reformation and industry were in vogue, what could be more natural than to save children from prison by placing them in reformatory and industrial schools? When these fell into disuse, approved schools emphasized the merits of education (it being, by the 1930s, no longer considered socially dangerous to teach literacy to the children of the poor); and, approved schools having themselves in time acquired stigmatic connotations, with what, other than 'community homes', could they be replaced in a decade whose twin social policy obsessions were with 'community' and 'family'?

But, archaic and dehumanizing or modern and sanitized, our arrangements for dealing with the sad and the bad have quite failed to stem a vast increase in recorded crime. This in turn has led to a considerable increase in the number of penal measures introduced to respond to it. Curiously, the more unsuccessful such measures have been in halting or detecting crime, the more resonant have been the calls for more of them. So far as welfare work is concerned, few studies indeed suggest that it has been effectively reductionist (M. Shaw, 1974, is one that does), and even fewer are sufficiently precise to give one confidence that they are replicable (see, for example, Martinson 1974; Klein 1979; H. Jones 1981). Such reservations have had little discernible impact on the proliferation of such services. Unless, therefore, it is to be assumed that there exists at the very highest levels of government a patience in comparison with which the response of Job to his tribulations appears both petulant and vituperative, it must be the case that the elimination of need and the reduction of crime, though doubtless desirable in themselves, are not prerequisites for the continued employment of the experts.

This thought is the starting-point for the ensuing consideration of the social and political purposes of the ever-growing presence of the experts in the juvenile court. Such an enquiry cannot be conducted satisfactorily within the limits we have had to set for it, but it is possible within that space to etch an argument which helps us begin to comprehend at least some aspects of the developing net of social control.

Power and control

The idea of power is one of our guides on this part of our enquiry, as it must inevitably be in any consideration of attempts to regulate the disruptions to social order brought about by deviants. We have already referred – and shall do again – to the emergence of State officials, the experts, whose duty it is to proffer advice on the disposal of the troubled and troublesome, and to the fact that this has increasingly been achieved by the legitimation of their knowledge. It is through this medium of expertise that contemporary social control is exercised, though this is but one means by which the employment of power more generically understood takes place, for at its broadest it refers to 'the possibility of imposing one's will upon the behaviour of other persons' (Weber, quoted in Bendix 1966: 290). This clearly allows for an abundance of situations in which power is exercised; the question of upon what precise bases (the source, nature, and means of implementation) the exercise of those intentions might be fixed (even in the face of resistance) is an empirical one, and offers a pathway into a perception of power as variegated, secured by a diversity of potential resources in a multitude of social relationships. While power may derive from a constellation of interests (that flowing from the class which owns the means of production is a particular instance of this), it has also to be understood as a process of securing the right to command, and establishing in others the duty to obey (Bendix 1966).

If Weber leaned more to the former of these analytical concerns, that is to say identifying the undergirding interests from which springs the exercise of power to meet certain objectives, it is to a more contemporary writer that we turn for help in comprehending in almost microscopic detail the mechanisms and 'strategical devices' by which power manifests itself. To Michel Foucault, power is an everyday experience, and he takes the fine sieve and camel-haired brush of the archaeologist to reveal the detail engraved on its surface. Power is immanent in social relations: all people exercise it and have it exercised upon them. Though to say this is to simplify, the notion that power is to Foucault what sex is to Freud and class to Marx gives the flavour of its centrality in his work (though for a fuller discussion of this feature of Foucault's work, see Smart 1985: ch. 3):

> 'There are certain categories of person – children, prisoners, the "insane" – whose ability to exercise power is severely limited, but few members of these groups do not find some means of exercising power, if only on each other. Power is not, therefore, to be identified with the state, a central apparatus that can be seized. The state is rather an overall strategy and effect, a composite result made up of a multiplicity of centres and mechanisms, so many states within states with complex networks of common citizenship. Factories, housing estates, hospitals, schools, families, are among the more evident, more formalized of such "micropowers".'
>
> (Sheridan 1980: 218–9)

Foucault is of no 'school', but his own master, and his theoretical allegiances have shifted, at times almost incomprehensibly, since his early work, based on his doctoral thesis, published in English in *Madness and Civilization* (Foucault 1967). It is quite incorrect to say, as Jones and Fowles do, that Foucault is a structuralist (Jones and Fowles 1984): he has repudiated both structuralism and post-structuralism as well as hermeneutics and existentialism (Dreyfus and Rabinow 1982) and Marxism (Smart 1983). The influence on his analytic framework of all these schools is evident to varying degrees, but none of them fully encompasses his elusive and dialectical mode of enquiry. He has successively used metaphors of archaeology and genealogy to describe his historical method, a method elegantly if paradoxically described by two leading Foucaultologists as 'interpretive analytics' (Dreyfus and Rabinow 1982: xxii). Foucault is, therefore, a *Foucaultiste* pure and simple; his method of enquiry is probably too idiosyncratic for it to be possible for *Foucaultisme* to become a school itself, but the intellectual thrust, the iconoclasm, the sense of irony which Foucault has brought to the study – not of history itself, but of what he terms the history of the present – have indubitably had a liberating function for a number of subsequent writers, particularly in France, but also in North America. Indeed, it is certainly true that 'to write today about punishment and classification without Foucault, is like talking about the unconscious without Freud' (Cohen 1985: 10).

Foucault's world is one of paradox. There is no 'State' except as a conventional reification, and there is no 'class interest' in the sense in which the vulgar Marxist speaks of such a notion. Indeed the very idea of a 'State' or a 'class' as a phenomenon whose logic can appropriately plot the path of analytic enquiry is a misleading one. Yet there is power, and power applied differentially within the social world; it is exercised, and has been historically, by kings on criminals and by psychiatrists on patients, and to deny it would be 'hypocritical or naive' (Foucault 1977: 276). Nor is there a huge conspiracy which rules our lives, from which, always in the name of class domination, comes very political act, its repressive or liberating surface revealing beneath it a set of practices concerned with nothing so much as the protection of privilege. The vulgar Marxist is deceived in this, in arriving at an answer and fitting the question into it. Yet if there is no organized conspiracy, and class domination is not a central issue, there are everywhere plots and power struggles, devices to seize more power, to have one's own way. Indeed nothing so significantly characterizes the world of social intercourse as machinations and manipulations of this very kind:

> 'According to Foucault the task of the genealogist is to destroy the primacy of origins, of unchanging truths. He seeks to destroy the doctrines of development and progress. Having destroyed ideal significations and original truths, he looks to the play of wills. Subjection, domination, and combat are found everywhere he looks. Whenever he hears talk of meaning and value, of virtue and goodness, he looks for strategies of domination . . . [Foucault] sees all psychological motivation not as the source but as the result of strategies without strategists.'
> (Dreyfus and Rabinow 1982: 108–09)

And there are paradoxes too in his method of enquiry. He cannot be the dispassionate observer studying the workings of humanity as if in a laboratory:

> 'A doctor can stand outside a patient and treat him objectively, but a practitioner of interpretive analytics has no such external position. The disease he seeks to cure is part of an epidemic which has also affected him.' (Dreyfus and Rabinow 1982: 202)

The meaning and logic of his own interpretations, therefore, are located in the same frame of reference as the object of interpretation itself, a tautologous process and internally contradictory. Yet not to interpret is to take at face value the interpretations of others and hence to interpret by default. It is an impasse which Foucault has sought to transcend by structuring his analysis around certain central symbols of human action: madness, sexuality, the creation of the institution. Taking one of these symbols he offers, not a new interpretation of it, for, there being no essential truth through which to penetrate, such an approach can do no more than uncover further interpretations, but an interpretation of interpretations, a metahistory of the symbol, its purpose and use. So to study hidden sexuality involves not the conventional skills of the archivist, uncovering for the first time what had hitherto been hidden, but an enquiry into the subject's own hiddenness, itself a highly visible phenomenon. *Why* should sexuality be hidden? What purposes does such a process serve? (Foucault 1979). Or, in relation to our own focus, *why* should there suddenly seem an upsurge of interest in reformation, in educating the young, in 'humanitarianism'?

In Foucault's world, a world without objective truth yet where subjectivism is incomplete and unsatisfactory, the material driving force is power. Power not just – or even principally – as a repressive force, imposed from above, designed to prevent, to deter, to halt, but power as a force for transformation, as having positive purpose, for shaping a world. This position is itself an assumption, justified by Foucault, convincingly or not, in part by the fact that his *locus* of enquiry is the surface action not the concealed pursuit of some abstraction, be it class interest or the investigation of the repressed psyche. As a hypothesis which is not only empirically unverifiable but also on occasion defended by Foucault with scant regard for conventional historical method, it does demand from its readers a degree of imaginative sympathy which is not always present. When it is lacking (see, for example, Jones and Fowles 1984) one observes the clash of two incompatible intellectual traditions. Our own position in this chapter is that Foucault's analysis of power and control (Foucault 1977) offers a helpful explanatory framework but does not in all respects explain happily or easily the development and practice of the English and Welsh child care and juvenile justice systems. Later in this chapter we begin to show why this is so. But as an analysis of the social purpose of supervision, it will serve rather well for the first part of our own enquiry.

To Foucault, conventional histories of penality, structured around the notion that it is steadily and progressively being 'reformed' (Gordon Rose's title *The Struggle for Penal Reform*, 1961, gives the flavour of this) incorrectly identify as the main objective of the process a humanitarianism which, if it exists at all, is incidental to the enterprise:

> 'one runs the risk of positing as the principle of greater leniency in punishment processes of individualization that are rather one of the effects of the new tactics of power.' (Foucault 1977: 23)

Tracing penal history triphasically – through torture and punishment to discipline – Foucault argues that it is not the compassion of the punisher but the logic of penality which has shifted. Torture was by no means a form of primitive vengeance, but 'a technique whereby minutely calibrated amounts of pain could be administered to the criminal's body' (Sheridan 1980: 140), to demonstrate not so much that vengeance was terrible as that the power of the sovereign (against whose body all crime was seen to be directed) was in all wise superior to that of the criminal.

In the second phase, under the influence of the Enlightenment philosophers, themselves the product of a society in which economic and political power had shifted to an emergent and affluent merchant class, crime took on a quite different form; it became a breach of the social contract which gave both rights and duties to citizens:

> 'His life is not now, as it once was, merely nature's gift to him. It is something that he holds, on terms, from the State. . . . The evildoer who attacks the fabric of social right becomes, by reason of his crime, a rebel and a traitor to his country. By violating its laws he ceases to be a member of it, and may almost be said to have made war upon it. The preservation, therefore, of the State is seen to be incompatible with his own continued existence.'
> (Rousseau 1762: Book II, ch. V, 1947 edn)

But exclusion or execution of this kind was by no means always deemed either necessary or legitimate. Beccaria maintained in 1764 that since man was not his own creator, his right to destroy life was circumscribed by the Utilitarian calculus that in so doing a greater evil must be thereby averted (cited in Tuttle 1961: 2). The possibility of reformation was beginning to take root, and with it a further significant change: a move from the willing severance of the social contract to a view in which a departure from a 'just' and free society could only be grasped as stemming from impaired reason (Donnelly 1983):

> 'What was now beginning to emerge was a modulation that referred to the defendant himself, to his nature, to his way of life and his attitude of mind, to his past, to the "quality" and not to the intention of his will. One perceives, but as a place yet unfilled, the

locus in which, in penal practice, psychological knowledge will take over the role of casuistic jurisprudence.' (Foucault 1977: 99)

So, with the onset of the factory system and its requirement for docile labour, came the penitentiary with its experiments in the exercise of power (Rusche and Kirchheimer 1939; Melossi and Pavarini 1981). Of course it would be analytically crude to perceive the penitentiaries as simply providing for the needs of the factories as though the creation of a whole penality stemmed from some idea among the industrialists and those who represented their interests that this would be the best way of managing their affairs:

> 'the slow growth of disciplinary technology preceded the rise of capitalism – in both a temporal and a logical sense. These technologies did not cause the rise of capitalism but were the technological preconditions for its success.'
> (Dreyfus and Rabinow 1982: 135)

Foucault speaks of France; the same is true in Britain and the USA. In both these latter countries the penitentiary became a laboratory in the exercise of power. The debates in nineteenth-century penology among adherents of the silent, solitary, and separate systems of prison management (S. Webb and B. Webb 1922) were structured around precisely this kind of issue (see, for example, Ignatieff 1978: 193 *et seq.*; Garland 1985; and, for a fascinating account of the systems as portrayed in Dickens's novels, Collins 1962: *passim*). Was it preferable to seek to change the character by means of solitary contemplation or by a controlled exposure to temptation, in laboratory conditions?

It was with the experimental possibilities of the *Panopticon* (Bentham 1791) that Foucault was especially fascinated. The full title page of Bentham's work makes plain that the plan was far more than a technical suggestion for building a prison: it represented, in Foucault's terms, a central symbol of power.

> '*Panopticon; or, The Inspection-House*: containing the Idea of a New Principle of Construction applicable to any sort of Establishment in which Persons of any Description are to be Kept under Inspection; and in particular to Penitentiary-Houses, Prisons, Houses of Industry, Work-houses, Poor-houses, Manufactories, Madhouses, Lazarettos, Hospitals and Schools: with a Plan of Management adapted to the Principle.' (Bentham 1791)

The inmates of the Panopticon could, at any time, and unbeknown to them, be observed in their cells and be liable for reward or punishment according to their behaviour:

The macro level: welfare work and the State

'Ideal perfection, if that were the object, would require that each person should actually be in that predicament, during every instant of time. This being impossible, the next thing to be wished for is, that, at every instant . . . he should *conceive* himself to be so.'

(Bentham 1791: Letter I)

The technology of the Panopticon created, where the actual exercise of power was impossible, an illusion of power. But beyond that the Panopticon represented to Foucault the very essence of a *disciplinary society*, where power was exercised not merely by inspectors on inmates, but by senior on junior inspectors as well; and potentially, as the ranks of inspectors multiplied, and as the categories of prisoner diversified, power would be exercised at such a multiplicity of levels that for all but the very highest and the very lowest ranks the exercise of power would become almost literally indistinguishable from subjection to it:

'Another very important advantage, whatever purposes the plan may be applied to, particularly where it is applied to the severest and most coercive purposes, is, that the *under* keepers or inspectors, the servants and subordinates of every kind, will be under the same irresistible control with respect to the *head* keeper or inspector, as the prisoners or other persons to be governed are with respect to *them*. . . . It presents an answer, and that a satisfactory one, to one of the most puzzling of political questions – *quis custodiet ipsos custodies?*. . . . It is this circumstance that renders the influence of this plan not less beneficial to what is called *liberty*, than to necessary coercion; not less powerful as a control upon subordinate power, than as a curb to delinquency.' (Bentham 1791: Letter VI)

The minute calibration of power, therefore, was to become a protector of the powerless against the abuses of their superiors. Its effect was to locate power in the hands of fewer, doubtless wiser and more moral persons. But the essence of this power was not its negativity, its repressive potential, so much as its generative force; its concern was not so much – or not only – with the elimination of the undesirable as with the promotion of the desirable: with a positive transformation.

'Power is not simply repressive: it is also productive. It is here that the role of the body becomes crucial. Power subjects bodies not to render them passive, but to render them active. The forces of the body are trained and developed with a view to making them productive.'

(Sheridan 1980: 219)

Of course the disparity between the theory of the prison laboratory and the reality of prison life was immense in Victorian England, and the avoidance of recognition and communication impossible. The experimental systems were, even at their height, being attacked as unrealistic, their intentions unenforceable:

> 'Indeed, the system savours somewhat of absurdity no less than unnatural severity; for it is preposterous to place several hundreds of criminals in association, and yet expect them not to communicate by words or signs. . . . "The posture of stooping", observes Mr Kingsmill, "in which the prisoners work at picking oakum, gives ample opportunity of carrying on a lengthened conversation, without much chance of discovery; so that the rule of silence is a dead letter to many".' (Day 1858: 254)

This avoidance of the disciplines of the penitentiary leads us to a further point. Once the target of power had expanded to the extent of controlling the total lives of these 'hundreds of criminals' by means other than total solitude, power itself came to succeed not only by the achievement of compliance but also in the means afforded it for further expansion by resistance itself. When power takes on as a target that which it cannot conceivably subdue – crime, sexual behaviour – the successful resistances which emerge come to justify the still further spread of power. But there is, of course, a paradox here, for resistance to power not only has the effect of expanding its application but also and simultaneously of circumscribing it, a circumscription which features, we think, insufficiently in Foucault's analysis. Yet the idea that power spreads ironically through its own failure is central to his analysis; we can certainly see too that the failure of the separate and silent systems to prevent contamination in the 1850s came to justify the development of the reformatories; the failure of the reformatories to do the same led to the placing of the youngest thieves in the industrial schools; the failure of the prisons led to the Borstal and probation systems, to the development of discharge on licence and hence to the increasing penetration of power into the lives and families of the criminal. It is when the boy persists in his petty thefts in the face of parental admonition that are summoned in, simultaneously or consecutively, teacher, doctor, clergyman, psychologist, psychiatrist, psychotherapist, youth leader, agony aunt, social worker, probation officer, policeman, magistrate, residential worker, and prison officer. Each expert offers a different perspective and cure involving perhaps, the deep treatment of the boy, the broad treatment of his family and friends, or both. And the boy's failure or refusal to succumb to the best efforts of these experts comes to justify each successive penetration:

'It is through the articulation of points of resistance that power spreads through the social field. But it is also, of course, through resistance that power is disrupted. Resistance is both an element of the functioning of power and a source of its perpetual disorder.'
(Dreyfus and Rabinow: 147)

So often for the most benign reasons, power multiplies in an almost infinite series of permutations of rescue attempts until finally, starkly, a choice must be made. Foucault's friend and follower, Jacques Donzelot:

'Starting with a child's occasional infraction, or with official attention being drawn by well-intentioned persons or certified specialists to the danger he risks in his family owing to the inadequate supervision he is under, a procedure of control and tutelage is set into motion, which eventually calls on him to choose between a subjection to norms and an orientation to delinquency that is difficult to reverse.' (Donzelot 1980: 113)

So resistance, failure, the departure of the messy reality from the mechanistic ideal of the disciplinary city of Panopticon contribute to the development of a system of control, of the exercise of power, structured around the classification and management of deviance. Hence the analytic error in the work of the naive historians with whose thoughts we began this chapter. The logic of their successes – the closure of this institution, the ending of that practice – both cements and transforms the existence and meaning of those institutions and practices which remain. To the extent that the institutions and practices which have gone served a necessary social function, those which remain will themselves inexorably be remoulded in such a way as to serve those selfsame functions. Hence it is that boundaries blur, euphemisms abound, and cant is rife throughout the language and constructs of the social professions; hence it is that in our final chapter we shall come back again to the idea of community control, of the decarceration of the deviant, and suggest that the decanting process which this involves by no means leaves untouched the receptacle into which the offenders are disgorged.

But it is not just that social reform has unintended consequences, rather that because power is generative it reproduces the very processes it exists to classify, those processes in turn justifying yet more control – in modern cybernetic language a deviation amplifying feedback loop:

'although legal punishment is carried out in order to punish offences, one might say that the definition of offences and their prosecution are carried out in turn in order to maintain the punitive mechanisms and their functions.' (Foucault 1977: 24)

The professionals, bureaucrats, and turnkeys who are so maintained – this vast army of politicians, civil servants, law officers, academics, judges, barristers, social workers, and the like whose status and identity depend on their being experts in a subject in which they are persistently unable to make advances – serve the purpose of processing criminals, transforming and sanitizing them, creating a social activity of 'delinquency' which itself exudes a logic which requires yet more corrective action. So the question to ask about prisons is not the one which the reformers always ask: why keep such an ineffective, expensive, and inhumane system? It is: what is it about the prison which makes it both successful and necessary?

'For the observation that prison fails to eliminate crime, one should perhaps substitute the hypothesis that prison has succeeded very well in producing delinquency.' (Foucault 1977: 272)

The sphere of the social

Between the civil – an area of private relations – and the political can be observed a more amorphous sphere concerned with the establishment of norms of behaviour and attitude best called *the social* (Donzelot 1980, 1984). At one level the social is the creation of a secular society lacking adherence to the norms of a particular set of religious or ethical principles; at another it can be viewed as a reflection of the power of miscellaneous professional groupings; historically it can be traced through the gradual assumption by the State of private endeavours to control motherhood and child-rearing (Donzelot 1980; Ehrenreich and English 1979), the rise of universal education, the trade unions, and so on. But the analysis of the causes of the social is not our present theme, which is rather to define its characteristics and consequences.

Administratively the social is represented by the construction of numerous official but non-governmental boards and councils (often, and significantly, described as 'quasi-autonomous') which, deriving their authority from Parliament but empowered to use that authority in an interpretive way, transform the nature and purpose of law and government in certain areas of its activities. For example, the Race Relations Act, 1976 established a Commission for Racial Equality (CRE) to work towards the elimination of discrimination, to promote equality of opportunity and good relations generally among people of different racial groups, and to review the working of the Act. The Commission was given wide (though by no means uncircumscribed) powers formally to investigate any aspect of these terms of reference, and though its use of these powers has been successfully challenged (Griffith 1985: 101 *et seq.*) the Commission still embodies an extension of the role of law from proscribing the illegal to prescribing the desirable. While the notion of social legislation, the monitoring of which is carried out within the social sphere is certainly not a new one, and there could be no better example of it than the New Poor Law of 1834 (for an excellent study of the implementation of which, see Brundage 1978) the extent and nature of it have shifted significantly over the period since the 1960s.

A central irony of the social is that a norm-distributing sector should itself be characterized by such normlessness. The example of the CRE makes plain the extent to which its external boundaries with the political on the one hand and the civil on the other involve a high degree of interpenetration. But more generally among welfare professionals there is a distinct lack of basic agreement as to what their aims are and how they should go about meeting them. We have already seen some of their uncertainties in Chapter 2, and shall do so again in Chapter 5. These uncertainties should not surprise us, for it is quite necessary that the experts' power is somewhat uncircumscribed, their duties more of a springboard than an electric fence: if simple rules could be made one would not, as we have remarked, trouble oneself with the complexities of professional discretion. It follows from this that the discretion will be variably exercised, there being insufficiently clear expectations laid upon the experts or agreed amongst them for anything else to be possible. But within all this variability there exists one analysis of the nature and origin of social problems whose logic perfectly fits this very normlessness. This logic cries out that, the social being a world in which everything is inextricably intertwined with everything else, no finite mandate can exist for those who operate within it. If criminals are poor, if lead in petrol makes people ill, if capitalism itself causes people to become clients, then the professional's duty is to penetrate the world of the political to attack poverty, multinational oil corporations, even capitalism itself. And this penetration is undertaken by the professionals not *qua* citizens, driven by the social concerns which may have influenced their career choice, but *qua* professionals, as part of their own diffuse mandate. The social becomes, therefore, a force for transformation, concerned not with the private lives of citizens alone, but with their social and political rights; not with enforcing those rights only, but with extending them:

> 'Nous ne luttons plus au nom du droit, pour *le* droit, mais pour *nos* droits, nos droits sociaux, en tant qu'ils définissent les privilèges

specifiques ou les compensations locales accordés a telle ou telle catégorie de la société, en raison des préjudices singuliers qu'elle est censée subir du fait de la division sociale du travail. L'exigence absolue de justice s'est effacée au profit de querelles sur la relativité des chances dont beneficient les uns, des risques qu'encourent les autres. En même temps, la notion de responsabilité disparaissait lentement au profit d'une socialisation des risques de la vie considérés comme de simples aléas, socialisation qui n'impute plus a quiconque le malheur des autres, n'exige plus de quiconque leur bonheur.' (Donzelot 1984: 11)

'We no longer struggle in the name of "right" for an *absolute* right, but for *our* rights, our social rights in so far as they define particular privileges or compensations afforded this or that social group as a recognition of specific harms suffered because of the social division of labour. The demand for absolute justice has retreated in the face of squabbles about the good luck of some and the risks run by others. At the same time the idea of "responsibility" was being gradually replaced by a "socialization" of the risks of life usually considered mere hazards, a "socialization" which no longer blames one person's actions for the misfortunes of another, and which no longer expects anybody to contribute to the happiness of anybody else.'

But, it being the case that when boundaries blur they do so bi-directionally, as the social penetrates the political so does the political penetrate the social. Hence increasingly in social work 'professional' decisions are challenged by the politicians, for how can one extract from the political context of a struggle against racism a decision to place a black child with white foster parents? How can one dislocate a professional decision to provide a child with some expensive facility from the reality of economic retrenchments and declining support for local authorities from central government? This fusion of spheres, this expansion of the social, can easily have the reverse impact from that intended:

'if the judges accept ever more reluctantly to condemn for the sake of condemning, the activity of judging has increased precisely to the extent that the normalizing power has spread. . . . The judges of normality are present everywhere. We are in the society of the teacher-judge, the doctor-judge, the educator-judge, the "social worker"-judge; it is on them that the universal reign of the normative is based; and each individual, wherever he may find himself, subjects to it his body, his gestures, his behaviour, his aptitudes, his achievements.' (Foucault 1977: 304)

The discipline of the social therefore represents in one sense an extension of the function of classical law from proscription to prescription. The law prohibits certain kinds of child abuse and neglect, but the social professionals teach positive child-rearing; the law protects certain old people from themselves, but the expert preaches the virtue of 'preventative' community care and family responsibility. In another sense the social professionals' diffuse mandate enables them selectively to enforce the law. While they regularly ignore certain infractions committed by their clients (Pearson 1975a, 1975b), on other occasions they are zealous in the imposition of their norms. One example suffices to make the point.

A branch of the National Association of Probation Officers passed a resolution to the effect that all waiting rooms should have posted in them a notice saying that racist language was illegal and would not be tolerated. Quite apart from the question of the accuracy of the informational content, two points emerge. First, most probation officers would presumably be aware that if their clients were people who regularly took heed of notices posted on walls they would be unlikely to be in a probation office in the first place; and second, no resolution was passed to inform the clientele that defrauding the social security system or defacing the seats was illegal and would not be tolerated. The notice, therefore, was not rationally reductionist in intent but symbolic; and it was a selective application of the law which reflected 'social' norms and served to emphasize the powerlessness of the client not just in the face of the law but in the face of the norms of the experts themselves.

The development of social control, with a small segment of which we are presently concerned, is, therefore, by no means a simple process. In attempts to control, from the Panopticon and Victorian experimentation and the rise of the reformers to the modern development of the social, the reality has never begun to match the theory. The Panopticon could not be built for both economic and technical reasons; the silent and separate systems failed to prevent contamination; so did successive children's institutions; the curative impact of a therapeutic relationship has proved minimal; and the process of permitting additional discretion to the experts has extended control, certainly, but with it arbitrariness and inconsistency. The elegant idea that society is, or can be made, a smooth running machine has here as elsewhere been proved fallacious. Something has always gone wrong in practice.

Foucault and juvenile justice

Foucault's work has been subjected to a number of criticisms; certain criticisms indeed have been embedded in our own account thus far. In this section we review some recent comments on his work in *Discipline and Punish*, and in the following two sections establish our own position in relation to his analysis which, broadly, will be that his perspective is a necessary component of any serious analysis, but that it is of itself insufficient. Our own discussion will incorporate also some of Donzelot's work to the extent that it complements Foucault's. There are certain theoretical conflicts between these two writers, but we shall not be discussing them in this book.

Foucault, it has been said, distorts the historical data on which his analysis is based (Jones and Fowles 1984). The view is not without justification but betrays such a lack of sympathy with Foucault's method as to be reminiscent of nothing so much as Dr Johnson's bewildered attack on the Metaphysical Poets:

'The most heterogeneous ideas are yoked by violence together; nature and art are ransacked for illustrations, comparisons and allusions; their learning instructs, and their subtlety surprises; but the reader commonly thinks his improvement dearly bought, and, though he sometimes admires, is seldom pleased.'

(Johnson 1779: 20)

Michael Ignatieff in his *mea culpa* ('this exercise is necessarily an exercise in self-criticism') lists three main concerns: that Foucault is too dismissive of altruism and humanitarianism in human relations; that he ignores the constraining influences on the steady expansion of State power; and that his model of the State is precisely that of the smooth running machine which we dismissed in our last section (Ignatieff 1981).

The first of these points seems to address both the motives of the reformers and the nature of family life. We have argued that it is precisely the confluence of Christian altruism and self-interest which made them such an irresistible force. So Mary Carpenter (whose most significant book is a combination of distressing case history and almost cynical *argumentum ad hominem*: Carpenter 1851) was in a line of female reformers whose personal qualities were combined to such effect with their political acumen. Elizabeth Fry's Newgate campaigns demonstrated many similar traits (Whitney 1947) as did the pioneering work in nursing of Florence Nightingale (at least if Lytton Strachey's less than dispassionate account is to be believed: Strachey 1918). Ignatieff also argues that family relations cannot be reduced to power relations.

Quite so, but our reading of Foucault does not lead us to believe that he thought they could. The family and the State have always had a complex and contradictory relationship (Mount 1982), but Foucault's concern (which is taken very much further by Donzelot: Donzelot 1980) is more with the management of the family by the State. Welfare workers hence become the means by which the State simultaneously promotes the (objective) interests of the powerless child when parental power is abused *and* supervises families to ensure that they keep their children only when they are succeeding to at least some degree in producing the offspring they should. Thus:

> 'We must cease asking, What is social work? Is it a blow to the brutality of centralized judicial sanctions, putting a stop to the latter through local interventions and the mildness of educative techniques, or is it rather the unchecked apparatus of the state, which, under the guise of prevention, is extending its grip on citizens to include their private lives, marking minors who have not committed the least offense with a stigmatizing brand? Instead, we should question social work regarding what it actually does, study the system of its transformations in relation to the designation of its effective targets.' (Donzelot 1980: 98-9)

The second comment, that the exercise of power is not some simple activity undertaken by the State, is correct. Power, as we have already argued in this chapter, is, rather, ubiquitous, even kaleidoscopic. We take it to be related to David Rothman's view that:

> 'Foucault's analysis never enters into the everyday world of criminal justice. It is one thing to claim that the goal of surveillance dominated the *theory* of punishment, quite another to examine what actually happened when programs were translated into *practice*. There is much more room for maneuver than a Foucault could ever imagine or allow.' (Rothman 1980: 11)

This argument in fact takes us to the heart of the present book and the purpose of its conceptual framework. We demonstrated in Chapter 1 that a detailed analysis of juvenile justice's governing legislation shows that its exercise of power results as much from ineptitude and political compromise among conflicting interest groups as from conspiracy; and when we examine in greater detail the nature and extent of the supervision which follows it will become clear that, if we may put it a little unkindly, there is more of Pooter than of Kafka about it.

It is, however, possible that Ignatieff's second criticism is also related to his third: that it is a structural–functionalist error on

Foucault's part to believe that prisons, ostensibly futile, are in some secret way functional. We think – but such is the elusiveness of Foucault's position that we are unsure – that this is a misreading, though if it is, it is understandable: witness first Peter Lazlett's puzzled review of *Discipline and Punish* in the British magazine *New Society*:

> 'We lay down this book knowing almost nothing about why, how or even when all the fascinating changes he discusses actually happened.' (cited in Jones and Fowles 1984: 28)

Witness secondly, and perhaps tangentially, a *Times* leader written to commemorate Sartre and Simone de Beauvoir on the death of the latter: 'It scarcely mattered that the analysis was . . . (to Anglo-Saxon logicians) oddly lacking in identifiable premisses' (*The Times*: 19 April 1986). This could have been about Foucault. But our reading of him differs from Ignatieff's. Foucault's society is not a machine, and the power which the prison exudes is in its erraticism and inefficiency not the product of one. Rather, it is self-generative, creating its own logic, meaning, and purpose to the extent that we can only say that it is there because it is there, and it is expanding because it is its nature to do so. But the prison is itself but a materialization of power, and as such comprises both a vehicle for the exercise of that power by those whose interests it serves, and a moral symbol which affects us all (Dobash 1983). Even the most liberal of us, on being victimized in some minor way, wish (even if momentarily and shamefacedly) for prison for our assailant; and such is the power of the prison that when 'non-custodial alternatives' are devised, they often, to gain credibility, ape the prison itself. Prison is punishment manifest, a linguistic and conceptual code which we share, to the extent even that not-prison is some concession, some piece of lenience to be justified, argued over, and, when things go wrong, to become the basis of public recrimination. Such, then, is the power of the prison, a power based not on what the prison is, but on what it means.

It is not the historical origin of the prison which concerns Foucault, that being a matter for the archivist or historiographer. His concern, which he terms the 'history of the present' is with how the generative properties of the prison have manifested themselves. So there is nothing in Foucault to make us believe that prison is either internationally ubiquitous or inevitable. But apart from the decarcerative policy in Massachusetts in the early 1970s (Rutherford 1986) which seems to have been based on very particular political circumstances and matters of chance and personality which have nowhere else been replicated, where prisons are little used there tends to be a developed system of social control. This is so in the Netherlands (Tulkens 1979) and, even more decisively, in China: there the system rests on

> 'a communal form of social control that truly relies firstly on the family system, secondarily (and very importantly) on neighborhood and work-group levels of social control, and only as a very last resort on bureaucratic structures. . . . Common courtyard forms of architecture in the cities increases the sense of group visibility and dependence. There is no support for individual deviance from social norms or group pressure. A basic Chinese assumption about crime is the escalation hypothesis: little disputes left uncontrolled will lead to major problems such as divorce or assault. Thus everything is fair game for local social control, and such control is generally accepted as legitimate and necessary.
>
> (Klein 1984: 10–11)

Finally among Foucault's critics, Anthony Bottoms, in a most thoughtful paper, raises two main concerns (Bottoms 1983). First he argues that Foucault's work fails to account for the proportional increase in the use of the fine; and secondly that there is often an unjustifiable conflation of 'discipline' as training and 'surveillance' of the kind which can occur unbeknown to the surveyed. His analysis of the second problem is persuasive:

> 'as societal power in the form of "the bio-politics of the population" has developed (through welfarism, corporatism, technological developments and so forth) so individual discipline ("the anatomo-politics of the human body") has become less necessary to the penal apparatus. Adequate social control can in many instances be developed externally to the penal system in the strict sense.'
>
> (Bottoms 1983: 195)

Part of the answer to the first problem lies in this answer too. The fine involves a form of self-regulation in that for it to be paid, work and stability must normally be respectively sought and achieved. If the fine is not paid, imprisonment is always there: in 1984 21,800 people were committed precisely for failing to pay their fines (Home Office 1985). But this is only a partial answer; another part lies in the fact that the spread of power is *not* quite inexorable, but subject to just the kind of constraints and pressures – fiscal as well as ideological – to which Scull (1977), Ignatieff, and Rothman have drawn attention. The absolute rise in crime has not been matched by a commensurate rise in direct surveillance or discipline; but an absolute rise in such surveillance and discipline has, notwithstanding, occurred. This is not a view with which Bottoms himself would apparently argue:

> 'The foregoing analysis should emphatically not be read as an argument that disciplinary punishment is dead or dying ... disciplinary punishments appear to be proportionately much more common amongst juvenile offenders (the foregoing analysis is deliberately restricted largely to adults).' (Bottoms 1983: 196)

Some of these views are reflected in our own comments on the contribution to juvenile justice made both by Foucault and by Jacques Donzelot, which follow. These comments are divided into two: the next section considers the nature and purpose of supervision in the juvenile court; the following section discusses some of the roles played by the supervisor.

The nature and purpose of supervision

> 'Orwell's terrible image of totalitarianism was the boot eternally trampling a human face. My vision of social control is much more mundane and assuring. It is the eternal case conference, diagnostic and allocations board or pre-sentence investigation unit.'
> (Cohen 1985: 185)

This section considers supervision as *tutelage*, a concept borrowed from Donzelot, and then examines certain particular characteristics of supervision: its *suspensive nature*, its *conflicting normative base*, and the extent of its *self-perpetuating tendencies*. In a short concluding comment we re-emphasize that supervision cannot solely be comprehended at the level of abstraction, nor yet simply at the level of practice, but that the focus of analysis must be not only both of these but also the nature of the relationship between them.

The idea of tutelage: education and a form of moral apprenticeship to established expectations characterize the experiences of the young in any organized society. Equally universal is the fact that they learn these matters in less than straightforward ways. In the words of the most famous of moral tales, written with the single object of 'the vivid inculcation of inward purity and moral purposes':

> 'I used once to have fine theories about it. I used to fancy that a big fellow would do no end of good to one lower in the school, and that the two would stand to each other in the relation of knight to squire. You know what the young knights were taught, Monty – to keep their bodies under, and bring them into subjection; to love God, and speak the truth always. That sounds very grand and noble to me. But when a big fellow takes up with a little one *you* know pretty

The macro level: welfare work and the State

well that *those* are not the kind of lessons he teaches.'
(Farrar 1858: 79)

Indeed they are not, and accordingly the question arises of how the young may be controlled, exposed perhaps to more suitable mentors than big fellows like Farrar's Upton. In Donzelot's analysis, historically this involved a different approach for middle- and working-class families. For the former, what was required was the inculcation of certain norms of motherhood which would protect the young from the disruptive and immoral influences of the nursemaids and other servants – a form of 'protected liberation'; for the working classes, however, both problem and cure were quite different:

'The problem in regard to the working-class child was not so much the weight of obsolescent constraints as excessive freedom – being left to the street – and the techniques employed consisted in limiting their freedom, in shepherding the child back to spaces where he could be more closely watched: the school or the family dwelling.'
(Donzelot 1980: 47)

Whereas the 'protected liberation' of the *bourgeoisie* had its legal corollary in the notion of 'contract', which itself reflected a certain consonance – or at least a working agreement – between family and social expectations, the supervised freedom of the working classes, expressed as 'tutelage', reflected a discontinuity, meaning:

'that these families will be stripped of all effective rights and brought into a relation of dependence *vis-à-vis* welfare and educative agents.' (Donzelot 1980: xxi)

With due allowance made for a degree of Gallic hyperbole, the concept tutelage adequately enough characterizes the supervised freedom of successions of offenders from 'ticket of leave men' through offenders licensed from reformatory, industrial, and then approved schools, adult criminals on different licences, and of course youngsters subjected to care or supervision orders by the juvenile court. Supervision affirms or inculcates certain behavioural and attitudinal norms, and in so doing defines a boundary between that which is permitted and that which is proscribed. Supervision of its essence involves a continuing contact, a new form of authority which, in the patriarchal family, renders the father in particular actually redundant, a failed head of household, himself under supervision and hence censure. For the delinquent from a sound family a discharge, fine, or police caution normally suffices (Bennett 1979; Landau and Nathan 1983; Rutherford 1986).

Now there is, of course, a perfect logic in concentrating resources (which in such an open-ended enterprise are by definition insufficient) where they are most needed, where family is weakest. Doubtless many of the children and families under supervision are in the greatest distress or disorganization. Doubtless too the children are themselves sometimes desirous of being 'taken away'; and, equally doubtless, when they are so taken the very process of doing so simultaneously strips the parents of their control and also offers to the children new opportunities, life chances of which they had hitherto been deprived by the poverty, cruelty, or fecklessness of their parents. Indeed it is precisely this nexus of care and control which makes the tutelary process so powerful. The very act which enhances the vulnerability of the family unit extracts from that unit the child whose circumstances have been simultaneously cause and effect of that vulnerability, and offers new hope, not only to the child but to the family as well. If the child is removed – or in danger of being removed – from home, it is the family which is to be 'worked with' (as welfare workers tend vaguely to express it) in order that, if the 'work' is successful the child may return, or stay, at home.

Suspensive nature: it would, therefore, be an incomplete analysis which failed to acknowledge that strong positives are embedded in the tutelary process, albeit quite inextricably from control. But here we stumble on yet another paradox: that the giving of such an opportunity, to child and family alike, serves to justify the imposition of direct penal measures where the opportunity is not taken. This is what Donzelot meant when he spoke of tutelage leading to a choice between 'subjection to norms and an orientation to delinquency that is difficult to reverse' (Donzelot 1980: 113). To the offence in law is added the moral infraction of spurning the hand of friendship, of not behaving as a Dickensian waif should. Hence the great irony which faces us: if no chance were to be given we should cry out at the injustice, the inhumanity of it; but, once given, the chance becomes of its very nature a further form of power.

It is in the suspensive nature of welfare supervision that this power is embedded. The intention is to persuade the young to choose the *via dextra*; that it is a more intensive intervention than the caution, discharge or fine is the source of part of its power, that it is less intensive than custody is the source of the rest of it:

> 'It is in this cavity opened up by the suspensive character of the punishment that the educative measure takes hold . . . it is always by nature derived from prison.' (Donzelot 1980: 109)

Its effect is to blur the distinction between the 'assistancial and the penal' (Donzelot 1980: 109) in part by creating a series of additional steps between them. The White Paper *Children in Trouble* is explicit here:

> 'Existing forms of treatment available to juvenile courts distinguish sharply between those which involve removal from home and those which do not. The juvenile courts have very difficult decisions to make in judging whether circumstances require the drastic step of taking a child away from his parents and home. The view has often been expressed that some form or forms of intermediate treatment should be available to the courts, allowing the child to remain in his own home but bringing him into contact with a different environment.'
> (*Children in Trouble* 1968)

Of course, when later in the book we come to consider the operation of the experts' decision-making, we shall show that there are specific points, particular moments, when the professionals have to make a choice *between* care and control. At a conceptual level, though, it will be perfectly plain that the two are literally inextricable, in a feedback loop whereby to increase the actuality of the one by definition increases either the potential or the need for the other.

Conflicting normative base: it would, therefore, be wrong either to perceive the experts as mere tools of an ever more watchful State, or to ignore the fact that the process of which they are a part generates a logic which makes such a function an inevitable aspect of their activities. The manner in which the experts undertake their duty can itself modulate State control by the insertion into the process of a range of professional ideologies, affiliations, and cultures which, while extending the influence of the court, simultaneously transform it. We have seen how, conceptually, the very nature of 'the social' exercises a transforming influence, albeit an erratic and often arbitrary one, on the residual functions of law; and we can point also to the way in which the professionals *do* in their supervisory activity penetrate the families and communities of their clients; but in doing so they exercise certain professional values and ideologies which, in so far as these are autonomous of any clear and unequivocal agendas the State may have, mean that they are simultaneously representing and undermining the demands of the State, subverting while simultaneously furthering the processes of which they are a part.

Self-perpetuating tendencies: the simple criterion of 'success' being less meaningful than one might suppose, there is a dynamic in failure which leads to and justifies yet further penetration. There are three main reasons for this. *First*, the opaqueness of the task necessitates a multifaceted intervention and almost guarantees failure. The successful resolution of some simple but irritating problem – a squabble with officialdom, say – is seldom enough of itself but acts as a spur to greater efforts to solve bigger problems and hence, of course, to ultimate failure. Although welfare workers have, over the last few years, learned some lessons from this problem, and frequently now will close their cases when a success has been achieved, this is especially difficult when the court has made the order, when the disorganization is so great, the need so intense, or the behaviour so worrying. *Second*, the means by which these jobs are tackled varies too. Inevitably given the range of tasks to which they have on occasion to turn their hand, the experts will fall back on the use of their 'bag of tricks': they will, that is to say, be 'eclectic', drawing on an almost boundless array of interventive and therapeutic possibilities, each with its own justification: so intense contact will demonstrate concern, no contact (at times of office pressure or annual holidays, for example) will demonstrate trust. And there are task-centred casework, family therapy (of various kinds), groupwork (also of various kinds), behaviour therapy, psychosocial casework – the list of therapies in which the experts will have received an hour or two's training is extensive indeed; what is lacking is a set of clear guiding principles as to their use, to act either as a guide to them or as a check for their managers. *Third*, from all this emerges a new logic of failure. Human wickedness or misery, or just plain bad luck being, within this set of assumptions, remediable, it follows that curative failure is the result of some technical inefficiency. Perhaps one has penetrated insufficiently far the client's social world: one may have seen the mother but not the brother, the girlfriend but not the 'peer group' (as friends are usually described by the experts), the teacher but not the doctor. This penetration can be done indirectly, by those who are themselves the objects of penetration, a process which is the very essence of the disciplinary society. The expert may recruit a volunteer army of auxiliary supervisors from the client's own social world, all of them working in the client's best interests and most probably with his or her permission. The value of confidentiality being what it is, none of these subalterns will be told more than necessary either about the activities of the other supervisors or about precisely why they are doing what they are doing. In such a system the expert's power remains supreme.

But it would be wrong to see this spread of power only in such simple terms. Constraints exist which serve to limit any such expansion. One of these in the juvenile court is the instability of the relationship between the magistrates and the experts. The experts are necessary to the court, but the processes by which they transform their mandate into something reflecting their own values and aspirations involve regular but unpredictable conflicts with magistrates in many cases. Sometimes the conflict is open – a particular difference of opinion which can potentially be resolved by meetings and telephone calls. But more often such specific arguments are but surface manifestations of a more fundamental clash of value and purpose which shows itself in, say, general grumblings about 'excuses' in the experts' reports, the clothes they wear, even the kind of people they are:

> 'We are aware that many social work staff are very immature and inexperienced; many have themselves been brought up in schools and houses without any discipline, and often without respect for and belief in law and order.'
> (Baroness Macleod of Borve, cited in A. Morris *et al.* 1980)

Yet at other times or in other places the experts' relationship with the magistrates is close. Variations are immense (Anderson 1978), to the extent that it is commonly said that there is no single system of juvenile justice, only a host of local systems, each with its own policies and quirks. That such variation is possible given the limitations of the governing legislation has been demonstrated; there are other reasons too, to do with the selection and training of magistrates, but these are matters outside the concerns of this book (see, however, Burney 1979, for a consideration of these issues). But the effect of this unpredictability and instability on supervision is to ensure that it exists not as a consensual disposal based on the shared values and objectives of those who make and those who manage it. Rather, its force is constrained, albeit erratically and even seemingly arbitrarily, by these various conflicts which surround it. For example, our study of supervision orders showed that in spite of widespread periodic infractions, a supervisee was almost never returned to court as being in breach of requirements. While part of the explanation of this lay probably in the pointlessness of the exercise in many cases and part of it in apathy, part of it too reflected a general unease with the court and a mistrust of what the courts might do if the power to sentence were given back to them.

Of other constraints which stem from the organizational context in which social workers in particular supervise offenders we shall have more to say in Chapter 4.

A concluding note: it will be seen that we have been influenced by the writings of Foucault and Donzelot, but have not been uncritical recipients of their work. It will be appreciated also that our use of them has been limited. We have not engaged in full theoretical or epistemological debate with them; nor have we considered the general applicability of the extension of power thesis to Britain. This latter enterprise, however, needs seriously to be undertaken. When it is, a possible starting-point might be the history of the Justice of the Peace, which seems to contraindicate Foucault's hypothesis. The institution of the JP system (Justices of the Peace Act, 1361) was in part a resolution of the Crown's concern 'to keep order throughout the country on a local basis, and without the men in charge of the localities becoming too powerful' (Milton 1959: 15). By the seventeenth century the justices were empowered to transport for up to seven years, and even a single justice could deal punitively with vagrants. This power, however, declined in the eighteenth century, and the administrative functions of the justices were all but abolished in the nineteenth with the advent of our modern system of local government. Hence:

> 'A modern magistrate would be alarmed to think that he might have to order women to be hanged for having no means of livelihood, or men to have an ear cut off for being "sturdy beggars"; he would find it irksome and embarrassing to supervise the observance of the law requiring that the cloak of every man below the rank of Lord should be of such length "that the same may cover his privy Members and Buttocks (he being upright)".' (Milton 1959: 21)

Foucault's failure to address the minor social control which characterized his 'torture' phase leads him both to underestimate the 'minute and meticulous laws governing every aspect of the citizen's life' (Milton 1959: 21) at that time, and to overestimate the suddenness of the transition from one mode of punishment to another; thus the discipline of the Bridewells and the Amsterdam Rasp House, for example, dated from the mid-sixteenth century, while forms of bodily mutilation continued until well into the nineteenth (Spierenburg 1984).

This spurning of detail leads us to the first of the two more general points we have here to make: that Foucault's *level of analysis* is inadequate to support his thesis. The second point will be an observation on his *disdain to evaluate* the calibrations of power he describes; his contempt for the naive reformer can almost blind us to the obvious fact that a comparison of a probation order and being torn apart on the rack does lend itself to an analysis which has nothing to do with the efficient exercise of power.

Levels of analysis: the distinctions we have drawn between, say, different juvenile justice systems, or different courts operating within the same system cannot be the product of a *Foucaultesque* analysis, but emerge from more detailed enquiry into the operation of the systems. To the *Foucaultiste* such differences blend into insignificance at a level of abstraction which considers only 'power' or 'control'. The converse approach, that of abstracted empiricism (Wright Mills 1970) simply reminds us that 'details, no matter how numerous, do not convince us of anything worth having convictions about' (Wright Mills 1970: 65). Hence it is in the relationship between the two, those lines which etch a passage from the *minutiae* of experience to the grand structure, that fruitful analysis must exist:

> 'Intellectually these schools represent abdications of classical social science. The vehicle of their abdication is pretentious over-elaboration of "method" and "theory"; the main reason for it is their lack of firm connexion with substantive problems.'
> (Wright Mills 1970: 86)

We can, therefore, analyse juvenile justice exclusively at the level of abstraction – its power, its educative and welfarizing propensities, and so on – only at the cost of ignoring questions as to why this court is different from that, or this country from that; why some jurisdictions elevate consistency over flexibility (the 'auditor model') and others the reverse (the 'contingency model') (Hackler 1984). But conversely, to consider only these matters of detail is to fail to see the wood for the trees, to be excessively confident that various technical changes will solve problems of social structure and purpose. The problems of juvenile justice are part structural and part technical; they cannot all be addressed at the same level; it is not, then, necessary to distinguish the levels themselves?

Foucault helps us understand the functioning and purpose of power but not its precise workings; the expansion of State control but neither its contraction nor its variability. So when he observes

> 'for the moment one leaves to others than the judges of the offence the task of deciding whether the condemned man "deserves" to be placed in semi-liberty or conditional liberty, whether they may bring his penal tutelage to an end, one is handing over to them mechanisms of legal punishment to be used at their discretion'
> (Foucault 1977: 21)

he is not addressing the qualities of any particular system, and accordingly if his analysis is not modulated by more precise study, he may mislead. For example, in England and Wales the problem is not so much to do with leaving things to experts outside the justice system as the fact that, by becoming so intertwined with the judicial, the experts lack quite the kind of freedom to which Foucault refers. There is not, that is to say, a simple conflict between due process and administrative or professional justice, but an interpenetration which results in neither the judicial nor the executive retaining any separate identity, but becoming barely distinguishable from each other. And the more integral they become, the more the experts find themselves assuming judicial functions: their sentencing recommendations will increasingly include an assessment of 'culpability' and 'risk' as well as need, for example. So while in an obvious sense the experts remain non-judicial; and while we are clearly not suggesting that there are not conflicts *between* them and the magistrates, the battlegrounds where those conflicts are fought out are not clearly delineated, nor are they the same ones in different systems. There is a confusion of purpose and role in the juvenile courts which is explicable historically not only as a broad and international phenomenon but also in the particular circumstances of the English and Welsh legislation and administrative arrangements.

Evaluation: juvenile justice cannot be reduced, as Foucault attempts to do, simply to an analysis of power and control any more than it can be considered as a steady but inexplicable process of increasing wisdom and concern. Few of us presumably would wish to trade the sanitized arrangements of today for the barbarities of yesterday, and in our unwillingness to do so we are making an implicit evaluation which, unless it is incorporated in our analysis, leaves by its absence that analysis insufficient. The clearest pathway into this problem is by a reversion to the idea of tutelage with which the section began. If the essence of supervision as tutelage is its suspensive nature, it exists not alone but as a function of other options. If in one system the option is torture or execution and in another a few months in a fairly tolerable institution, then the nature of the supervision itself is quite different in the two situations, the power of the supervisor and court varying as the sanctions for non-cooperation vary. Perhaps it is easier for this rather obvious reality to be ignored by professors of history and systems of thought than by youthful offenders as they await news of the penalty to which they have been assigned.

Translators and negotiators: supervisors in court

The experts are not in court by some grace and favour arrangement, however marginal they may sometimes be made to feel. They are essential to the operation of the proceedings and they have the effect of expanding, albeit in erratic and unpredictable ways, the power of the court into the private life of the delinquent. It is of course the case that the experts are dependent on the court in a number of ways, for the court accepts or rejects their suggestions for sentence, punishes clients for whom the experts have sometimes come to feel personal sympathy and whom they wish to support in some way, and generally can, in a host of minor ways, extend to or deny them a range of courtesies and privileges of the kind which will make their working life fairly agreeable or fairly disagreeable.

In this final section of a rather long chapter, we isolate one particular function which the experts have in the court: we call it a function of translating and negotiating (and for a related discussion, see Carlen and Powell 1979).

Most young offenders can be fairly straightforwardly processed. Their offences being minor and their circumstances tolerable, they may generally be interchangeably disposed of by means of discharges, small fines, a few hours at an attendance centre on Saturday afternoons, and possibly a few weeks in a detention centre if they persist. Although the experts tend to become irritated by short custodial sentences, in fact disposals of this order need not detain practical people long or disturb them unduly: they are typical sentences for typical people in relation to whom the experts' function is merely to investigate and offer a fairly clean bill of moral and behavioural health.

It is with more complex cases that their role becomes central. Magistrates, it must be remembered, are lay people, selected for being, as Dr Johnson would have said, of 'sound bottom', with common sense and life experience (Burney 1979) and with attitudes which remain largely unaffected by their perfunctory training. Such people can make perfect sense of those offenders who are 'on the make'; and being in all probability parents or grandparents themselves, they can normally allow also for situations in which decent but harassed parents struggle to cope with the vagaries of adolescence manifested in the behaviour of their brood. But of course even such an obvious notion as this – that decent parents, so long as they can weather the storm, will generally produce decent offspring – brings in its wake a darker, more disturbing notion. For if parental decency so influences the behaviour of the young, the children of not-decent parents cannot be simply designated rational offenders, but also victims of circumstance. Magistrates, in short, encounter numbers of cases where it seems to them obvious that the explanation of the crime lies in circumstances beyond the offender's control. This is the first kind of case which requires translation by the experts and, once translated, ameliorative action which is within the purview of the expert but not, directly at least, of the court. After all, how often have the magistrates thought, as they survey the grubby miscreants who stand before them, that if only they could get to the parents all would be well? It is to the experts' knowledge of the art of teaching good child-rearing that they will turn on occasions such as this, but also to their analysis of what, in this particular family, has gone wrong.

A second category of complex cases involves those in which there is bizarre behaviour which they may find somewhat disturbing. The offender may indulge in sexual misdemeanour or torture animals, be too fond of fires or have a predilection for placing boulders on railway lines. Such behaviour is literally senseless to the magistrate whose explanatory framework allows principally for motivation-instigated criminality; nor is it quite satisfactory to consider it one of the acceptable mysteries of growing up. Again the experts translate such *bizarrerie* into a language which, if not fully comprehensible to the layman, at least gives an indication that somebody understands what is going on. This is a relief, partly because cognitive dissonance is itself stressful (Festinger 1957), but mainly because to identify the possibly dangerous offender as the province of a particular professional is to transfer both the dangerousness and the responsibility for managing it from oneself to another. By this process the experts metamorphose gracefully from translator to treater, being charged with offering a form of moral orthopaedics which will put right the complaint which they themselves have identified. The effect of this is to permit the court to deal simply with the routine cases by removing from its direct jurisdiction the complex ones. The fit is perfect, for the avidity of the experts to deal with the difficult case, or the person otherwise bound for custody, matches precisely the anxiety of the court to leave such delinquents to somebody else. When things go wrong, as by nature they will, not only do the experts provide a ready scapegoat if a scapegoat be sought, but also the failure of their best efforts itself justifies a more punitive response: after all, at least one has tried. The maintenance in the British criminal justice system of that neo-classical compromise (Taylor, Walton, and Young 1973) which blends responsibility with pathology needs precisely the tutelary to sustain it.

But we have spoken not only of translation, but also of negotiation. The relationship of welfare worker to court cannot be understood except as a continuing one. Some experts make their appearance and are never, or almost never, seen again. A psychiatrist, teacher, or psychologist sends a report and the court takes it or leaves it. This is not so with the welfare workers: because they both advise and serve the court they have to establish themselves as professionally credit-worthy and this necessity constrains their translating function. Because at quite fundamental levels of ideology there are rifts between many magistrates and many welfare workers, in particular cases the experts are likely to discard modes of explanation which the court may consider indiscreet, even inadmissable. In this sense they are fortunate indeed to have their varied bag of tricks, for so many stories are there which can be told that the averagely resourceful expert should be able to find one which both suits the court and fulfils the objective of the report. The matter can be frustrating, of course, notably for the revolutionary socialists among the experts who are, on the face of it, likely to find the paradoxical relationship between their role and their belief system difficult to disentangle. Two Marxist probation officers observe:

> 'Criminal acts are viewed purely as a particular aspect of an individual's behaviour and not as a more widespread social phenomenon with social, economic and political causes. Probation officers operate within that *individualized system of criminal justice* and maintain that perspective. They must remain within the limits of relevance set by the court . . . the poor housing situation of an individual offender can be described and may evoke sympathy but comment about the way in which market forces systematically disadvantage certain groups would be unacceptable.'
>
> (Italics original. Walker and Beaumont 1981: 23)

So the continuity of relationship between courts and experts (which itself exists at an organizational as well as individual level) to a degree symmetrizes court demand and expert opinion by setting an agenda of what is acceptable and what is not. How far such symmetry extends into the realities of supervision is, of course, a different matter. Certainly in court the experts utilize a range of strategies to achieve their various ends, much as other relatively powerless people typically do when confronting the more powerful. So discordant information is filtered out of reports (Carlen and Powell 1979; Thorpe 1979), and positive information highlighted for strategic reasons. Indeed so neatly can an expert's report launder a complex and messy reality that it can make the precise details of the youngster's offence seem almost to have been predestined from the day of conception.

These, then, are the experts in court, many of them expressing in their dress or demeanour the sense in which they negotiate the relationship between court and defendant: they may be *in* court but their appearance often indicates that they are not precisely *of* it. They represent *par excellence* the blurring which takes place in the domain of the social between the *gravitas* of the judicial process and the life of the working-class defendant. Translator, negotiator, supervisor, educator, processor, carer, controller – all these roles exist within the domain of the social, all of them are at some time and to varying degrees played by the experts.

Yet in practice as we have seen, it has not worked so neatly. Reality is more erratic, even anarchic, and we have begun to understand why. The experts' tasks are self-constraining, riddled with paradox, irony, ambivalence; their relationship with the court is varied and unpredictable: certainly they are locked into no cosy conspiracy with the court to control ever more insidiously and effectively. Failure does indeed justify more penetration, but supposing that too fails, as often it must? What do we derive from such failures but unread dossiers, identified but unmet needs, known but unpunished infractions? It is not, perhaps, so much that the Emperor has no clothes as that we have the clothes, but have quite lost sight of the Emperor.

4 The mezzo level: conduits of care – welfare organizations and the supervisory State

'Whilst [social services] departments are not simply outcrops of some universal self-generating bureaucracy neither are they associations of uncontrolled self-supporting "professionals". Whilst they are not simple obedient agents of social control, neither are they unrestrained instigators of social change.'

(Brunel Institute of Organization and Social Studies 1974: 19)

'Probation work is a clear example of a marginal occupation. Probation officers are in an ambiguous position with regard to two systems of control: the legal and the social services . . . The probation officer is frequently caught among the wishes and demands of probationer, judge, department administrators, police, social service agencies, and influential members of the community.'

(Thomson 1984: 111)

The deviant, disadvantaged, or distressed may experience welfare work through particular encounters with specific workers which they may characterize as helpful or not, useful or not, and so on. But the nature and content of these encounters emerge not only from the personal characteristics of the workers, but also from the policies, practices, priorities, resources, and culture of the bureaucracies which employ them. Organizations variously constrained to meet need, censure the wayward, and contain the disagreeable will formulate workload priorities for their staff in ways which most readily show them to be discharging their mandate in a manner pleasing not only to employees and clients but also to the various outside interests which influence their activities. The time to be spent on particular problems, the interpretation of permissive legislation, the procedures to be followed in specific instances, the resources available for various provisions – home helps, meals on wheels, intermediate treatment, day centres – all reflect policies which, though possibly influenced by the professional staff, are by no means determined by them. Yet decisions of this kind impact profoundly on the nature of the experiences of the clients as they sit, in the interviewing room or at home, with their welfare workers.

Equally, as employing agencies the organizations exercise different levels of control over their staff according to the nature or politicality of the work they may be doing. Quite obviously in child protection cases all social services departments have procedures, manuals, and close monitoring arrangements at both inter- and intra-organizational levels, and the matter is also very seriously addressed in probation offices. That such prioritization reflects principally external pressure need hardly be emphasized: children who may be at risk of violence, after all, receive so much more urgent attention than, say, elderly people who may be at equal or greater risk of self-injury that simple humanitarian concern cannot be an adequate explanation. This vulnerability to outside pressure of welfare organizations – social services departments in particular – is the central theme of this chapter. It is a matter which extends beyond the area of child abuse to permeate also the agencies' responses to a wide range of duties, among them the supervision of young offenders.

As David Howe has observed, then, we cannot decontextualize professional practice from the organizations within which it takes place: it does not have a separate life of its own (Howe 1986). A similar point can be made about the impact of the agencies on the supervision orders made by the court, and which their staff have to manage. A supervision order, though it originates in the juvenile court, takes its meaning from the organizational processes which turn it into reality: it is not only what the court orders but also what the supervisors do. It is an almost universal experience for tensions to emerge, covert practices to develop in relation to the management of the orders, and various forms of occupational deviance to occur (Pearson 1975a, 1975b). Although some of the deviance may reflect private activities by the front-liners who supervise the orders, it would be naive to assume that the non-reporting of undetected offences and the failure to return to court recalcitrant clients, for example, are anything but implicitly if not explicitly sanctioned activities within the agencies themselves.

But the matter is not simple. The organization does have its differences with the court, which mean that the latter frequently fails to get what it wants from the supervision order. At the level of practice, the organization makes particular demands of its front-line workers. But different and contradictory processes also occur which undercut the transformational impact of the organization itself. First, in relation to the courts, though squabbles and manipulations of the kind we have been describing are indeed everyday occurrences, behind them lies a broad consensus which ensures that the disputes take place against a background of shared assumptions about the very nature of delinquency. More precisely, courts and agencies are the products of those assumptions, their very existence and meaning being framed within a discourse which, for example, takes delinquency to be an individual act requiring individualized treatment. It is in this sense that *the agencies convey as well as transform ideology*, and we explore the issue as the first of two themes to be developed in the next section.

The second of these themes involves the analysis of the organizations themselves, *sui generis*, as *open systems* variably vulnerable to pressures from different external sources, but also containing within themselves a conflict of traditions – notably between the Poor Law and autonomous professionalism – which is worked out in practice between competing operational models of agency service and independent practice. By separately discussing social services departments and the probation service we shall show that whereas the latter has effected a feasible resolution of this problem, social services departments remain vulnerable both to attack from without and to dissension from within.

The welfare organization, then, is neither a passive container of active professionals nor a force which destroys professionalism itself. If, as Maurice Kogan and James Terry have observed, one does not want (we would say need) professionals to act as professionals, one would hardly go to the trouble of employing them (Kogan and Terry 1971); hence David Howe overstates the matter when he suggests that the organization 'determines' practice (Howe 1986); it clearly emerges from the organization but exists in a dynamic relationship with the demands of managers. In this chapter we trace the line through court mandate, organizational imperative, and agency practice as a means of accounting for the nature of the supervisory practices we observed in our study.

At this point, however, we must confront a particular linguistic problem. We have been speaking, and shall continue to speak, of 'the organization', or 'the agency' as though to imply both that it represents an homogeneous, even organic, whole, and that the front-line worker is somehow outside of it. This is not our intention: any complex organization contains conflicts both among different levels of staff and different categories of staff – between senior and middle management, for example, and between the professionals and the administrators. Equally, to address the front-liner, the person is *within* this mêlée, both influencing and influenced by it. When in this book we speak of 'the organization' we shall be referring to the formal policies and less formal official expectations which emerge from it and which may be subverted at any level. This, we know, is unsatisfactory to the organizational theorist, but we can only plead that one has to draw the boundary somewhere, and our boundary reflects the fact that our main interest in welfare organizations is in the extent to which their policies and norms have a transformational effect on the court order, and the ways in which those policies and norms are passed on to and further transformed by the front-liners. Readers with a more detailed interest in welfare organizations will doubtless look elsewhere for fuller discussion (see, for example, Billis 1984; Blau and Scott 1963; Brager and Holloway 1978; Hardiker and Barker 1981: ch. 4; Hasenfeld and English 1974; Kakabadse 1982).

Welfare organizations: two themes

Welfare organizations as carriers of ideology: when the juvenile court makes an order transferring responsibility for the management of a youngster to a welfare agency, it effectively removes that youngster's social label of 'defendant', replacing it with a new label, 'client'. We know that to the already stigmatized the process of 'becoming a client' is typically further stigmatizing (Rees 1978; Page 1984), and that the positive professional ideologies of 'respect' and 'confidentiality', for example, are constantly undermined by the status, history, and function of the agencies of which the professionals are a part. Clients bring expectations to their encounter with the agency which reflect their folk-knowledge of that agency, its predecessors, its existing clientele, even the building in which it is housed – the spectre of the 'Bastille', for example, has repeatedly haunted former workhouses to whatever subsequent use they may have been put. As a general principle, the more stigmatized, the closer to the residuum, a particular client is, the more he or she is likely to perceive the agencies in negative, censorious terms.

Stereotypes are not, of course, immune to change, and are repeatedly modified or confirmed by the day-to-day practices which occur within those parts of the organization which the new client encounters (see, for example, Hall 1974). But a folk history of stigma, back through national assistance to public assistance and the 'means test man', is not easily erased, and nor, given the residual income maintenance functions which the social services department at least has assumed, is there strong reason why it should be (Handler 1973). To develop this point somewhat we return to the Charity Organization Society, whose rationalism we mentioned in Chapter 2, as a case study in the developing culture of the welfare agency.

The Charity Organization Society (COS), founded in 1869, represented a point of convergence of two contradictory trends in Victorian thinking: the concern to give alms to the poor for the relief of distress, and the belief that to do so undermined the moral qualities necessary for personal success (Stedman-Jones 1971). The COS was in part the philosophical child of the revisionist philosophy of John Stuart Mill, whose *Utilitarianism* had been published in 1861, and to whom the Greatest Happiness Principle was no private psychology but encapsulated higher social duties which included charity:

> 'It is better to be a human being dissatisfied than a pig satisfied; better to be a Socrates dissatisfied than a fool satisfied. And if the fool, or the pig, are of a different opinion, it is because they only know their own side of the question. The other party to the comparison knows both sides.' (Mill 1861: ch. 2)

But of at least equal influence on the society were those thinkers such as Barnett and Lock, whose acceptance of the more stringent tenets of classical Utilitarianism remained generally firm. Indeed the society's early years and predominant influence coincided precisely with the popularity of Samuel Smiles, whose *Self-Help* had first appeared in 1859, but whose later books, *Character* (1871), *Thrift* (1875), and *Duty* (1887) were yet to come. The society, in short, operated within a profoundly individualistic frame of reference.

But the danger remained that, corrupted by the example of the clever pauper ingeniously extracting funds from the emotionally vulnerable wealthy, the labouring classes would become demoralized and diverted from life's stern disciplining. To give, according to this ascetic approach, required not an emotional response to the apparently simple property of destitution, but a 'scientific' reaching beyond the observable, to assess the person beyond the facade, to judge the genuineness and character of the supplicant. This was revealed best by a historical or biographical account of the person's pathway to the present: how past vicissitudes had been conquered; how far previous moral fecklessness had contributed to present misfortune; what balance existed between catastrophe and complicity in this person's impecuniousness. Biography became essential to assess character and evaluate signs of progress or resolve. Where such signs were apparent the reward was a charity which, unlike admission to the workhouse, left relatively intact the supplicant's civil and citizenship rights.

Hence in that private forerunner of State welfare provision, a system of files, records, and documentation emerged not for either benign professional or neutral administrative reasons so much as with a view to moral accountancy. The evaluation of a claim needed no longer to depend upon the moment of contact with the agency – the nature of the problem, the appearance of the supplicant – but extended into a cumulative picture of *this* person's achievements, previous disbursements received, and so on. The power of the agency hence incorporated past as well as present morality, and a morality exhumed by personal questioning, visits, enquiries of relatives and neighbours. But even though knowledge of claimants was central to the application of professional power, it was but the other side of the coin from the agency's concern for the acuity of its staff, so that what was known and recorded reflected an 'objective' truth, not some personal idiosyncracy of the person who knew and recorded it. Emphasis upon functional roles rather than the individuals occupying them marked the bureaucratization of welfare.

The Charity Organization Society represents an ideal type of the transformation of charitable or philanthropic endeavour into a tutelary process. The regulation of the lives of the poor by monitoring and the giving or withholding of alms reflected not only the penetration of bourgeois values into the lives of the residuum but also, more subtly, a recognition of the fact that those values already existed among the respectable working class, and had to be inculcated in the undeserving poor:

> 'it is a serious overestimation of the role of the state to assume that its sanctioning powers were the exclusive source of the social division between criminal and respectable. The strategy of mass imprisonment is better understood in class terms as an attempt by the authorities to lend symbolic reinforcement to values of personal honour which they themselves knew were indigenous to the poor.'
> (Ignatieff 1981: 174)

Hence the COS involved not only colonizing the poor but also buttressing the honour of the respectable by delineating boundaries between them and the disreputable; a process, in short, of classification. But it is by studying the form rather than the content of the society's activities that we can glean a better understanding of contemporary welfare organizations – the accumulation of knowledge by, and its transmission among, people who are functionally interchangeable; the creation thereby of the reification or objectification of that knowledge; the link between knowledge and power; knowledge which is 'special', or expertly processed, remote somewhat from the discourse of the laity.

In spite of the COS's eclipse by the collectivist responses to social need of the twentieth century, there remain sufficient numbers of 'residual' problems to justify the continued individualization of supplicants. So the COS's legacy is principally that of method: the holding of information on individuals, the establishing of files and cases, the social history all continue, and testify to the Society's role as a progenitor of rational and bureaucratic welfarism. The individualism and uniqueness of each case were established through the mechanisms of assessment and classification; the eschewing of the impressionistic and the endorsement of privileged knowledge prefigured the later experts, even if arcane psyknowledge (Donzelot 1980) had not yet taken the place of the moral certainties of characterology.

But the reality of the COS's power lay not so much in its vaunted rationality as in the vast gap which existed between rational theory and capricious practice. Certainly to its supplicants, 'cringe or starve' seemed the choice, a phrase which itself encapsulates a view of a disjunction between rational and fair ideal and moralistic and arbitrary reality. The COS's agents seldom if ever attained the wisdom of Solomon, and such wisdom, such omnicompetence, would have been essential were they to have made correctly the kind of judgements which they claimed the legitimacy to make. Rather, the very capriciousness of the almsgiving heightened the power of the donor and weakened that of the recipient. Capriciousness destroys certainty, the linearity of cause and effect, the process by which all the players know the rules. Capriciousness meant that the only option open to the poor was to apologize, to assume they had erred, to repent – in short, to cringe.

Now the purpose of this case study is not to suggest in some simple way that no 'progress' has been made; that the moralism of the society permeates the professionals of today. But nor can the agencies of today quite divest themselves of either the method or the purpose of the COS. In method, as we have seen, they replicate and extend the doctrine of individualization in terms both of professional practice (collecting social histories, noting detailed explanations of events) and of organizational procedures (caseloads, allocations, files which render the professionals interchangeable, which make knowledge the property of the agency). In purpose they classify, process, judge, and act upon judgements to the extent that any professional ideology of 'non-judgementalism' is circumscribed almost out of existence into philosophical approaches barely sustainable in practice (see, for example, Stalley 1978). Of course judgements must be made, and they must have social consequences: how could it be otherwise when resources have to be allocated responsibly and accountably; when private information innocently given may form the basis of a report to a court? How can knowledge not be power, and how, conversely, can the possession of power not lead to the demand for, and acquisition of, knowledge? That the practice is carried out courteously and in a friendly manner is of itself desirable; but the means *by which* it is done cannot deflect the reason *why* it is done.

The agencies constitute a process of bureaucratizing their clients' lives consistently with these methods and purposes. Problems, needs, triumphs, failures become translated into 'file' knowledge, individualized and dislocated from the wider social and economic processes which generate them. It is in this sense that the agencies regulate disruptions in public order, that they transfer the ideology of delinquency from courtroom back into society, where by processes of monitoring, befriending, cajoling, and generally making work for idle hands they seek to impose good behaviour on that minute proportion of young offenders who come their way. But the irony of this individualization is that it is itself an organizational routine: when everybody is individualized, nobody is individualized, and the ultimate logic of file-knowledge is the identical processing of innumerable cases: interchangeable clients dealt with by interchangeable professionals.

There is also a sense in which the internal structure of the organization can reproduce, legitimize, and consolidate the allocation of more general social roles. One of these is the issue of gender. A majority of front-liners are women, subordinated to male managers, but also, by virtue of their necessary contact with clients, conveying a particular imagery of what women 'do'. The imagery is ambiguous; at one moment women may be seen as responsible for this part of the apparatus of control, at another as softening the control itself by being interposed between it and the people being so controlled (Heidensohn 1985: 172–73). The ambiguity reflects, therefore, not only the paradoxes of welfare which we have discussed, but also broader paradoxes to do with the dualisms embedded in women's social roles.

It is in these ways that welfare organizations are conduits of care. They share the court's individualistic perception of delinquency; they reflect that perception in their own structure and practices; and the historical tradition in which they are located is predominantly (though not exclusively) negative: the Poor Law and police court heritages of the two agencies have been too little acknowledged by commentators. The agencies' procedures operate too at a level of irony: as we have seen, to individualize the person behind each face queuing up in the waiting room is such a routine procedure that its consequence is to individualize no one.

Within the organization, however, exist two contradictory elements which modulate this function of conveying ideology. First, although the ideologies of individualism held by the court are indeed carried into the supervisory process, at an *operational* level there exist the conflicts and jealousies, the suspicions, to which we have earlier alluded and which militate against the possibility of a closely collusive relationship between court and agency. The practicalities of the day-to-day management of a statutory order differ markedly from the practicalities of passing sentence and having done with it, and almost inevitably lead to elements of concealment and minor deviance; equally the role of the organization differs from and is in some respects more restricted than that of the juvenile court: the former has no deterrent or prophylactic mandate, for example, and the exercise by the court of its powers in a punitive way not infrequently engenders hostility within the agencies. Further, the agencies are even less concerned with what the offender has done than with what he or she is. So embedded in the juvenile justice system is the welfare agency, of course, that this is no qualitative shift: that comes earlier in the process, usually at the moment the police decide to take action and a kindly, concerned juvenile bureau officer knocks on the front door. But though at this later stage the sentencing act which creates a tutelary process is a quantitative not a qualitative shift, a shift it nevertheless is, as the court's action becomes a springboard for further interventions of a kind which, as we shall later see, are somewhat unpredictable.

The second conflict is that between the negative stereotyping and the professional value and aspiration of the front-liners. The organizations, it will be recalled, are not *simple* successors of poor law provisions, but contain within them different, contradictory traditions based on professional counselling and quasi-therapeutic child care theories. These traditions are embedded in the professional ideologies of the front-liners themselves and reinforced in their training (which, to make the point even more explicitly, is usually studiously referred to as 'education and training'). The struggle of the professionals, whose motivation is on the whole benign and ameliorative rather than controlling, to carve for themselves a 'space to care' in an organization which all too often seems antithetical to such an objective (Hardiker and Barker 1981) is a matter to which we shall return later. Welfare work is, however, an 'interstitial profession which serves both the client in need and society at large' (Compton and Galaway 1975: 472), and, in that it serves the former only to the extent permitted it and in the manner laid down for it by those representatives of the latter who employ its practitioners, its capacity to provide for its clients in the way those practitioners might wish is considerably restricted.

Welfare organizations as open systems: if the Charity Organization Society represents for us a paradigmatic instance of the links between organizations, ideologies, and the social structure, it will be obvious that similar links exist today. Welfare organizations are part of a broader social context and penetrated by a range of external influences (E. Roberts 1982; Hardiker and Barker 1981). These influences affect their functioning at levels both of policy and practice, and though they cannot be said to *determine* all such policies and practices (complex human organizations being notoriously immune to any such certainties), they do impact upon them profoundly:

> 'An open system exists, and can only exist, by exchanging materials with its environment. It imports materials, transforms them by means of conversion processes, consumes some of the products of conversion for internal maintenance, and exports the rest. Directly or indirectly, it exchanges its outputs for further intakes, including further resources to maintain itself. These import–conversion–export processes are the work the enterprise has to do if it is to live.'
> (Miller and Rice 1967: 3)

So while to the professional supervising the delinquent, the desired output might be either the psychically adjusted or the materially better-off client, with a reduction in delinquency having less centrality, to the impinging systems the desired export is reformed ex-delinquents. That such a demand is unrealistic will be obvious; equally obvious from our own argument thus far will be that, unlike the manufacturing system which produces commodities attuned to the demands of the environment or it perishes, the welfare organization is not dependent on this kind of 'success' for *survival*, because it fulfils certain social functions by its very failure: it intrudes, classifies, monitors. But surviving by failing is an uncomfortable way of earning a living and leads to a range of strategies which we begin to describe in our next section. For the moment, however, our concern is with the nature and level of the demands of the environment on the organizations. They exist at two levels – the level of *broad socio-political realities* and *precise legislative sanction*. The relationship between the two is a complex matter beyond our present scope, and details of the agency sanction afforded both social services departments and the probation service are available elsewhere (see, for example, Jarvis 1974; G. Roberts 1981). Our concern here is with the nature of the relationship between the welfare organizations and the broader socio-political realities which impinge upon them.

At this point we introduce two illuminatory concepts. First, Dingwall, Eekelaar, and Murray have helpfully presented the organizational task as a *charter*, a notion embodying a fusion of the legislative and the interpretive:

> 'By establishing governing charters under the control of the public or their elected representatives, state intrusion into citizen's [sic] homes may be legitimated. The chain of moral accountability is the essential corollary of the preservation of liberal ideals. Inasmuch as it is broken or eroded, surveillance becomes oppressive rather than facilitative, coercive rather than regulatory. . . . While the professional has only to square his or her conscience, the bureaucrat or bureau-professional must attend to a line of external constraint.'
> (Dingwall, Eekelaar, and Murray 1983: 120–21)

The charter defines not only the framework of rights and duties which constitute agencies' sanction, but also a set of roles they must play and judgements they must make. It will be recalled that of their essence these judgements are not always amenable to rule-making, nor can they be in some rationalist way value-free. The essence of a child abuse scandal may well not be simply incompetence (though that is not to deny its existence) but a different interpretation of the charter between members of the organization and its environment: it is, after all, one thing to export an unreformed and unrepentant delinquent, quite another to export a dead child. But when, as in such an instance, a charter embodies the necessity of a judgement being made among competing values or conflicting rights, in the absence of clear and broadly accepted operational guidelines the outcome must be acrimony, uncertainty, and variant decision-making. Jasmine Beckford may have been a child in trust (Blom-Cooper 1985), but the balance in a charter between the child protective duty and the duty to respect family rights is easier determined with the benefit of hindsight than at the time. Hence this comment:

> 'While our personal conclusion must be that agency staff are over-respectful of parental liberties and that "justice for children" may require more rather than less state intervention, we recognise that these deficiencies, by our standard, do not represent failings by the individual agencies so much as the inherent limitations of the licences and charters which we, as citizens, have granted to them.'
> (Dingwall, Eekelaar, and Murray 1983: 207)

But the idea of a charter means that individual welfare workers cannot legitimately shirk the controlling functions mandated to their agency, whether they involve child protection, the management of community service orders, or the supervision of young offenders. They may, of course, lobby to change the charter, but pending change, or if they are unsuccessful, they are obliged to do their duty. It is in this sense that welfare work exists within a preordained discourse out of which it is an idealist illusion to pretend there is a path (Webb 1981; and from a different perspective, Davies 1985).

The second concept is that of *organizational resolve*. The charter given to organizations does not represent any broad social consensus, nor is it always clear. Both probation and social services agencies are subject to conflicting pressures and demands – the latter, as we shall show, very much more than the former – and out of the plethora of external pressures and internal conflicts not only about specifics but also, existentially, about the entire nature of the enterprise of welfare, the mass of people who ultimately comprise the organization have by some means to determine, negotiate, or have imposed upon them a set of operational policies and practices by means of which to tackle the tasks and fulfil the roles embodied in their charter. The extent to which this is done we term organizational resolve: it is that which brings an organization to approach a particular problem in a particular way, which determines how far the different levels and types of workers who make up the organization agree about the purpose and method of an intervention; how far conflicts can be contained; how far there is goodness of fit between the organizational practices and the demands of the environment which receives the organization's exports (Kakabadse 1982). In looking at, successively, probation and social services agencies, we shall show that organizational resolve is a useful vehicle by which to analyse certain similarities and differences between them.

So all welfare organizations contain conflicting models of service delivery, and it is preferable to analyse what might otherwise, and more individualistically have to be interpreted as coincidental mass incompetence in terms of organizational or structural factors of this kind. For example, in our study of supervision orders (Harris and Webb 1983; Webb and Harris 1984) we saw on the part of social workers in particular an apparent abdication of control which reflected more than anything a conflict between the preconstituted role of welfare work which we described in the last section and the 'professional' ideology of practice of the front-liners; a disjunction, that is to say, between an *agency service* and an *independent practice* model of service delivery, the one reflecting hierarchical models of accountability, the other autonomous social workers acting in a client-centred way on the basis of professional values and knowledge. Although in the day-to-day world a truce can often be sustained between them, it is by definition at points of difficulty that the cracks appear, and stark choices are presented to workers between what *should* be done (for which knowledge they might draw on books of practical ethics, such as Leighton, Stalley, and Watson 1982, or Rhodes 1986), and what the agency's charter decrees *must* be done. This conflict accounts in part for the sense of alienation among social workers in particular detected by researchers (DHSS 1978; Hadley and Hatch 1981; Glastonbury 1982).

If organizational resolve is vulnerable to these conflicting ideologies (which hide behind them fundamental questions such as 'what kind of social worker am I?') it is vulnerable also to two further and related matters. The first lies in the very answer to the question just posed: 'what kind of social worker am I?' has numerous possible answers which range from community activist to overt social controller. Hence the diversity of answer which can be given – and justifiably given as well as theoretically defended given welfare work's abundant pluralism – leads to yet further questioning, an overarching *Angst* which finds its expression in occupational uncertainty and an acute awareness of the paradox involved in working for a profession which is so singularly unable even to define what it does.

Then also comes the matter of professional knowledge, which contributes to welfare work's relatively low insulation from lay opinion. Seen by some as censorious interlopers and by others as paid excusers of moral failure, welfare workers are ready scapegoats for numerous ills. Those who claim expertise in the intangible domains of relationships, parenting, and delinquency will inevitably clash with a culture which expects of its experts certainty and specific output. 'Everybody' knows something of the concerns of welfare work, and, as we remarked before, sometimes claims greater prescriptive certainty than the experts themselves. There is no barrier of arcane knowledge, no agreed expertise.

Such realities impinge variously on the two agencies. For the *probation service* the matter, though not simple, is the less fraught. Linked as it is through employing committees dominated by local magistrates to the Home Office of central government, the service stands largely outside of the more volatile politics of local government. As that arm of the criminal justice and penal systems which reaches out to the world of reformation and community control it does, of course, have acute and painful dilemmas with which its practitioners grapple (Harris 1977), and the dilemmas have their echoes in equivalent services overseas: hence Fogel notes that 'The struggle to disentangle help from control is ubiquitous in Western Europe' (Fogel 1984), and Conrad that 'no one person should attempt to combine surveillance and service . . . these two functions must not be assigned to the same agency' (Conrad 1984). But of course such a move – however conceptually neat or professionally desirable one might think it to be – would leave probation with the need to be given a new charter; and as it happens, the 1980s have seen the English and Welsh probation service resolve its conflicts not by separation of function but by the development of a new operational ideology which has significantly heightened its organizational resolve. The development, described in Chapter 2, of the ideology of decarceration has provided a common denominator between the professionals and the managers (Boswell 1985). Though there remain pressures from many probation officers to revert to a more 'caring' service, these now appear to have little political influence in the face of pressure and resource allocation which are designed to further the objective of decarceration (Haxby 1978). The controlling probation service sought in the mid-1970s by the revolutionary tactics of the Younger Report has, then, arrived more gradually, encouraged by the selective allocation of resources. Hence the service's general adherence to the demands of the Statement of National Objectives and Priorities (Home Office 1984) has ensured a relative lack of conflict with the Home Office. At a more local level, though relations with courts vary, and there is a particular problem to do with the use of recommendations in social enquiry reports, the service generally has come to be seen as providing a useful resource for courts. It has, therefore, been able to secure substantially more organizational resolve than has generally been the case with the social services departments.

Social services departments, unlike the probation service, are not deeply penetrated by a single system, but rather encounter an abundance of demands, many of them conflicting – from elected members of the local authority, members of the public, community activists, the local Press, and voluntary organizations in particular. Their position, as bureau-professional organizations within the local authority sector dealing with politically fraught issues of rights and duties makes them highly visible. Whereas the Home Office is nothing if not cautiously conservative, local government can be volatile. Elected members may take a back seat in professional matters but they may lead from the front; they may see the department as a vehicle for a front-line attack on racism, sexism, capitalism, or the nuclear arms race (for examples of some of these hopes for it see Jordan and Parton 1983); or they may regard it as a necessary evil, to be starved of resources in order to facilitate fixing a low rate. They may have views on residential care, trans-racial fostering and adoption, the involvement of the community in the care of the elderly; they may initiate or oppose joint-funded projects with the National Health Service; they may determine research and training priorities for their staff as well as recruitment policies.

This vulnerability reflects two issues, not only the politicality of the *location* of social services, but also the weakness of the framing of welfare as a professional activity. Since, as we have already observed, boundaries do not blur in one direction only, the lack of definition within the sphere of the social (Donzelot 1980) which encourages many welfare workers not just to help the poor but to attack poverty, not just to protect but to seek to extend clients' 'rights', equally leaves welfare work vulnerable to penetration from outside. And the social services department is particularly well placed (a privilege it increasingly shares with the education department) to become a political football. The issue of community social work is a case in point:

> 'First, there are those who believe that it could be mobilised into political pressure groups to obtain a massive increase in statutory resources. Secondly, there are those who believe that the community model would generate a sufficient volume of informal care services to justify drastic cuts in statutory funding.'
> (Pinker 1982: 261)

These conflicting pulls, this politicality, are both cause and consequence of a lack of organizational resolve within the departments themselves.

But in addition to being, by their nature and location, thus permeable to multiple influences from without, social services departments face uncertainty and dissension from within. One source of uncertainty is the very multiplicity of the duties enshrined in the charter. There is a plethora of goals, of competing demands, and the combination of infinite need and finite resources can become organizationally debilitating to the extent that the work is never done; further, the fact that to address one need is to set aside another leads to yet more pressure from the set-aside clients. Such is the nature of social workers' own commitment to ideals, that the pressure is quite liable to be orchestrated from within the departments themselves by those front-liners who seek to champion the cause of the neglected clientele.

It is aspects of this nature of social work which lead to the second source of dissension from within. Drawing as they do on the American-influenced model of independent professionalism, social workers typically take on their clients' battles as their own, sometimes to the extent of seeing themselves actually penetrating their own employing agency as emissaries on their clients' behalf. Though all professionals will seek to influence some aspects of their activities, the impact of social workers' attempts to do so is considerable. This is partly, of course, because of the *extent* of it, but that is an effect more than a cause of the agency's vulnerability. The problem of knowledge-status is more central. Such is the competing range of theories about, say, mental illness (all of them passed to social workers in simplified form) that any debate about it will include one set of arguments in support of anti-psychiatry, another in support of the value of psychiatric symptomatology. Although neither side ever actually wins the argument, each one pursues the case as though it is not only a difference of opinion but also a personal *credo* which is at stake. When the organizational charter includes an obligation to enforce sanctions alongside an occupational disinclination to do so; when the status of the knowledge on which an instruction from a senior to a junior professional might be based is so doubtful; when theoretical debates are frequently mere metaphors for the expression of deep-seated ideological conflicts; when the most junior members of the organization claim autonomy for 'professional opinions', the potential for the convincing exercise of organizational resolve is not especially great.

Conclusion

As a conduit, the welfare organization represents the *locus* of a convergence of different and conflicting traditions; it embodies both conflict and consensus with the court. It effectively provides the means by which the logic of the individualization of criminality is taken to its natural conclusion – a form of supervision and control. But in carrying that ideology it in effect transforms it. This transformation is in part a reflection of the practicalities of managing people who have already proved to be unmanageable, and involves a series of accommodations to a reality which it would be beyond the court's sphere of knowledge to comprehend. But also it transforms as a result of a number of separate pressures to which it is subject – pressures both from outside the system and from its own professional staff. These external pressures impinge differently in kind and degree on the two welfare agencies, but create a situation of considerable instability for the social services department in particular. Internal stresses for the organization result from the clash of traditions, the organizational and the professional, which, we have argued, take on different manifestations in the two agencies. In probation the conflict has been in good part resolved around the common objective of decarceration, an objective which simultaneously ensures the growth of the organization *and* provides a professional legitimation for probation officers themselves. But in social services departments there is no such device, and this lack, combined with the vastly larger and more complex charter to which the organization works, creates a distinct lack of organizational resolve. That this problem presents acute difficulties not only for the organization, but also for the front-liners will become apparent in the next chapter.

5 The micro level: the experts at work

'But, at the outset, we encounter this difficulty: Ought the moral reform to exclude the physical suffering and the shame which accompany punishment? If so, is the penal sanction to consist, not in the menace of an evil, but in the promise of a good? The effect of such a proceeding, it is evident, would be completely to overturn the motives of conduct, since the worst part of conduct would be rewarded by especial care on the part of the State; untouched by any agency of physical suffering, the criminal would receive as the sole consequence of his crime, the privilege of gratuitous instruction.' (Garofalo 1914: 256)

This chapter completes our conceptual analysis of the supervisory process by examining just what it is that the experts themselves do in their day-to-day encounters with their clientele. The chapter as a whole falls into two main parts: first we complement the argument in Chapter 4 that the intra-organizational conflicts within welfare agencies cause particular difficulties for the experts themselves, by exploring some of the ways in which the professionals experience and cope with what we term 'occupational uncertainty' (Webb and Harris 1984). We then report empirical findings which are relevant to our theme in this book. First we shall describe the clients themselves – their class membership, offence behaviour, family patterns, school conduct, and the like – to defend empirically the argument that many of the people subject to supervision orders are really remarkably ordinary; and secondly we shall describe the rather different supervisory practices of the two agencies responsible for managing the orders to illustrate just how capricious are the demands made of the youngsters themselves, how dependent not on their behaviour or needs, but on chance, the agency to which they have been allocated, and doubtless, within the agency the particular supervisor.

By this means the empirical study parallels the theoretical exegesis of Chapters 3 and 4. Just as Chapter 3 demonstrated the imposition of arbitrary power over more and more offenders, so does the first part of the empirical report indicate the apparent, albeit implicit, censoriousness to which the supervisees are subject; and just as Chapter 4 showed how in practice that power was variably and spasmodically implemented, how it was refracted through the filter of the agency to the extent that its reality was almost unrecognizable from the *Foucaultesque* theory of the matter, so do we see the objects of supervision by the two agencies subjected to significantly different expectations.

This chapter's empirical component relates to the boy offenders in our main sample; the subsample of girls, in relation to whom there are additional matters which also require addressing, is the subject matter of Chapter 6.

Occupational uncertainty

Welfare workers are subject to a cruel irony: what for many of them are the very reasons for their occupational existence – the alleviation of problems, the expression of altruism, a commitment to social justice – have been denounced as a sham, with welfare work itself held to be covert coercion, an ideological practice individualizing structural problems and blaming their victims.

In the academic establishments where they are formulated, these criticisms are seldom that bald, but in the vulgarized form in which they are received by welfare workers they can easily appear destructive and demoralizing. Even community care, the epitome of deprofessionalization, returning power and responsibility to the people, becomes in this analysis a mere exercise in the extraction of yet more unwaged work from women.

Nor, of course, is the political right any friend of welfare workers; indeed such is the revolutionary fervour rhetorically attributed to them by some demagogues of the right that one might be forgiven for believing that the phrase 'social worker' has been inadvertently inserted in a speech intended to refer to the 'socialist worker'. But welfare work has also been arraigned not just on these moral and economic grounds but also as empirically ineffective and professionally spurious (Brewer and Lait 1980).

To neither set of criticisms can welfare workers make a confident reply; indeed the experience of listening to them trying to explain and justify their existence to those outside their own professional and assumptive worlds is typically a dispiriting one. Doctors and lawyers find it, obviously enough, much simpler to say what they do – indeed everybody knows what they do; but beyond that they manage more straightforwardly to deal appropriately with the various conflicts of loyalty or crises of conscience which they encounter. Doctors have to deal individually with structurally caused diseases; lawyers have to prosecute defendants with whose position they are in personal or political sympathy. But in these cases the professionals concerned develop coherent practices for dealing with such problems, and seem better able than welfare workers to separate the individual action from the issue to be raised with the professional association or in the correspondence columns of *The Times*.

Welfare work is a more weakly framed activity, characterized less by coherence than by the necessary but conceptually unclear function of plugging gaps left by the more strongly framed activities of other professionals. Teachers, doctors, housing officials, and policemen all have relatively clear job descriptions but encounter problems in the lives of the people with whom they deal which, severe as they may be, fall outside that description: professionals should not normally, after all, become embroiled in matters outside either their competence or their jurisdiction. But welfare workers have no such circumscription: in particular cases they may be adjuncts to almost any of these professionals because their role may impinge on the functions of all of them. They may be interpreting what the other professionals are saying or exerting pressure on the professionals themselves to do something different; and they may be collecting evidence from others to take action consistent with their own statutory powers. They provide homes for the old and for children, they have to authorize compulsory admissions to mental hospitals; but they are not experts in gerontology, child development, or mental illness. They have a nodding acquaintance with all these areas and much more besides, but their role remains nebulous, their niche hard to define.

How, then, do welfare workers respond to these assaults from outside which can so devastatingly fuel their own existential uncertainties? Both the meaning of the question and its answer lie in the nature of *the social*, that sphere within which we have seen them to operate. In the amorphousness of the social lie far more possible actions than there do clear rules for selecting among them. Though this is true for social professionals other than welfare workers – health workers are an obvious case in point – the flaccidity of the welfare workers' knowledge combined with the nature of their task and the power they exercise create particular problems for them, and of course a high degree of unpredictability and vulnerability for their clients (Howe 1980; Sheldon 1978). The rules to which these experts are subject come from legislation and agency policy; but except in particular and controversial areas these are blunt instruments: they confine the discretion of the experts in that they set certain boundaries around their rights and duties, it is true; but they do relatively little to govern the way the experts structure their day-to-day decision making. As we have already observed, their capacity to do so is strictly limited: if rules could be made, the experts would be both unnecessary and undesirable.

Faced with these uncertainties (and their concomitant opportunities for diversity and idiosyncracy) the experts naturally enough present a fragmented and internally inconsistent set of ideas about what their work is and about how best to go about doing it. Of course diversity and informed debate are appropriate attributes of any profession, and we take for granted that they will exist among welfare workers too. But such variations are not quite what we have in mind. The nature and degree of fragmentation seem sometimes to leave unclear quite what is the core activity against which these deviations are to be measured, as the experts create for themselves a private coherence, a cognitive and assumptive structure by which and through which to identify their own professional selves. Such fragmentation, though we think it especially characteristic of social services departments (for reasons which will by now be obvious), is not a matter from which the probation service is immune either.

Fragmentation takes many forms: it may be principally professional or political (an unsatisfactory distinction we know, for how, in the sphere of the social, can we separate the two?) But some experts will find their occupational coherence through a flight into crypto-therapeutics, as though a thorough grasp of the Milan Method of Family Therapy or Transactional Analysis could truly provide it; others, ironically, have embraced the idea of retributive sentencing (to the inadequacy of which one might have thought their very presence stood eloquent testimony) and due process, becoming adherents of the 'back to justice' movement. Others gain their gratification from an association with more prestigious professionals such as consultants and judges, basking thereby in a modest quantity of reflected glory; others again busy themselves by becoming aligned with members of the oppressed classes.

So there are probation managers who argue that the job is to control offenders on behalf of the community (Griffiths 1982) and involves the unquestioning acceptance of authority (Bibby 1976); there are conservative or liberal academics attacking the role of critical theory in welfare work training (Davies 1985) and advocating the selection of less questioning students by courses (Munday 1972). And there are probation officers who say this:

> 'It is through the union that probation officers can make links with other workers and with wider struggles within the state. Organization in the working-class form of the trade union facilitates these links. It also helps probation officer escapes from an esoteric

identity as "the neutral professional" to a recognition of their status as sellers of labour power, having common cause with members of the working class. These links enable us to connect with, and contribute to, broad and fundamental struggles over social justice, distribution of wealth, eradication of poverty and provision of welfare services.' (Walker and Beaumont 1981: 194–95)

This might seem a relatively ambitious mandate for the humble probation officer, but the strategies for achieving such laudable goals seem designed less to bring about these transformations than to excite the maximum hostility among managers and magistrates. Indeed perhaps a more discreet revolutionary would have disseminated them to the faithful by word of mouth rather than committing them to print:

'It is wise to guard against unnecessary criticism. Management scrutiny tends to concentrate on written records and the keeping of up-to-date minimal records is an important safeguard. Often work with clients will have to be justified in the sort of language management prefers – references to esoteric social work theories, the needs of the relationship and professional judgement will prove useful.'
(Walker and Beaumont 1981: 186)

In short, business as usual, albeit justified conspiratorially. One would expect nothing else given the discourse within which probation work is located: the central irony of attempting to insert a praxis rooted in Marxist materialism into probation practice is that the very notion of so inserting it is quite irredeemably idealist given the specific and subordinate place occupied by welfare work generally within the social formation (Webb 1981).

But the sum effect of all these fragmented interpretations, these personal syntheses, is paradoxically to create yet further uncertainties: the professional co-existence of such incompatible beliefs and purposes, lacking as some of them do even the most basic agreement about the core of the job can have no other effect. But its cause is explicable hardly at all in terms of the private psychopathologies of the individuals concerned, and for academic social scientists to believe that the answer lies in selecting a different kind of person is clearly absurd: people are moulded by the processes of which they become a part, and where those processes are themselves unclear, where there are multiple paths to heaven, none, in the relativisitic extremes of welfare talk, preferable to another, diversity will inevitably occur.

The diversity, then, emerges from aspects of the welfare workers' role, task, history, and knowledge; it is inseparable too, as we argued in Chapter 4, from the traditions of which they are a part.

'No poet, no artist of any art, has his complete meaning alone. His significance, his appreciation is the appreciation of his relation to the dead poets and artists. You cannot value him alone; you must set him, for contrast and comparison, among the dead. . . . The existing order is complete before the new work arrives; for order to persist after the supervention of novelty, the *whole* existing order must be, if ever so slightly, altered.' (Eliot 1951: 15)

The more secure the tradition, the more it can accommodate and respond to change and diversity. Probation, hence, manages better to retain its central meaning while incorporating a wide range of differences of perspective within it. With a secure base, diversity and debate challenge, stimulate, and are essential for development. Without such a base – and the reader will recall the multiple and conflicting traditions of the social services department – diversity can all too easily become dysfunctional: either the enterprise is diverted into putting into operation some new fad – whether of organization or professional activity – or it is impugned for failing to address competently some new and pressing social necessity. But it is simultaneously insufficiently secure to incorporate this new exigency and insufficiently confident to decline to do so. Its practitioners, therefore, are vulnerable to prolonged and repeated states of self-recrimination, which cause them to doubt ever more centrally the value of their professional work.

The consequence of all this is occupational uncertainty, its practice, once the specialisms and the fragmented commitments and the conflicts with agency expectations have been allowed to run their course, is that paradoxical process of *routine individualization* which we mentioned in Chapter 4, whereby simultaneously everybody and nobody is individualized. Routine individualization exists as the very child of the social, between, at the one extreme, the non-discretionary application of specified rules, and at the other, the *truly* individualized response to every problem, the flexible, creative practice which, though part of welfare work's professional persona, is altogether unrealistic among bureau-professionals whose lives are measured out in files and cases, and who have little option, at least after the first flush of enthusiasm has worn off, other than to approach each new client with the question: 'what type of case is this?' (Giller and Morris 1981).

By 'routine individualization' we mean the application of individual or organizational procedures which, though perfectly sensible to those who apply them, are typically less so to those who are subject to them. The considerable differences between the routine individualizations of the two welfare agencies illustrate clearly that these practices have their origins in factors other than logic or rationality, in the private and unpredictable cultures which have emerged in the agencies themselves, as the unstable heirs of disparate and conflicting traditions. Routine individualization, as we shall demonstrate in the next section, finds its way into social enquiry practice. We found in our study that recommendations for supervision orders were rarely amplified by reference to what would actually be done if an order were made; nor did courts blanch from making orders without such justifications. But the significance of this is that 74 per cent of our sample of boys were trivial or medium offenders with no more than two previous convictions, and 46 per cent were first offenders of whom fewer than one in five had committed a serious offence. The very free-floatingness of the supervision order, then, links with the uncertain processes by which it comes to be recommended to make it an aspect of the tutelary process. In the next chapter we shall show how this tendency is especially manifest in the case of girls, but in that of boys too variety of purpose and method, wide-ranging power, lack of coherent tradition, theoretical flaccidity and the experts' simultaneous vulnerability to generalized criticism and imperviousness to precise accountability, combine to make the supervision order just such a form of surveillance.

Now all these uncertainties make of the order too a disposal *suspensive* not only in its imposition but also in its implementation. Two separate processes are at work here. The court, in making the order, has in mind that non-cooperation will lead to a return to court and a more punitive response. But the uncertainties of the supervisory role mean that this very seldom occurs in spite of the widespread failures among a majority of clients to conform to the letter of their orders. Indeed, in our study the most conforming clients were generally those of whom least was demanded.

This may seem a curious point to make: after all, does not the potency of power itself exist in its application, either in its subduing of opposition or, in *Foucaultesque* ironic vein, in failing to do so and hence justifying more of it? How can the failure to report a recalcitrant supervisee to the court constitute a further form of power?

The answer to these questions must itself be equivocal: after all it is perfectly obvious that to return every offender to court on every minor infraction would indeed constitute power manifest. But such is not the only kind of power. The effect of the simultaneous sabotaging and sustaining of the process of which they are a part by the experts is to transform rather than diminish the power to which their clients are subjected. It is to add a second layer of suspensiveness to an already suspensive order, to suspend suspensiveness itself, and to create of the experts themselves a filter through which decisions are to be made as to whether the power of the courts is to be invoked. This is itself a form of power: as any schoolboy once knew, while to be caned was painful, it was hardly more so than the daily rough and tumble of the playground or the rugby field; and in a curious sense to be caned was a relief: one had experienced, survived, and so, oddly, triumphed over the worst that could be done to one, and certainly no second caning would be so fearsome. But *never* to have been caned was to be subjected to a fear of the unknown – a terrible threat and the most cogent of reasons for generally behaving oneself. Much the same applies with the supervision order. The powers of course in respect of breaches of supervision are less than awesome: a fine or an attendance centre order is a mere pin-prick, after all. But to have the unrealized possibility of a return to court hanging over one's head is likely to be a rather greater inducement to conformity.

The power of the supervision order, then, lies not in some efficient policing practice whereby the least deviance is brutally avenged; we have no stories of children being incarcerated for being ten minutes late for an appointment. On the contrary, so far as we can tell with some offenders missed appointments are so common that they are hardly even commented upon by the supervisors: and every excuse is doubtless accepted. There are analogies with a study of the management of child abuse:

> 'the structures of the organizations involved and the practical reasoning of their members have the effect of creating a preference for the least stigmatizing interpretation of available data and the least overtly coercive possible disposition. Officially-labelled cases of mistreatment are, quite literally, only those for which no excuse or justification can be found.'
>
> (Dingwall, Eekelaar and Murray 1983: 207)

This is occupational uncertainty epitomized; but it is, nevertheless, the application of a peculiar, paradoxical form of power, not quite its abdication. For the power is not something which the experts *can* abdicate: it is there not because they have taken it, but because its exercise is, in turn, imposed upon them. Studies suggest that however the experts may conceptualize their activities in terms of 'care', this reality of power, this sense of control is an ever present one for many clients (Morris and Giller 1977; Morris and McIsaac 1978; Parker, Casburn, and Turnbull 1981). As the agents of somebody else's power, the experts' capacity to negotiate its exercise, though real, is by no means uncircumscribed. There *are*, of course, good professional practices for making sense of this negotiating potential: it is

The micro level: the experts at work

certainly neither our intention to belie the value of openness and clarity (of the kind advocated in, for example, the experts' own literature on 'contracts': see, for example, Cordon 1980) nor to suggest by omission that some experts do not handle their role very much better than others: everyday experience of welfare professionals confirms one's impression that vast differences in skill and ability exist. But the literature of the experts, or their 'value talk' (Timms 1986) would lead one to believe that such professional strategies are enough. This cannot be.

Clients on supervision orders exist in the space between what has been done and what is able to be done to them. A simple, if somewhat defective, analogy demonstrates the meaning of this. Most of us who drive motor cars at some stage commit minor infractions, normally matters of parking or speeding. That we are so seldom apprehended is a consequence both of the near ubiquitousness of the deviance and of police decisions to concentrate their resources elsewhere. We offenders at large are vulnerable, therefore, not only to bad luck but also to a change in policing which (doubtless for some internal, and hence obscure, reason) leads the police to wish to punish drivers speeding through the town in which we live. When we are caught and fined, seemingly arbitrarily, for an offence which we and millions of others have previously committed with impunity, we cannot, according to the principles either of strict logic or strict morality, complain at our lot, but unless we are extraordinarily phlegmatic we are likely to rail at the gods notwithstanding.

Motoring offenders are not, of course, alone in being thus vulnerable: Young has shown a similar phenomenon amongst marijuana users (Young 1971); prostitutes, shoplifters, importuners for immoral purposes, and the like, as offenders whose crimes are not only grossly underreported but also easily detected, are equally liable to be dealt with thus. A supervision order which imposes on youngsters who are *already* known to have broken the rule of law further rules to which the rest of us are not subject – to keep appointments with a supervisor, to attend school, to lead an honest and industrious life for example, and for a period generally as long as two years – precisely ensures that at some stage they will fail. This in turn creates amongst the supervisees a dependence for their continued freedom on the expert. No strict injustice occurs: the offenders should keep appointments just as motorists should obey speed limits. But the vulnerability remains and is in no way abolished by the relative unlikelihood of supervisees actually being called to account for their omissions and commissions.

Occupational uncertainty, then, has implications for workers and clients. In this section we have traced the origins and processes of the vulnerability: in the intra-organizational conflicts of which the experts are a part, in the unpopularity with others (including those radicals whom the experts might have expected to be their supporters) of welfare work, in welfare workers' own anxieties and indecisions and so on. But these uncertainties have implications not only for the psychic equilibrium of the experts themselves but also, as we have gradually moved on to see, for the fate of their clients. We have offered a model in which we see power over the clients exercised by people who feel uncertain, even resentful, about having to exercise it, but people also who are vulnerable to pressure from outside and who may operate within a cluster of differing and sometimes competing professional ideologies (see, for a further discussion of this issue, Hardiker 1977; Hardiker and Webb 1979). The rules which govern the exercise of supervision are unclear to the clients, however comprehensible they may be to the supervisors in terms of organizational routine and culture. But because that routine and culture are themselves vulnerable to attack from without or within, they may change; and this uncertainty increases the powerlessness of the clients still further. Even the non-exercise of power is, as we have argued in this section, an application of power; and when that non-exercise is itself perhaps subject to a policy change, a directive from government, a complaint from a judge or a shift in the interests of the experts themselves, the uncertainty of the experts and the discomfiture of the clients are further augmented.

Supervising freedom

> 'A departmental committee . . . found that some boys had been placed on probation with a condition that for two years they should not enter a cinema; also that a young offender of 18 was directed not to smoke for the year of his probation and during that time was to remain indoors every night after nine o'clock. He was also directed to attend church once every Sunday. Another case was discovered in which a man and a woman found guilty of a joint crime, were directed not to speak to one another. Within a month of their probation they were married and how this tangle was sorted out is not reported.' (Mullins 1957: 27)

This section is divided into two parts. The two together comprise a compressed summary of part of our empirical data on boys; data on girls are included in Chapter 6. Since the book is not intended to be a research report, the section is relatively brief, and selected to illustrate empirically the themes which we have been discussing thus

The micro level: the experts at work

far. The methodology of the study is included in Appendix B. It will be recalled that the total sample is 971 boys aged 14 to 16 on supervision for an offence for the first time; 701 of the boys are supervised by probation and 270 by social services. Because, however, the source of our data was the welfare records of the youngsters, there are a number of omissions. Where records are incomplete or in some other way doubtful in relation to particular issues, we have discarded dubious material, and are reasonably confident of the accuracy of those data included. We were fortunate to have such a large sample; even with discarded files, our database for any one question never dropped below 700, which makes the study by a very long way the largest ever undertaken on the supervision order.

The first part of this section focuses on the supervised population itself, giving details of the kind of person who was placed on supervision; the second offers an analysis *by agency* of the supervisory process. The thrust of the first part will be that the population is remarkably ordinary, that many of the sample are supervised almost be default, that few demonstrate great need or present great risk. In the second part we shall demonstrate empirically some of our earlier theoretical and conceptual points about the differences between the agencies.

The supervised population: in our theoretical exegesis thus far we have painted a curious picture of an almost dilatory exercise of power by experts over very considerable numbers of the working-class young. We have described as *the social* the realm within which the supervision takes place, and have portrayed it as a norm-distributing sector, but as being itself characterized by a host of conflicting and competing norms. We have also shown how it is that this conflict of norms, of which the flaccid knowledge-base of the experts who inhabit the social is a part, has created an unpredictability, even capriciousness, which renders the experts relatively impervious both to control from above and to accountability to their clients. 'Capriciousness' is perhaps the wrong word for that which we wish to convey, for it smacks a little too much of malicious whimsy, a kind of social Russian Roulette. The capriciousness of which we speak is more benign in intent than that, albeit that elements of the Russian Roulette – perhaps with plastic bullets, though – remain. Impressed upon us, as we survey the scene, is the Nietzschean axiom that 'the consequences of our actions take hold of us quite indifferent to our claim that meanwhile we have "improved"' (Nietzsche 1886).

The supervisees were certainly ordinary in their personal and social characteristics. Although a disproportionate number were from one-parent families (one in five, against a 1978 average of one in nine: Central Statistical Office 1980: 81), some 80 per cent of the youngsters were from complete families with two parents. Of those from one-parent families the vast majority, as one would expect, had a father absent, and in about half these cases the mothers were in waged work, most of them in unskilled jobs. For these families money was clearly likely to have been rather tight, and if we add to this 20 per cent of the total those other financially precarious units where the father, though present, was unemployed, we find that at the time the order was made about 40 per cent of the total sample had one parent either absent or unemployed. This figure would substantially underestimate the impecunious circumstances of the families, since quite clearly many more would have had, or would come to have as the order continued, experience of parental unemployment. The overall economic tenor of the boys' homes was unskilled or, less frequently, semi-skilled. Fewer than 8 per cent of the boys (a total of 76) had one or both parents in 'white-collar' jobs, and it is likely (though not certain from the way we collected the figures) that a proportion even of these few cases would have had the other present in a lower-status occupation. Almost all the boys, then, came from working-class homes, in many of which the work situation would have been characterized by subordination, and where there would have been a reasonably high degree of financial uncertainty brought about by low wages or unemployment.

Being working class was the most marked characteristic of this group; within the class the sample was not especially atypical: certainly we uncovered no greater picture of social dislocation than one would expect to find among the working class more generally (see, for example, Townsend 1979). In short, with the exception of the single-parent indicator, the sample was of fairly 'typical' boys from fairly 'typical' working-class homes. The vast majority of the sample (78 per cent) were still at school, and almost all of the remainder were engaged in some form of employment or training, with only 3 per cent of the total sample being classified unemployed when their orders were made. This does seem a remarkably low figure, but it must be remembered that in 1978 the total unemployment figure was no more than 1,475,000 (Central Statistical Office 1980: Table 5.15).

It is also possible that, aware of the fact that to be unemployed might be disadvantageous in court, a number of the boys obtained some form of employment prior to going to court — though we have no means of verifying this. Certainly as a group the sample existed almost entirely within the financial and emotional orbit of the family. Of those at school, almost all were in normal secondary education, with only 10 per cent either in special schools or remedial streams. We were able to inspect school reports in 759 cases of boys still at school; of these, as many as 54 per cent had good or average records of attendance, with the remainder characterized by varying degrees of absenteeism. But when we undertook a further analysis of the poor attenders, we found them no more likely to have been involved in serious than in trivial infractions. Nor, in spite of the generally negative tone of the school reports in the files, did it seem that as a group they were deemed especially disruptive or aggressive by their teachers.

This normality in education is worthy of brief note, since it has long been believed that some association exists between social failure and delinquency (see, for example, McDonald 1969; West 1969; West and Farrington 1973; though for an indication that the nature of this relationship is unclear, see the research review in Rutter and Giller 1983: 199 *et seq*). What we suspect has happened is this. The more disruptive or spectacularly unsuccessful pupils are likely to have come to the attention of the authorities at a younger age than our cohort, and to have been made subject at that time to either supervision or care orders. What may be interesting about our sample is that our selection procedure, by eliminating all but those offenders who are being supervised for the first time as young persons, has filtered out the more difficult youngsters and served to highlight the existence as supervisees of a large number of predominantly unproblematic adolescents.

This ordinariness extends into their offending behaviour, where relatively few of the sample could be said to be either serious or recidivist delinquents. We dealt with the *seriousness of the present offence* by creating a tripartite division into trivial (property offences of less than £10 value and common assault were the main matters here); medium (property offences of £10 to £100 and assault occasioning actual bodily harm); and high seriousness (property offences of over £100, grievous bodily harm, and malicious wounding). We also had an aggregation system whereby multiples of trivial offences became 'medium' or 'high' seriousness offences and so on. In this simple categorization, 30 per cent of the offenders had committed only trivial offences, 52 per cent medium; and only 18 per cent were high seriousness offenders.

But perhaps this rather surprisingly modest criminality was balanced by previous records, and the more trivial offenders had the longest records? Perhaps the serious offenders were more likely to be first offenders? In fact neither of these hypotheses is borne out to any marked degree: the range of first offenders in all three categories was

42-9 per cent with the highest number of first offenders coming into the middle seriousness category and not, as one might have expected, into the highs. There seems to be no significant additive influence in previous court appearances, and the range for recidivists (three or more previous findings of guilt) was only 7-10 per cent. In short, only a minuscule proportion of these supervision orders were in respect of persistent offenders. Quite clearly, therefore, as an 'alternative to custody' the supervision order in 1978 was almost completely irrelevant, and was rather drawing into the tutelary complex far larger numbers of marginal offenders who could almost certainly, as we are about to demonstrate, have been dealt with otherwise. There was no discernible proportionality about the orders, and this almost complete lack of tariff status means that they were being interpreted variously through the routine procedures of report writing and sentencing. When only 7 per cent of the serious offenders in our sample had three or more convictions, but 42 per cent of trivial offenders were also first offenders, there is presumably only one conclusion to be drawn.

We did generate one significant relationship which indicated a modest proportionality: between criminal status and the length of the order. We isolated the rather large numbers of trivial first offenders from all other supervisees, generating a status of 'not serious' for the former and 'serious' for the latter. On this very generous measure we did find that the former were rather more likely to receive one-year orders, but the two-year order remained modal for both groups: so 58 per cent of 'not serious' and 70 per cent of 'serious' cases received two-year orders, apparently as a routine disposal. Interestingly, almost no use was made either of the six-month order (which was newly available in 1978) or, at the other extreme, of the three-year order, which was clearly at this time going out of fashion. The lack of anything very specific to do in many cases, to which we refer later, may have gravitated against a six-month order, however, since if what was wanted was, as we believe, generalized supervision rather than the specific achievement of particular goals, then a two-year order would see all these youngsters out of school and into work; it would also involve their being subject to a court order as they went through the peak crime age of 15 to 16, though we do not suggest that this thought was specifically in the magistrates' minds.

A substantial minority of the supervisees were previously known to one or other of the statutory agencies (22 per cent to social services, 16 per cent to probation, almost none to both). We could find little reference in the files to contact with voluntary organizations such as the Family Service Units, which proffer professional guidance to the poorest, most disorganized families; nor were there many references to contact with the Child Guidance Service. We were keen to test whether previous contact with a welfare agency was associated with supervision orders being made, and here our finding was interesting and complex. We tested for previous contact with one of the agencies by seriousness of the offence. There was a patterned relationship between them which involved 59 per cent of trivial offenders, 55 per cent of medium offenders, and 51 per cent of high seriousness offenders having had prior contact.

Now the possible explanations of this finding are, first, that the same objective need which brought the offender into contact with the agency also justified the making of an order at this stage; and secondly that the contact itself had an amplificatory impact: that once one was caught in the net, in the net one stayed. For the first possibility to be plausible, we should want to see a persuasively argued report setting out a range of problems, a set of strategies for dealing with them, and a reason why it was necessary to have a formal order for these strategies to be pursued. But when we came to look at the experts' reports written on the offenders whom they knew, not only did we not find such strategies spelt out, but also we found that the report writers were marginally less likely to have recommended supervision for them at all than they were for the offenders who came to them new. (Supervision was recommended in 69 per cent of cases where there was prior contact, and 73 per cent where there was not.) Though we make nothing of this difference, we can certainly claim that at the very least offenders known to welfare agencies were no more likely to be recommended for supervision than were others; yet clearly magistrates were still making the orders.

This in turn is partly explained by the fact that rather more reports on previously known offenders were written by social services departments whose 'strike rate' in our study was significantly lower than that of probation (only 60 per cent of social services' clients had been recommended for supervision compared with 74 per cent of probation clients). Now it might be thought from this that the social enquiry report itself, by revealing intimate family matters on the basis of information acquired in the course of the previous contact, raised such concern among magistrates as to encourage them to make an order. This may be so: we can neither prove nor disprove it. But that such a consideration is at most no more than a subsidiary one is revealed by our analysis of those reports where a supervision order was made but not recommended. Of these reports, almost 40 per cent made no recommendation at all. This figure was partly explained by an especially heavy tendency in one social services department to eschew recommendations; but when this agency was discounted 'no recommendation' remained the largest single conclusion (at 31 per cent of the remaining total). Of the remaining unsuccessful recommendations, almost all were for low tariff disposals, with only 6 per cent for care or custody.

But when we analysed the cases for which no recommendation was made, we found that quite contrary to our expectations, the experts were significantly less likely to make recommendations in the case of more serious offenders: recommendations were made in 90 per cent of trivial cases but only 75 per cent of serious ones (using our tripartite classification). Quite clearly the popular view that not to make a recommendation in a serious case is to consign the offender to custody is not entirely correct; equally the finding suggests that magistrates see in the supervision order a feasible and desirable means of community control, as well as – or rather than – a form of social welfare.

When we add to this finding one which we shall further discuss below, to the effect that only a minority of reports which did recommend supervision spelt out what would happen if an order was made – what professional strategies would be utilized to solve problems or ensure control – we do have a situation in which a large number of rather ordinary working-class youths are being subjected to supervision for (mainly) two-year periods either without having been recommended for it or, if recommended, without any indication being given as to what would happen to them or why. The youths gave no great sense of having personal needs (we amplify this point later), and many of them seem not to have committed any offence more serious than the kind admitted to in self-report studies by up to 90 per cent of adolescent boys (Belson 1975). Somehow, however, they worked their way through the vagaries of the police cautioning and input systems (Ditchfield 1976; Oliver 1978) to be placed on supervision. Yet the more serious their offences, the less enthusiastic the experts were about supervising them. It was matters of this kind which we had in mind when we talked about the supervised freedom of the working-class young. We described the process as a kind of benign capriciousness, for in truth there is little or no malice about it. But therein lies the very source of power, for who could object to having a youngster overseen by a kindly probation officer or a youthful social worker in order to steer him through adolescence? Yet it is by these very means that the offending boy's world is penetrated, his family – and almost twice the national proportion of one-parent families appeared in our sample – worked with if it seems desirable to do so, the boy himself given, perhaps, compensatory 'treats', helped to find a job, guided to an adult life of contented conformity. This is supervised freedom indeed, but of a particular British kind. It has been called a 'Micawber approach' to the matter, a process of monitoring, chatting, 'forming a relationship', and 'being around', sometimes predictably, sometimes unexpectedly, in the hope that some time, some day, something which needs to be done will just turn up.

The process of supervision: although this subsection of the chapter is structured around an analysis by agency of the supervisory practices of probation officers and social workers, in strict terms we are not offering a precise comparison between them. For example, in five of our six research areas the local agreement between the two agencies was that the young person (aged 14 to 16) in our sample would normally be supervised by probation. Hence in all but that one 'deviant' area, social services' clients comprised those who would normally have gone to probation; and conversely, of course, in the one area the same point applied to probation officers' supervisees. The main reason for the allocation of supervisees in this way was that the supervising agency had either had previous dealings with the client himself or with some members or members of his family. Accordingly it was not surprising to find that significantly more social services clients had had previous contact with their supervising agency than had probation clients (Harris and Webb 1983; Webb and Harris 1984). This was so even though, as we previously remarked, we excluded all cases where the client had previously been subject to a supervision order.

This means that in looking at the practices of the two agencies we are not simply comparing like with like. There may be a greater distribution of social need among social services clients, though we have no reason to believe that there is any simple dichotomy here: probably more significant is that for a number of them intervention was already occurring in the family, and the making of a supervision order on a son was simply the provision of a different kind of legislative backing for work which was continuing anyway.

These are real differences and mediate any firm conclusions. The existence of need within the family may, for example, go some way towards explaining the greater tendency to which we shall draw attention later, for social workers to visit clients and families at home. But two points suggest that the answer is not that simple. First, the tendency towards more home visiting must be placed in a context whereby the contact between social worker supervisors and their clients of any kind is less than that between probation officers and their clients; and secondly, it is only for a minority of social services cases that home visiting could be considered to be anything like intensive. Only 17 per cent of clients, for example, were visited at home on more than ten occasions on a two-year order, and while this was almost exactly twice the percentage of probation clients who received this degree of home visiting, the proportions remain small. However much young offenders supervised by social workers might have been regarded as candidates for the 'welfare' element extended by the supervision order, this was not apparently translated into practices designed to meet particular needs.

It seems unlikely then that supervisory patterns are some simple and rational response to problems. If this were the case, we should expect some sense of urgency on the part of social workers to make contact after the order was made. On the contrary, though, *Table 1* shows that social workers allowed significantly more time to elapse between when the order was made and first seeing their clients than did probation officers, who themselves seldom demonstrated any great sense of urgency in the matter. No less than one-quarter of social services clients were not seen for thirty-six or more days after the order was made. *Table 2* points also to a highly significant difference in the frequency of contact between worker and client with social workers involved in markedly less contact with their supervisees than were probation officers.

Social workers' tardiness in this respect was extended to the first three-month period of the order. This three-month test is an important yardstick: welfare workers tend to say that it is the first few months of a statutory order which are crucial: the relationship is made or it is not, the tone of the proceedings is set. Accordingly we selected two levels of contact frequency over the first three-month period: a low one (three meetings) and a high one (eight meetings), and tested how many social workers and probation officers met their clients on three or fewer occasions (52 per cent of social workers and 26 per cent of probation officers) and eight or more occasions (13 per cent of social workers and 23 per cent of probation officers). In each case the difference was significant, especially strongly so on the low incidence test ($p < 0.001$). These figures are for two-year orders; when we tested for one-year orders we found a similar disparity, with 23 per cent of probation officers seeing their clients on three or fewer occasions, as against 48 per cent of social workers.

The trend for social workers to have significantly less contact with their clients than probation officers continues throughout the order. For example, on two-year orders 69 per cent of social services clients were seen on fifteen or fewer occasions compared with 42 per cent of probation clients ($x^2 = 34.52$, $df = 1$, $p <= 0.001$), a pattern of difference reflected, though less markedly, in the case of one-year

Table 1 Number of days between order being made and first contact by agency of supervision

number of days	probation		social services	
		%		%
0 – 7	189	(30.9)	52	(25.0)
8 – 14	135	(22.1)	48	(23.1)
15 – 21	120	(19.6)	30	(14.4)
22 – 28	53	(8.7)	16	(7.7)
29 – 35	41	(6.7)	13	(6.3)
36 +	73	(12.0)	49	(23.5)
total[1]	611	(100.0)	208	(100.0)

$x^2 = 18.50$; $df = 5$; $p < 0.01$

Note: [1] In all tables, 'totals' reflect the usable files for any particular item, and for this reason are smaller than the sampled population.

Table 2 Frequency of contact by agency of supervision

frequency of contact	probation		social services	
		%		%
0 – 5	69	(11.2)	51	(22.9)
6 – 10	105	(16.9)	57	(29.9)
11 – 15	128	(20.8)	49	(21.9)
16 – 20	117	(18.9)	27	(12.1)
21 – 25	83	(13.4)	16	(7.2)
26 – 30	40	(6.5)	14	(6.3)
31 +	75	(12.1)	10	(4.5)
total	617	(99.8)	224	(99.8)

$x^2 = 41.39$; $df = 6$; $p < 0.001$

orders. Using here ten visits as the break between a high and low incidence of contact, 63 per cent of social workers' clients fell into the latter category compared with 35 per cent of those supervised by probation officers ($x^2 = 10.60$, $df = 1$, $p <= 0.01$). Of course contact alone is not enough to judge the adequacy of what takes place between worker and youngster and it would clearly be of limited use to make a fetish of this. However, when there is relatively little contact with the client or any member of his social world it is difficult to maintain that anything constructive at all is happening. The only possible exceptions to this are when although the welfare worker is not seeing the client, someone else is carrying out supervision on his or her behalf, which the welfare worker is monitoring and supporting; and when the welfare worker has located a specific problem in the client's social world, and is working on that for the benefit of the client, following Baker's dictum, that is to say, to go not 'where the pain is' in conventional therapeutic terms, but 'where the pain is caused' (Baker 1983). In relation to the first of these possibilities we did indeed find that social workers were significantly more likely to involve the parents in the supervision of the child (32 per cent of cases as against 18 per cent of probation cases) and also the school (14 per cent against 9 per cent); although neither set of workers made more than minimal use of other community figures as surrogate supervisors. This finding supports the possibility that in the midst of their confusion social workers were struggling to articulate a model of supervision conceptually distinct from the criminal justice model embraced (albeit uneasily) by probation officers.

It would, however, be wrong to draw too stark a contrast between the habitual explanations adopted by the two agencies responsible for supervising young offenders: *Table 3* sets out the various problems typically identified by social workers and probation officers, from which it is clear both sets of workers share an occupational ideology which sees juvenile delinquency as legitimately and appropriately explained by the family nexus. Indeed the rank correlation between the items referred to by social workers and probation officers is highly significant (*re* 0.948) and indicates a tendency to 'weight' the items similarly. None the less there are, within this similarity of 'profile', differences in the frequency with which they report the problems, and in all but two of the items (8 and 9) the incidence of reporting such problems by social workers is significantly greater than that of the probation officers. It is not that social workers hold one view of delinquency and probation officers another – that the former are the sole exponents of the family dynamics model of causation – but rather that the strength of attachment to this explanation is somewhat greater for social workers than it is for probation officers.

If there is an element of need apparent in the lives of those youngsters encountered by social workers which makes the 'welfare' concerns of the supervision order the rationale for it as a disposal, there was little evidence of this being said in so many words in the social enquiry reports presented by them. We were interested to see to what extent reports, when they did recommend supervision, set out a proposed 'social work strategy'. The concern which magistrates have expressed about giving a 'blank cheque' to social workers (Berlins and Wansell 1974; House of Commons Expenditure

Table 3 Cases seen to exhibit various 'problems' by agency of supervision

	agency of supervision							statistical values	
	probation ($n = 701$)				social services ($n = 270$)				
	yes	(%)	no	(%)	yes	(%)	no	(%)	x^2	p
1 disruption caused by separation	108	(15.4)	593	(84.6)	79	(29.3)	191	(70.7)	23.94	< 0.001
2 significant separation from parents	333	(47.5)	368	(52.5)	169	(62.5)	101	(37.4)	17.73	< 0.001
3 chaotic household	33	(4.7)	668	(95.3)	32	(11.9)	238	(88.2)	15.48	< 0.001
4 problematic parental disciplining	276	(39.4)	425	(60.6)	136	(50.3)	134	(49.6)	9.59	< 0.01
5 history of economic hardship	108	(15.4)	593	(84.6)	64	(23.7)	206	(76.3)	9.04	< 0.01
6 deviant family norms	62	(8.9)	639	(91.2)	39	(14.4)	231	(85.6)	5.98	< 0.02
7 problematic school behaviour	144	(20.6)	557	(79.5)	72	(26.8)	198	(73.3)	4.23	< 0.05
8 parental criminality	64	(9.1)	637	(90.9)	34	(12.6)	263	(87.4)	2.42	N.S.
9 absence from school	214	(30.5)	487	(69.5)	95	(35.2)	175	(64.8)	1.93	N.S.

Committee 1975) might be diminished were the experts to describe in some detail what they had it in mind to do if an order was made. A specific recommendation for supervision linked with an identifiable welfare work strategy was found in just 30 per cent of the social enquiry reports prepared by probation officers, and only 13 per cent of reports written by social workers, a difference which is statistically significant (x^2 = 28.57, df = 1, $p <$ = 0.001). The 'welfare objectives' – which presumably the workers concerned might see themselves as having some competence in addressing – do not come across too often, and with notably less frequency and saliency in the case of social workers. It is unclear whether this arises because they are in fact less clear than probation officers about the purposes of supervision or simply that their court report technique finds them less adroit at spelling out the sorts of things that magistrates feel should be expressed.

Finally, in both agencies we found a remarkable tolerance of clients' failures to conform to the requirements of their orders. Supervision orders typically require offenders to report to their supervisors as instructed, to be available for visits to their homes, to attend school, and to lead an honest and industrious life. Although our comments on this tolerance must be seriously mediated by a significant change in the law during our research period (it being possible to take breach proceedings only against clients subject to supervision orders made after 17 July, 1978) (Children and Young Persons Act, 1969, section 15(2A) as inserted by the Criminal Law Act, 1977, section 37(2)(3)), it was previously possible for supervisors to initiate care proceedings in cases where supervision had broken down (Children and Young Persons Act, 1969, section 15(1)).

About twice as many probation as social work clients appear to have breached their orders at some time. On one-year orders breaches were recorded by 69 per cent of probation and 36 per cent of social work clients; on two-year orders the figures were 73 per cent and 38 per cent. The likeliest explanation of this is that very much more was demanded of probation clients than was demanded of social work clients; a subsidiary possibility is that probation records were more complete than social work ones, though here and elsewhere we omitted all records with apparent omissions: over 100 cases in this figure. We noted 460 cases where a probation client had missed office appointments and only 91 social work instances; 13 per cent of probation clients on two-year orders failed on eleven or more occasions as against only 1 per cent of social work cases. Against this, however, over half of social work clients were asked to report to the office on five or fewer occasions on a two-year order, as opposed to less than a fifth of probation clients, and only 9 per cent reported on sixteen or more occasions (as opposed to 39 per cent of probation clients).

Yet in spite of the frequency of failure to conform in both sets of client, only nine probation clients and one social work client were returned to court for breach proceedings, and in only ten probation and four social work cases were clients recalled for care proceedings.

In short, the picture is of each agency struggling to make sense of the unclear task it has been asked to perform. We are not arguing that the situation is straightforward for probation and not for social workers, for while it *is* the case that probation practice is closer to what courts expect, it is not precisely what courts expect; nor is it the case that probation officers do not themselves struggle with the problems inherent in having to serve two masters. Rather it is that there exists within the probation service a set of routines for the supervision of offenders in the community; those routines have developed over many years and are based on office reporting interspersed with home visits and occasional group activities. When supervision orders were introduced in the 1969 Act, therefore, there was a series of tried (if not tested) practices on to which the new task could be grafted, and the supervision order seemed to present relatively few new problems for probation officers. Supervision orders were assimilated into existing practices and those practices constituted a fairly strong tradition of court-based supervision.

In the case of social services, however, the very fact that they were being asked to take on part of the probation service's work indicated that something different was required, but the legislation and departmental guidance to local authorities were not such as to elucidate quite what it was. But social services departments had a huge task already in creating a unified culture from a range of different traditions, some of which they might wish to continue (such as the tradition of a professional casework service with a distinct knowledge and value base) and others of which (such as the Poor Law origins of welfare services for elderly and handicapped people) they might wish to repudiate. So for magistrates and others in some simple way to 'blame' social workers for their practices with young offenders or for their ambivalence about the court is to miss the point that such characteristics cannot be located in the personality defects of the workers, the 'ivory tower' training they are said to receive, or matters of that kind: magistrates, police, justices' clerks, lawyers, and probation officers may not like it, but social workers themselves are not necessarily the correct targets for their spleen.

This then is the situation in which social workers found themselves in 1971. They had been given hitherto undreamed of resources; they carried with them – and had themselves encouraged – the hopes of politicians and public. But their organizational base was new and chaotic (Satyamurti 1981) and their knowledge base rather light. The ideas that they did have – that catering for the welfare of offenders and helping put their families and communities to rights would make a significant impact on both the quality of their lives and on their offence behaviour – were quickly to be disproved empirically and rejected ideologically by the liberal and radical intellectuals who might have become the gurus of a new welfare age. The social workers had considerable power but little tradition or experience on which to base its exercise. As time went on they had to make sense not only of a new situation, but also very quickly of the collapse of part of the very theoretical and conceptual structure on which their existence was based. Only if we grasp this central point can we begin to understand the complexities of their task and the contradictions of their situation.

Conclusion

This short empirical report both justifies and explains the historical and conceptual analyses which preceded it. These analyses sought to unfold some of the dimensions of meaning of the supervision order, and by so doing to demonstrate the impossibility of understanding this particular provision without stepping outside the day-to-day world of the practice guide and the rhetoric of the experts. The logic and purpose of the present can only be grasped – and even then doubtless tenuously – through an understanding both of how it has been historically shaped and of the processes which occur between the drafting of the tutelary provision and the encounter in the interviewing room in which the tutelage occurs. We have sought thus far to offer at least a glimmering of understanding of both these processes which, it is hoped, both illumines and is illumined by the account of the experts at work.

In approaching the matter thus, we are aware of certain dimensions which are lacking. Readers will say, if welfare work is their commitment, that we have been in some way 'unfair'; that the processes we described in relation to supervision orders which for the most part terminated in 1980 no longer apply now; that no credit is given for 'practice advances' which endeavour to meet just the kind of problem we have been outlining: the use of 'contracts', the reluctance to write reports on first offenders, the practice of reserving supervision orders for higher tariff delinquents.

Although we hope our final chapter will go some small way towards answering these criticisms, it will not, we concede now, go very far,

The micro level: the experts at work

for no reason other than that to do so would involve either a very much longer or, more probably, a different kind of book. Material describing practice innovations is, however, on the whole readily available to practitioners, in the pages of the weekly welfare work press, for example, or in materials made available to their employees by departments to do with the writing of social enquiry reports. We are aware of such materials and use them in teaching; nothing in this book should be read as questioning their value, but their availability to the experts themselves discourages us from repeating them here. What has been lacking, we believe, is the kind of analysis we have attempted to offer, and this book can be read by those practitioners who have been interested enough in what we have to say to have stayed with us this far as a kind of gloss on the 'nuts and bolts' publications with which they will be all too familiar. We do think that some of this literature – much of it written by academics like ourselves, or by managers, or specialist practitioners – presumes too much: its cries to try harder or learn something new have the effect above all of asking people already in a whirl simply to whirl faster, or perhaps in a different direction. To the extent that the professional problems with which this literature seeks to deal are decontextualized and dehistoricized, they become matters with which the front-liners themselves are told to deal, but which it is in fact beyond their remit to change.

But for practice improvements to occur it is certainly necessary for the experts to develop at least the kind of working distinction we essayed in Chapter 1 among those aspects of their work which are buried in the very logic of its structure, those which may be amenable to micropolitical pressure, say from their professional associations, and those which are simply the fall-out, the unintended consequences of the paradoxes or contradictions to which they are subject, and which can be remedied without undue alarm either by a modest and uncontroversial legislative amendment or even by the development of particular practice principles. In relation to the possible criticism which we earlier forecast for ourselves – that we have failed to acknowledge that the welfare workers are getting much better at this kind of thing now – we are happy to agree, and the reforms to which we alluded in passing are, we think – with perhaps some slight reservations – steps in the right direction. More, however, could be done – by no means all of it by welfare workers – and we return to this and other related issues in our final chapter.

For the moment, however, we turn to an analysis which complements the empirical study reported in this chapter. The supervision of girls highlights also particular constraints to which the experts are themselves subject.

6 Censure and sex: justice and gender

'There are few types that come before the juvenile courts that are more difficult to handle and more in need of expert diagnosis than some of these over-sexed adolescent girls.'   (Elkin 1938: 119)

'Varium et mutabile semper
Femina'   (Virgil, *Aeneid*, Book IV)

Within the last decade, certain traditional assumptions about women's crime and its treatment have come under critical scrutiny from criminologists and penologists influenced by feminism. The first of these assumptions, which, since it impinges only tangentially on the concerns of this book, we shall mention and then leave, relates to the causes and incidences of female criminality itself. Crudely, the assumption is that women have traditionally been law abiding but, in their liberated state, have become more like men: twentieth-century Renaissance Woman, having thrown off her shackles, is opportunistic and self-seeking, a kind of female Edmund the bastard:

'Let me, if not by birth, have lands by wit;
All with me's meet that I can fashion fit.'
                              (Shakespeare, *King Lear*, I ii)

In truth, however, the female beneficiaries of the women's movement come generally from a different class from that whence derive most women criminals (Box and Hale 1983, 1984). The experience of working-class women over the last ten years has been of increasing economic marginalization, as personal and family unemployment impact upon them and as social policies have often failed to meet the needs of the increased numbers of one-parent families. Hence, whether or not women's crime has increased (either at all or disproportionately to that of men) is probably, as Anne Campbell observes, an unanswerable question (Campbell 1981: 235), but where such crime occurs it needs to be understood in the context of 'a consumer-oriented and status-conscious community that is continuously [sic] conditioned by aggressive mass media advertising' (Box and Hale 1984: 477). The issue then is not so much to do with the changing position of women and their 'liberation' in particular as with a shift in the economic and cultural climate to which women are obliged to relate.

But two further assumptions have also been heavily criticized: first, that female crime is a pathological manifestation of women's emotional vulnerability, and second that in consequence women are offered leniency and treatment by courts, not the harsh penalties meted out to men. In this chapter we avoid entirely any debate about the 'causes' of women's crime itself, but do address the manner in which the agents of the control to which the women are subject translate their own typifications into some form of action.

In this enterprise we are guided partially by those 'labelling' perspectives which substituted the social genesis of delinquency for aetiology. Labelling theory, by its emphasis on social control as the means by which deviant and delinquent statuses were ascribed, broke with the essentialist doctrine which had hitherto stood so securely as the focus for criminology. The characteristics of criminals no longer occupied the enquirer's mind, but rather the nature of rules created, endorsed, and sustained by this or that set of moral entrepreneurs. Stressing the relative and contingent nature of all rule-breaking behaviour, labelling theory also opened up the prospect of a detailed examination of the underlying assumptions, interests, and typifications of those censuring particular forms of behaviour. The control culture itself became a legitimate object of ironic enquiry as an agency which, through its rules, laws, and attributions, 'created' the very deviance which it simultaneously sought to extinguish by treatment or reformation.

This general perspective, then, (though not 'labelling theory' in its strict application) (Plummer 1979) infuses the present enquiry. As the feminist criminologists have reminded us, however, these changes in perspective have developed principally in relation to male criminality. Only more gradually has the recognition of the fact that the pursuit of an objective 'truth' in these matters is a vain one extended also to the study of female offenders. Increasingly, however, the focus of female criminology has shifted to the nature of women's involvement with the criminal justice and penal systems (see, for example, Morris and Gelsthorpe 1981), and the question of women and crime has become more centrally one of women and social control (Hutter and Williams 1981).

> 'Most sociologists of deviance have been so fascinated by the processes of defining deviants and becoming deviant that they have got over-excited. In this state they largely tend to ignore the much larger and more complex problem of the production of conformity.'
> (Heidensohn 1985: 108)

Rather as positivism and penology once made up an uneasy alliance with intersecting foci but distinctive assumptions (Garland 1985: 126 *et seq.*), so do labelling perspectives and penology share a concern with the management of the socially deviant, but with the former professing a detachment from the administrative concerns of the latter. Labelling perspectives invite, too, an enquiry into how far and in what fashion the nature and pattern of sentencing may convey both the formalizing of precepts about behaviour and the interpretation of statute. In relation to both, it is said that the law subjects women to a form of control reflecting familialism, propriety, and conventional gender practices (Smart 1976). Paradoxically from this perspective any discretionary latitude, whether manifested as greater harshness *or* as greater leniency, reaffirms certain preferences principally because 'Typifications of deviant and conforming women . . . have effects on agencies of control and on the public' (Heidensohn 1985: 107). Hence leniency comes to be extended to one women because of her demonstrably competent motherhood, and harshness applied to another in order that she can be appropriately remoralized (Carlen 1983; Nagel 1981; Sachs 1978). Any discriminatory practices of the criminal justice system become, therefore, not mere maladministration but reflections of the deep structure of material and moral interests to which women are subject. In this view, juridical practices resonate with those patriarchal interests which are securely embedded within the social order (McIntosh 1978). The particular treatment of women and girls before the law has, therefore, been one way in which gender issues have been brought into mainstream developments within criminology and penology. Both precepts and practices (which frequently, as we have observed, exist in ironic counterpoint to each other) are capable of being exposed for abandoning the principle of equal citizenship. In juvenile justice, as we have seen already and shall do again, this process works through the latitude extended to both courts and experts in the manner in which they conceive of and approach their respective tasks.

It is, of course, almost tautologous to affirm that social status and ascription are reflected in the precepts and practices of the criminal justice system, for the latter emerge precisely from the nature of, and interests embedded in, the former. Changing statuses are reflected quite clearly in such phenomena as the rise of the fine (see, for example, Rusche and Kirchheimer 1939) and the development of community service orders. And the status of women must equally be reflected in their treatment by the courts. So their historical status as property emerges not only in, say, the mutilation of adultresses (which is certainly traceable to King Cnut's reign in the eleventh century) but also the gradations of fines imposed on male fornicators as long ago as the seventh century, which reflected the value and status of the woman or girl concerned (Hibbert 1963: 18; for a further discussion of this general subject, see Dobash, Dobash, and Gutteridge 1986: ch. 2). It can be seen also in the sexualization of witchcraft in the sixteenth and seventeenth centuries in particular, in which women were interrogated, examined, and tortured in order to establish whether they had had carnal relations with the Devil. The residue of all this exists in certain discriminatory legislation of today, most obviously in the refusal of courts to countenance the possibility of wife-rape (see Smith and Hogan 1973: 324–26).

As we have earlier shown, in the juvenile court, saving and correction are ushered in to regulate the lives of the delinquents with the child's best interests (as defined by the experts) guiding the rehabilitative enterprise. But inasmuch as this definition is interpretive, it represents also a moral evaluation of need. In this *ensemble* of legal welfarism and assumptions and attributions about gender, delinquent girls find themselves subject to a particular regulatory censure. Because of the exceptionalness of their criminality, such girls have become, as the Victorians would have it, 'unsexed', departing not only from the legal code but from gender expectations about the appropriate behaviour of the sexes. Delinquent girls are thereby subject to the attribution of multiple waywardness: not only formal, legal infraction, but also that of being a gender deviant (Campbell 1981; Hiller and Hancock 1981; Shacklady Smith 1978; Terry 1970).

Whereas the 'ordinariness' of rule breaking by boys and its continuity with what is normally expected of them can be readily grasped (boys will, after all, be boys), amongst all the images upon which the puzzled observer can draw when approaching these 'unusual' girls, 'there is no conception of the "normal" exuberant delinquency characteristic of males' (Heidensohn 1985: 95). The idea of delinquent girls thus creates a dissonance not only with the control culture's preference for obedience to the law, but also with its demand for adherence to more diffuse norms. Because it seems 'obvious' to regard girls' delinquency as 'a perversion of, or rebellion against, their natural female roles' (Shacklady Smith 1978: 75), greater behavioural compliance is demanded of them.

Since offending is so frequently viewed both in statute and in occupational ideology as evidence of problems in the offender's life, criminal proceedings can provide scope for welfare interventions over and above the punishment of the infraction:

'as with all kinds of legislation couched in fairly general terms, the personnel whose task it is to implement it are left to interpret the provisions, as they see fit, in the context usually of prevailing values, attitudes and expectations.' (Hiller and Hancock 1981: 101)

Nevertheless, it would be quite wrong to assume from this that the theoretical hegemony of those arbiters of normalcy the psychiatrists is unproblematically extended into the juvenile courts. With the sole (and major) exception of the control of girls' sexual behaviour, the differences between the treatment of boys and girls are of degree and not kind. Crudely put, psychiatric interpretation is not always used for girls, but it is sometimes used for boys. The balancing out of the rational and the determined within the neo-classical compromise can be legitimately but not exclusively analysed along the dimension of gender, but very much more detailed empirical study (of a qualitative, interpretive kind) will be necessary before we gain any real understanding of the processes of juvenile justice in relation to its treatment of girls. Certainly, however, the court's very *raison d'être* decrees that it cannot abandon notions of *mens rea* in the case of girls any more than it can in that of boys, though the flaccidity of the roles of the courts and the experts who operate within them does permit certain girls to be subjected to *additional* forms of censure over and above that which results from their delinquency; and it also permits a widening of the net to include more and more non-delinquent girls who are *merely* gender deviants. Girls are the objects of the superintendence aimed at young deviants in general, but are bound within this by a particular inflexion which reflects the typifications of the agents of the control culture: they are hence subject to a stronger form of that tutelary process which is also directed at working-class boys. Thus, for example, as community corrections expand, '*girls* with little prior system contact are a particularly vulnerable group for further processing by the new programmes' (Cohen 1985: 55).

Magistrates regularly juggle need and risk, and in the case of girls the balance so often, to a paternalistic eye, seems skewed in the direction of the former, that well-intentioned remedial action is liable to be taken sooner rather than later, with delinquent girls quickly passed on to the ministrations of the experts. Hence the crucial nature of that expert role of translating messy reality into a coherent story: if 'femaleness' to the magisterial mind jars with 'criminality' a story must needs be told to explain their co-existence in the status and behaviour of the defendant presently before the court. But to assume that the effect of this is simply to redefine the criminality as pathology is to miss the point that the discourse within which the interaction of court and expert occurs itself restricts the range of 'acceptable' explanations of delinquency which can be put. The medicalized explanation – except in the extremest and most unusual cases – exists within the neo-classical framework of the court's interpretive structure: it may help us understand *how* something can happen, but it cannot remove entirely the offender's culpability (Longford 1961). And it is within the conflicts between these two notions that the judicial process operates, for girls as well as boys, but with possibly different inflexions. As in the case of boys again, in the conflict between these ideas lies the space for moral judgement to be made, stereotypes to be constructed, and control to be exercised. It is in this sense that the juvenile court's treatment of girls reflects less a qualitatively different set of theories about crime than a different form of gender-related prescriptions.

So when we move away from elaborate theories of psyche, somatotype, and atavism to the practices of the courts, we see anything but a confident assertion that female crime is the consequence of some innate or genetic deficiency. We see rather confusion and conflict, and out of these a vacuum emerging which is always liable to be filled by stereotypical disposals. But underlying it all is a tremendous *uncertainty*: Winifred Elkin, for example, in this chapter's lead quotation, found what she termed 'over-sexed adolescent girls' *difficult* to deal with. This was not because she applied a different set of theoretical ideas to the management of girls: indeed her comment that 'Most mistakes of the juvenile courts are due to a failure to realise the strength of the emotional urges that are so frequently to be found behind an act of delinquency' (Elkin 1938: 129) relates to boys as well.

So it is not quite that courts are operating confidently according to a separate set of theoretical constructs in the case of girls, but rather that their intrinsically uncertain and unstable practices vary when analysed on a number of dimensions, including that of gender. In the case of boys and girls the neo-classical compromise contains notions both of culpability and constraint. There are, it is true, psychiatric penal establishments for women, including Cornton Vale Prison (Dobash, Dobash, and Gutteridge 1986), and the 'new' Holloway was constructed on psychiatric principles, albeit that these principles have been regularly subverted in practice and are now less in fashion (Mott 1985: 48–50). On the other hand there are also psychiatric institutions for male prisoners, so the distinction is not a simple one. Dobash and colleagues, in the course of supporting their thesis that women's crime *is* typically seen in psychiatric terms, cite Camp's lay study of Holloway as observing that the 'great majority of women offenders need some form of medical, psychiatric or remedial treatment' (Dobash, Dobash, and Gutteridge 1986: 124), but they miss the significance of Camp's own confusion by omitting to set this kind of opinion alongside contradictory comments he makes elsewhere, such as this common-sense view about the aetiology of prostitution:

> 'The reason why girls go "on the game" has been the subject of many solemn enquiries by sociologists and others, and has resulted in a great deal of nonsense being talked. So-called "broken homes" are often a contributory factor, as may be a traumatic sexual experience, such as rape or incest, suffered by a girl when very young. But basically the reason why most girls become prostitutes is for no more complex reason than to earn money – and to earn it at ten or twenty times the rate offered by more conventional work.' (Camp 1974: 118)

A similar confusion surfaces in Ann Smith's obviously muddled paper predicting that women's liberation would lead to an increase in women's criminality:

> 'On the rare occasions when they have held such power in the past, women have not shown themselves to be able to resist the temptations of bribery, corruption, fraud and embezzlement any more than men. In the struggle for success in an increasingly competitive world one can expect to find many more women coming before the courts accused of such offences.' (Smith 1974: 160)

Yet that prediction is still combined with this prescription:

> 'Even if, with greater opportunity to express her personality and abilities within society, and greater equality with men, she encounters new stresses and temptations, it is all important that society should not forget that when a woman comes in conflict with the law she needs to be treated more than to be punished.' (Smith 1974: 157)

In the commonplace world of courts and institutions, then, female crime is viewed neither as *unaffected* by individual psychopathology nor as solely explicable in terms of it. These conflicts play themselves out in the sentencing arena much as they do with boys, but, as we observed before, with different emphases. John Watson's comment makes this clear:

> 'There are today people who disbelieve, or profess to disbelieve, in punishment as an effective factor in the reduction of crime. A proposition to that effect was advanced recently by a well-known

psychiatrist in the correspondence columns of *The Times*. I recommend to this type of theorist a short course of practical instruction in a busy juvenile court. There he will observe that the magistrates are faced with not a few psychological problems: but he will also encounter, perhaps to his surprise, the boy (*less often the girl*) who presents no psychological problems and requires no psychiatric treatment. . . . What he needs is a short, sharp unpleasant experience to bring him to his senses . . . fear of consequences is a low motive for good behaviour; yet, human nature being what it is, the fear of punishment remains an effective factor in children's upbringing.' (Italics added. Watson 1950: 202)[1]

Our own contribution to the literature is also in the sphere of the juvenile court, where confident analysis of the treatment of offenders by gender is substantially militated against by the fact that boys and girls together share the status of children: in their function of distributing norms, the courts and the experts seek to socialize the unruly young not only, and possibly not principally, into gender appropriate roles, but also into child appropriate ones. The obvious overlap between these aims may lead us to anticipate that while we will uncover certain assumptive and strategic differences, they are unlikely to be dramatic. The one area, however, where there does seem to be a stark difference (though even here we later offer two caveats) is in the regulation of sexuality. In one sense the feminist criminologists are right to relate this difference to conventional double standards of sexual morality (Campbell 1981), but they are not quite correct analytically in seeing this attitude as a simple *cause* of the regulatory activity: it is equally its means, justification, and consequence. As we have seen, Foucault's analyses of sexuality and crime control were structured around the notion that failure to control itself *justified* control. Power emerges not merely through the effective elimination of the controllable but by a failure to eliminate activities which cannot be disposed of. Crime and sexual behaviour are good enough instances of this, and they converge in the cases of those delinquent girls who offend not only against the law but also against the behavioural norms to which their gender makes them subject. So to debate whether girls are treated 'leniently' or 'harshly' is rather to miss the point. In certain situations some girls will be treated differently from boys on the basis of normative expectations to which they and not boys are subject. Whether this is harshness or, as some

---

[1] It must be remembered that at this time a detention centre for girls was being planned. Moor Court Detention Centre opened in 1962 but, after a fairly unhappy history, was closed on official advice in 1969 (Home Office 1968, 1970).

of the magistrates we have been citing earlier would say, an opportunity from which they will benefit, is, of course, a matter for individuals to determine: different views will reflect different political philosophies.

What is clear, though, is that the State's attempts to curtail the sexual activity of girls make them subject to an intense degree of social control; the inevitable failure of the State significantly to affect their sexual behaviour creates its own rationale for yet more control and for ever finer calibrations of that control which already exists (Foucault 1979). Girls' sexual behaviour becomes translated into the social process of sexuality whereby the more attempts are made to extinguish the phenomenon, the more deceit and dissimulation result, the detection of which paves the way for yet more repression. It is thus perfectly natural that for the best of intentions more should be done to curtail the activities of non-delinquent girls:

> 'Actually the girls who habitually stay out dangerously late are often those who are beyond control and who are not guilty of a *legal* offence. In these cases it is only possible to make a supervision order, in contradistinction to a probation order, and no conditions can be attached to it. That means that in many of the cases where a curfew would be most useful, it cannot be applied. It is unfortunate that the courts should be hampered in this way in their attempts to deal with these uncontrolled adolescent girls.'
> (Italics added. Elkin 1938: 180)

Later, Elkin returns to the same point in a context which makes plain that the main impact of the expansionary powers of the 1933 Act, to which we referred in Chapter 1, was on girls. But these powers were still not enough; more were needed:

> 'The much wider powers given to the courts under the care and protection clauses of the 1933 Act, combined with the raising of the maximum age from 16 to 17, resulted in a marked increase in the number of girls brought before the courts who are drifting into bad habits and bad company. It is nearly always essential in these cases that the girl should be got away from her normal surroundings, and as things stand at present that means there is no alternative except to commit her to an Approved School, unless she is willing voluntarily to go into a home.' (Elkin 1938: 263)

So the answer to this problem of girls who are 'extremely over-sexed, and the one thing they are craving for is the satisfaction of their desires' (Henriques 1950: 175) is not only more power, but also more gradations of power by which means the children experience State control not in a few large steps but in many small ones, the very smallness of which may make them easier to take.

But even this process is not simple or unproblematic, and clearly the care and protection girl should choose her court with care. Barbara Wootton, in characteristically robust vein, writes:

> 'I just could not persuade myself that a night or two a week with a personable American was so immensely more degrading than forty hours or more of unskilled and uninteresting work in a factory.'
> (Wootton 1978: 158)

Like much else in the analysis of social processes at work, our story contains inconsistencies, idiosyncracies, and paradoxes. Girls *and* boys are subject to the imposition of State power for reasons which would not permit such intervention had they been adults. We have tried to show that within this generalized powerlessness, girls are doubly vulnerable, and that in particular this vulnerability relates to their sexual behaviour. Boys seem not to be dealt with for this reason, though even here we must make two caveats: first that it is possible that similar control is imposed on homosexual boys (though there is no substantial literature on this); and secondly there is evidence that sexual behaviour by boys *already in institutions* (whether homosexual or heterosexual) is liable to censure. Here is an extract from a case record of a 14-year-old boy in a Youth Treatment Centre:

> 'His behaviour became progressively more violent, usually in response to teasing by other boys, and he was described as depressed and vulnerable. On two occasions he took a drug over-dose in apparent suicide attempts. He was known to have had sexual intercourse with a promiscuous 13 year old girl, but there are no other reports of sexually precocious or unusual behaviour, or of aggressiveness towards women. . . . A concensus [sic] of opinion indicated that there was a likelihood of J. committing a serious offence when his immediate needs or desires were not gratified, probably a sexual attack on a female.'
> (Cited in Cawson and Martell 1979: 92-3)

Girls and juvenile justice: a brief literature review

The juvenile justice system is, as we have argued, a subsystem of that broader nexus of State control which comprises also the child care and criminal justice systems. But it also contains within itself a number of separate but interacting parts, and a detailed empirical study of discriminatory practices in juvenile justice would have perforce to analyse interactions between the consumer group under consideration and the police, courts, experts, and institutions. In relation to girls, there is insufficient evidence at any of these decision-points for us to state categorically that particular forms of discrimination do or do not occur, though the drift of the literature we are about to review (and of our own study, a report of which follows), is that some girls *are* more quickly sucked into the tutelary system than boys. But it must also be said that this literature is of variable quality and covers a considerable time-span in an area in which practice may be changing quickly. Nor do the gender differences which do emerge tell a simple story.

The police largely control the system input by virtue of the wide discretionary powers they enjoy. In the case of juveniles, to the decision made by the constable on the beat as to whether to notice officially some infringement is added the bureaucratization of the aptly named 'juvenile bureau' which constitutes a second tier of decision-making and operates according to rather different principles in different parts of the country. American studies of police arrest decisions in respect of women offenders generally have suggested that there is a greater possibility of 'chivalry' being extended to older and white women who conform to gender stereotypes than to girls and black women (see, for example, Visher 1983), but more significantly for our purposes, in England and Wales girls aged 14 to 16 are consistently and significantly more likely to be cautioned by the police than are boys: the figures have been fairly constant for some time now, showing that approximately 45 per cent of boys and 70 per cent of girls of these ages are cautioned rather than prosecuted (*Criminal Statistics: England and Wales, 1984*). The interpretation of this is by no means clear. Even if we dismiss Carol Smart's curious argument that this represents discrimination against women (because, there being fewer women than men offenders in the population as a whole, *therefore* fewer women have been cautioned – Smart 1976: 138) we still have Landau's study which suggests that any differences are explicable in terms of legal and non gender-specific extra-legal variables (Landau 1981). The most plausible explanation of this would be that a higher proportion of girls than boys cease offending after one or two apprehensions, with a consequent depressing of the court input figures; though this hypothesis requires empirical testing.

In relation to juvenile courts the picture is equally unclear. Carol Smart and Anne Campbell both argue that girl property offenders are more leniently treated than boys except where there is evidence of sexual misconduct. Smart is of the opinion that a process of 'sexualization' occurs whereby a girl offender who is *also* a sexual deviant may find her offence 'overlooked in favour of proceedings based on sexual (mis)behaviour' (Smart 1976: 23); Campbell makes a similar point, emphasizing, as we have in this book, that discrimination occurs more in practice than in precept and, therefore, reflects the broader purposes of the juvenile court:

> 'Girls who breach the code of sexual morals evoke a more punitive response . . . the majority of these discriminations are not enshrined in legislation itself but occur in its implementation.'
>
> (Campbell 1981: 212)

David May's study of decision-making by a Scottish panel showed that girls were more likely to be placed under supervision or in an institution and less likely to be fined than boys (May 1977), and Cohn's New York study found that sexually delinquent girls were three times more likely to be institutionalized than were boys, and typically on a probation officer's recommendation (Cohn 1970). Historically, girls have been more likely than boys to be made subject to three-year probation orders (Elkin 1938: 172) and in a Cambridge study from the 1950s, girl first offenders were significantly more likely to be put on probation than were boys (27 per cent against 8 per cent: Radzinowicz *et al.* 1958: 39).

Girls do, then, seem more likely to be sentenced to tutelage, and this conclusion will be borne out by our own study reported in the next section. But around the decision as to whether or not to prosecute, the evidence does not conclusively support the view that there is an eagerness to charge girls in order to push them into the system. At worst Landau's study suggests that they are treated much the same as boys, and at best the cautioning figures in *Criminal Statistics* suggest, *prima facie*, preferential treatment. Once within the system, girls are also significantly (and consistently) more likely than boys to be absolutely or conditionally discharged (*Criminal Statistics: England and Wales, 1984*) as well as sentenced to welfare disposals, though it also seems clear that under particular circumstances (which may, though our data cannot establish this, include the question of sexual conduct) the supervisory and tutelary complex is given freer rein. It is also of course the case that for girls the tariff is shorter than for boys: there were no attendance centres for girls in our research year, so girls were always liable to 'jump' the tariff (Parker, Casburn and Turnbull 1981: 70) into what Parker and his colleagues consider the paternalistic arms of the supervision order. But how far this tutelary effect is an intent among the decision-makers as well as a consequence of their actions must for the present remain moot.

The picture is yet further complicated by the existence of considerable gender bias in respect of the total numbers of children in care. If the tutelary process operated strongly on the dimension of gender we should expect to see proportionately more girls than boys in care for a range of reasons, many of which, in Smart's terms, concealed the 'sexualization' of their behaviour or situation. But in fact there is a significant imbalance in the direction of boys. This imbalance is noticeable in infancy and increases with age, so that depending upon the bench-mark chosen, in a care population of a little less than 100,000 there is a statistical excess of boys of between 8,000 and 16,000 (Lawson and Lockhart 1985: 179). This imbalance holds in all categories both of care orders and receptions into care except where the moral danger criterion is used (Children and Young Persons Act, 1969, section 1(2)(c):

'we might not be too surprised to see the preponderance of males in the categories covering criminal cases, proven guilt, truancy, and in the breakdown of parental control. . . . We might even see the preponderance of females in the moral danger categories . . . as reassuring evidence that social workers are not atypical in their attitudes towards sexual hazards. But unless we believe that children in broken marriages are more likely to be male than female, or that having more boys than girls was a predisposing factor in marital breakdown, we might be puzzled by the results in the "divorce" category.'   (Lawson and Lockhart 1985: 178)

These researchers suggest the possibility that the number of girls going into care is less than that of boys going in because boys are more difficult to control or more liable than girls to behavioural or learning disorders. In this context, therefore, the evidence for a committed, feminist argument that there is systematic and *generalized* discrimination against girls seems weak, though there are clear indications that *particular* forms of discrimination have occurred historically and probably still do in still to be defined circumstances. Overall, however, it seems probable that both boys *and* girls are subjected to a considerable amount of somewhat variable and unpredictable control.

The evidence on the institutionalization of girls again remains weak so far as current evidence is concerned, though certain cautious extrapolations can be made. The Ingleby Report (1960) pointed out that whereas 95 per cent of boys in approved schools were offenders, the figure for girls was only 36 per cent, and Gordon Rose, like other writers, points to the sexuality of the girls in approved schools as being more central than their crimes:

> 'As might be expected, most of the girls are committed as non-offenders: in fact, the number of non-offenders runs at about one and a half times that of offenders. . . . Perhaps the most outstanding characteristics of the girls who come into approved schools is their history of sex experience. We have no means of knowing if this exceeds that of other girls of a similar age and background, but one cannot help thinking that it does.' (Rose 1967: 40)

This preoccupation with the girls' sexual conduct is reflected in a monograph to which Rose draws attention, *Girls in Approved Schools*, produced in 1954 by the Association of Headmasters, Headmistresses and Matrons of Approved Schools, which points to a high level of sexual experience and venereal infection among the girls admitted. Helen Richardson's study compared the sexual experience of girls in her sample with the rates described in a large representative sample of girls published shortly earlier (Schofield 1965). Richardson found significantly higher rates of sexual activity among the approved school girls, and in particular far higher rates of *casual* sexual contact, rather than sexual activity in the context of a longer-term relationship (Richardson 1969: ch. XVIII).

More recently, in Ackland's study of girls in residential care the large majority saw themselves there not for 'punishment' but for various family reasons, including 'non-school attendance, not getting on with parents and getting into trouble' (Ackland 1982: 43), though the ambiguity of 'getting into trouble' makes confident analysis difficult; and Petrie's study of girls in a Scottish List D school showed both that concern over sexual misbehaviour was the overriding reason for institutionalization, and that this concern was associated with notions of an 'inadequate' family (Petrie 1986).

There is a nagging suspicion that while there may be (and we are not entirely sure from our data that this view is correct) a measure of sexualization of problems amongst girl offenders, there may equally well be circumstances where quite 'objectively' the young girl is being exploited by men. Since sexual activity of this sort is not a freely entered contract for the girl, 'protection' might stand as the sometimes 'rational kernel' to the disciplinary activities of the State. In this context, of course, to regard 'the State' as simply discriminating against girls would be crudely negativistic, when its *failure* to provide refuge for the confused or abused young, or to offer where necessary substitute parenting would itself provide cause for complaint by feminists. The State cannot seriously be analysed as a monolithic or unambiguous oppressor of girls; more relevant is to consider the processes by which its *practices* in relation to them become so very expansionist, and how it is that they create the kind of tutelage which we have identified in the management of supervision orders.

Girls on supervision

In the course of our study of boy offenders on supervision, we generated a subsample of 241 girls aged 14 to 16 who, like the boys, had been placed on supervision for an offence for the first time in 1978. Almost all such orders made in that year in our six experimental counties are included in this report. Girls are proportionately significantly more likely than boys to be placed on supervision for offences, though the numbers are of course very much smaller. But in our research year 22 per cent of girls dealt with for indictable offences were made subject to supervision orders as opposed to 14 per cent of boys. A total of 1,800 supervision orders on 14- to 16-year-old girls were made in 1978 (*Criminal Statistics: England and Wales, 1984*), so that our sample constitutes 13.4 per cent of all orders made in that year. Clearly if we were to find patterned differences between the girls' offending behaviour and that of the boys, we should have at least some evidence of discriminatory sentencing. This one would expect to be especially important as an index of social control should the girls transpire to be even less criminally involved than the boys, not least because as we demonstrated in the last chapter the boys themselves were really remarkably ordinary.

We need hardly add that the decision to analyse our data by gender and present it separately reflects not an attempt to marginalize the matter of girls' delinquency, but an acknowledgement that gender is likely to be a significant dimension in the juvenile justice process, and accordingly that particular attention can usefully be given to girl offenders. Overall the data demonstrate that discretion and

Table 4 *Seriousness of offence by gender*

	boys		girls	
		%		%
trivial	256	(29.7)	84	(38.7)
medium	454	(52.7)	114	(52.5)
high	152	(17.6)	19	(8.6)
total[1]	862	(100.0)	217	(100.0)

$x^2 = 14.76$; $df = 2$; $p < 0.001$
Note: [1] 'Total' on all tables reflects usable data and excludes 'missing cases'.

preconceptions about girls' delinquency do appear to give particular form to the judicial process. *Table 4* shows there to be a statistically significant difference in the seriousness of the offences committed by the boys and girls in the study. Although the modal offence category for both was medium seriousness (Appendix B) a greater proportion of the girls were placed on supervision for trivial offences. A specific offence within our 'trivial' category illustrates this point: a theft of property up to a value of £10 accounted for the criminality of 15 per cent of boys but 26.6 per cent of girls. Girls were also more likely than boys to be placed on supervision for only one offence, as *Table 5* shows.

Table 5   *Whether or not convicted of more than one offence, by gender*

	boys		girls	
	%		%	
convicted of more than one offence	434	(45.3)	84	(35.4)
convicted of one offence only	524	(54.7)	153	(64.6)
total	958	(100.0)	237	(100.0)

$x^2 = 7.52$; $df = 1$; $p < 0.01$

Perhaps of more significance in documenting what appears to be a pattern for girls to be moved up the tariff more quickly than boys are the data shown in *Table 6*. Criminal 'record' will – other things being equal – bring about a more severe disposal, since it reflects a previous indifference to milder punishment. However, it is clear from these data that previous offence behaviour is much less salient among the girls on supervision than it is among boys; whereas 46 per cent of the boys in the survey were subject to a supervision order on their first court appearance, this rose quite dramatically to 75 per cent of the girls, pointing again to the apparently more rapid deployment of a supervisory sanction for girl delinquents.

Table 6   *Number of previous court appearances by gender*

	boys		girls	
	%		%	
none	437	(45.9)	174	(75.0)
one	294	(30.9)	40	(17.2)
two or more	221	(23.2)	18	(7.8)
total	952	(100.0)	232	(100.0)

$x^2 = 65.24$; $df = 2$; $p < 0.001$

The tendency towards a noticeable difference between the treatment of boys and girls in the making of what, in their eyes at least, might be seen as the same disposal is suggested further in the following tables. Here, as in Chapter 5, those young offenders who were both subject to a supervision order for a trivial offence *and* without previous convictions have been compared with the remainder of the study population. It should be noted that because of missing data, the 'leakage' of useable cases increases as more conditions for each are sought and this explains the totals which are smaller than those of *Tables 4–6*. Of the girls' files, 78 per cent are useable for the remaining analysis and similarly 73 per cent of boys.

Table 7 indicates that those on supervision with a modest criminal biography were more likely to be girls than boys; almost a third of the former and slightly under one-seventh of the latter. This susceptibility to supervision for what on the face of it may seem slender reason is not, however, boundless. If it were, proportionally more girls than boys with modest criminal biographies would be expected to have found themselves on two-year rather than one-year orders. This proved not to be the case; about two-thirds in both instances were placed on supervision for two or more years, and there was no statistical difference between two particular sub-populations ($x^2 = 0.27$, $df = 1$, ns).

Table 7 *Supervision order by criminal status and gender*

	boys		girls	
		%		%
'not serious'	105	(14.76)	57	(30.0)
'other'	606	(82.24)	133	(70.0)
total	711	(100.0)	190	(100.0)

$x^2 = 23.21$; $df = 1$; $p < 0.001$

In general, the length of the supervision order tends, albeit rather weakly, to reflect the seriousness of the offence committed and previous convictions, and it operates in this manner for boys *and* girls: in both cases virtually identical proportions of boys and girls with more serious criminal biographies (75.8 and 77.4 per cent respectively) were subject to an order of two years or more. It is almost as though the courts were seeking to claw back some of the proportionality lost in the making of the supervision order in the first place: the pursuit of welfare as a self-evident 'good' was apparently tempered to some degree by traditional considerations of justice.

In submitting social enquiry reports to the court, welfare workers stand as professional advisers on sentencing, tendering their considered view about the most appropriate disposal, but giving due weight to the young person's welfare in so doing. Recommendations thereby convey the welfare worker's own sense of what should be the response to a young person's infraction. In our study it appears that they did not substantially discriminate among delinquents in terms of the gravity of their offence when recommending supervision: *Table 8* makes plain that supervision was recommended in almost identical proportions of 'serious' and 'non-serious' cases both for boys and girls:

Table 8 *Recommendations made for supervision, by gender and 'criminal status'*

	boys not serious	boys other	girls not serious	girls other
	%	%	%	%
specific recommendation made for supervision	74 (75.5)	410 (71.3)	40 (75.1)	86 (68.3)
no recommendations made	23 (24.5)	165 (28.7)	14 (24.9)	40 (31.7)
total	98 (100.0)	575 (100.0)	54 (100.0)	126 (100.0)

Those placed on supervision were considerably more likely to have been involved in trivial than in serious offending; given the greater proportion of girls than boys characterized by modest criminal biographies, it is not surprising that the overall link between gender and petty criminality is stronger for girls than for boys. Since the girl offenders did not in the main possess the 'formal' requirements for a moderately high tariff disposal the decision to recommend a supervision order would seem to lie in the 'needs' revealed by the routine professional practices of social workers or probation officers.

Although the question of the objective status of these needs must be suspended, their precise determination being contingent upon, for example, the professional ideologies of the welfare workers and what their agencies are constituted to address (Smith 1980; Dingwall, Eekelaar, and Murray 1983), it is none the less important to see how far the offender is viewed as possessing personal or social difficulties which may be addressed through welfare work involvement. After all, locating and specifying problems and needs are part and parcel of the professional remit of the welfare worker since it is through such practices that otherwise 'irrational', 'anti-social', or unaccountable behaviour can be made publicly intelligible (Hardiker and Webb 1979; Philp 1979). In other words, the supervision order would be serving welfare objectives should needs be identified and met through welfare work, even if in terms of 'justice' the offence alone merited a lesser disposal. Although to critics of welfare sentencing this might seem unjust, it would nevertheless point to a sense of purpose in what was being recommended rather than to the manipulation of the report to express from a position of power deeply embedded 'feelings' about the nature both of girls' offences and of girl offenders themselves.

Nevertheless despite recommendations for supervision orders being made on girl offenders largely irrespective of the seriousness of their offence, it is difficult to see quite how they were linked to a coherent welfare response. In the course of the research project, social enquiry reports were coded to see whether clearly identified welfare work strategies had been proposed; if they had then this would stand as some 'justification' for recommending supervision, a rational response to identifiable disruption in the young person's life, in relation to which welfare work might make a constructive intervention.

Clearly stated reasons were more likely not to be made than made, and this applies to both boys and girls, something which has doubtless contributed to the sense of unease sometimes expressed by the magistracy about the vagueness of the content of these reports (Webb and Harris 1984). None the less, *Table 9(a)* indicates that at least in the case of boys involved in minor misdemeanours, welfare workers were significantly more likely to spell out a professional strategy to accompany their recommendation than when writing about more serious offenders. This was not the case with respect to girls, however, as *Table 9(b)* makes plain.

This is not a straightforward finding to interpret. The fact that for both boys and girls the numbers in the 'not serious' band are small advises caution; on the other hand this categorization was deliberately constructed to include only the extreme of the distribution curve. A youngster who had committed a 'trivial' offence (most frequently a property crime involving up to £10 worth of goods) *and* who was making a first court appearance could reasonably expect, *mutatis mutandis*, to be discharged or nominally fined. A recommendation for supervision would, in such a case, be quite disproportionate to the

Table 9 *Specific welfare work strategy in social enquiry report by criminal status*

	(a) boys 'not serious'		'other'	
		%		%
welfare work strategy in enquiry	42	(40.0)	173	(28.5)
no strategy	63	(60.0)	433	(71.4)
total	105	(100.0)	606	(100.0)

$x^2 = 5.21$; $df = 1$; $p < 0.05$

	(b) girls 'not serious'		'other'	
		%		%
welfare work strategy in social enquiry	19	(33.3)	42	(31.5)
no strategy	38	(66.7)	91	(68.4)
total	57	(100.0)	133	(100.0)

$x^2 = 0.07$; $df = 1$; n.s.

offender's 'normal' place on the tariff and, one would assume, should be strongly defended in a report.

When boys and girls are taken together, that no professional strategy was outlined in 101 out of the 162 'not serious' cases is of itself remarkable, and it is against this baseline that the even greater likelihood of no such strategy being outlined in the case of girls has to be set. There are two possible explanations for this. First that the nature of the understanding between court and expert is such that the former takes it on trust that the latter knows what to do, and the latter does indeed know, but prefers not to say (whether for reasons of 'confidentiality' or for some other motive). This is not, as we have remarked before, to suggest there is a conspiracy between them: rather a shared understanding about the nature of the relationship between the State and children which effectively shifts the burden of proof from the former – that a case must be made for a disproportionate penalty – to the latter – that it must be demonstrated both in relation to the offence and to the lifestyle that the state need not intervene extensively. The power that is exercised is exercised in the child's best interests, but well-intentioned power, as we have already observed, is quite the most difficult with which to deal.

The second possibility is that the supervision order is more likely to be made by a *need–push* than by a *solution–pull* mechanism. We do know (Thorpe 1979) that social enquiry reports are extraordinarily variable in content and presentation, but that they also frequently contain a catalogue of problems to do with faulty relationships, inadequate adjustments to social situations (school, work), poverty, low self-esteem, and the like. There is, it need hardly be said, a considerable disjunction between the nature of many of these problems and anything that an expert can do to solve them, beyond simply sounding sympathetic and understanding. It would be plausible to extrapolate from our data that many supervision orders are need-push ones which are made by courts (and recommended by experts) on the basis of human misery or mischief of some kind, but without a clear analysis of what if anything can be done about it. Need–push supervision becomes in this analysis the very child of the social, the cause, means, justification, and product of the exercise of power, the rationale for the abandonment of proportionality, the stepping–stone to an intervention which is both intensive and extensive, but with no clear limits imposed upon it by the boundaries of any professional technology. There is, that is to say, no clear distinction in the sphere of the social between problems which can be solved by the expert and states which must be endured by the sufferer. When the problem is there but has no technical solution the experts are still used, even though no one actually knows what to do. But the experts are neither merely private therapists nor professional friends, for as we have been arguing throughout, they embody the power of the State. That three-fifths of boys and two-thirds of girls in our study who were trivial first offenders were subject to supervision orders without any indication of what would be done in the course of them is, for whatever reason it occurred, a remarkable transfer of responsibility to the social professionals. This is the more so when to this transfer we add the finding described in the last chapter that in very few of these cases were the needs themselves sufficient to necessitate intensive intervention: our analysis of contact patterns between supervisor and client indicated that for girls as well as boys a casualness pervaded the proceedings which is hard to square with such a potentially intensive penetration being ordered on such flimsy evidence.

Discussion: social control, deviant girls, and welfare

The findings reported here refer to one disposal only and apply to girls in particular rather than women offenders in general. Extrapolations to the full span of sentencing and the entire age spectrum must inevitably therefore be limited and cautious. This is important to bear in mind. The little evidence we have suggests that adult women offenders are generally subject to neither harsher nor more lenient sentencing than men when seriousness of offence and criminal record are held constant (Nagel 1981; Farrington and Morris 1983), though it is possible that within this apparent equality of disposition the actual practices of the sentences reflect evaluations of the woman offender's gender competence (Carlen 1983). For girls, these practices seem more overt.

Though benign in intent, such strategies have been criticized for the suspension of justice entailed, though only rarely has the point been made about the amplified impact that this may have on girls in particular, (Campbell 1981; Casburn 1979; Hudson 1983). It is the penological consequences of being a delinquent, female, child which, through our data, we have sought to explore, consequences which have significance in the weakness of the framing of welfare work knowledge, its relative lack of insulation from popular discourse, its failure to secure a real measure of epistemic autonomy. When this openness is conjoined with statutory and occupational requirements which are themselves imprecise, it is not surprising that social welfare activity can sometimes appear *ad hoc* and expedient. If we 'excavate' supervision, we can secure a greater sense of this precariousness. It implies authority, but authority which is benign, resting upon a sagacity of life experience rather than upon technical expertise. Assistance is extended to those who, on their own and because of a variety of deficiencies (moral, cultural), have failed or refused to participate fully in civil society. And all this, which involves substantial lay rather than specifically professional qualities, occurs within the ministration of befriending, the contingent offering of pseudo-mutuality. Supervision in these guises is a mundane task, easily appropriated by common sense and the everyday, so vague that almost anything can go.

Although the remit of the supervision order is diffuse, that of supervision as tutelage is very specific; its concern is with moral departures and their necessary correction and socialization. Ironically the very latitude allowed to the supervision order makes it responsive to the hidden and reified arrangement of things; within a multiplex of lay and professional assumptions about the extreme atypicality of female delinquency which official statistics and criminological accounts apparently endorse, the girl offender becomes an obvious target for having her self-evident needs compulsorily met. In focusing upon social deviancy to a greater degree than on legal infraction and criminal history, the practices of juvenile justice here involve the court not so much in pronouncing judgement on crimes as examining individuals: 'There is *a dematerialization of the offense* which places the minor in a mechanism of interminable investigation, of perpetual judgement' (Italics original. Donzelot 1980: 110). For delinquent girls the rehabilitative ideal which informs liberal penal policy is given a very specific inflexion. The reform which marks, in Pearson's phrase, their 'return to utility' (Pearson 1975b) is accomplished with singular emphasis being placed upon their performing not so much as socially competent *citizens*, but as demonstrably orthodox *girls* (Hudson 1983; Heidensohn 1985).

We can see then how the intersection of the welfare organization's charter with the occupational ideologies of the welfare worker creates a form of 'expert' whose practice is at some remove from a knowledge and skills-based authority. The expert is such because of the exercise of discretion, and it is the inaccessibility of what that is based upon which consolidates the welfare worker's power. It is because of this that we have earlier spoken of control emerging not from well-orchestrated manoeuvrings but from the inconsistency, irregularity, and unpredictability which make up capriciousness. Because 'welfare' legislation vests authority and discretion with the experts, in this are inevitably admitted their professional ideologies as they endeavour to assess 'just what sort of case is this?' (Giller and Morris 1981). But such ideologies are not exhaustive and the lacunae which 'knowledge' cannot encompass come to be addressed by extra-professional assumptions, often based in common-sense morality: hence problems arise in accommodating those atypical offenders who stand outside the purview of that habitual knowledge which makes for the routine, relatively unproblematic handling of cases (Sudnow 1964). Women offenders, whether young or old, do not fall easily into the familiar categories of crime, save perhaps that of themselves *being* self-evident 'problems' with no more to be said. Not surprisingly there is an absence of clarity in problem formulation and recommendation making by welfare workers, and a vulnerability to restricted representation which it has been suggested is a common feature of women's experience within the judicial system (Carlen 1983; Dell 1971): the person charged with speaking for the deviant is muted because there is no clear and agreed framework within which to offer an account of the wayward's actions.

All young offenders are liable to be sentenced on the basis of their welfare needs, and are accordingly subject to a certain distortion of proportionality and an imposition of tutelary power. The findings reported in this chapter suggest that the girls in our study were, however, subjected to a 'double dose' of such tutelage which sought to resocialize them into not only an acceptable role of childhood, but also of girlhood. The literature we have reviewed hypothesizes that this can be explained in good part by a concern about their sexual behaviour, and our own data offer possible empirical support for this view, though they do not categorically confirm it. Nevertheless the findings of the study (which, so far as we are aware, is the largest scale one yet undertaken in this area) do indicate certain significant differences between the criminal histories of the boys and girls sentenced to supervision, and suggest that the tenuous proportionality sustained in the case of boys between crime and punishment is even further attenuated in that of girls. But whether the overt intent of the courts and the experts is to monitor girls' behaviour, or whether such monitoring is rather the effect of an almost complete dearth of ideas as to what is to be done, the effect of these processes is a disproportionate exercise of power over girls. What has been termed 'the behaviour of law' (Black 1976), at least in this small corner of juvenile justice, has had the effect of impacting more centrally on some citizens than others, and on the basis, so far as we can tell, less of either the need they present or the risk they pose than of their gender.

7 Towards the future

'Recently, a New Mexico judge sentenced an offender convicted of passing bad checks to three years' probation. As a condition of the sentence, the offender was forced to wear an "electronic bracelet" on his ankle for 30 days. The bracelet permitted a private security company to monitor the offender's movements everywhere he went. If the offender moved more than 200 feet from his telephone, a central computer was signaled by the bracelet. . . . This unusual sentence was said by the judge to be inspired by a *Spiderman* comic he had read.' (Albanese 1984: 24)

'I do wish that the future was over.' (Gilbert Harding 1953: 224)

Final chapters are notoriously hard on both readers and authors. They tend to fall into one of two categories: either they simply stop, as though the author could stand no more (in which case the reader, having eagerly turned the page only to discover the bibliography, feels justifiably cheated) or they offer a list of recommendations of which most if not all fall into precisely the traps that the rest of the book had been devoted to analysing. Into which of these categories (or indeed any other category) this chapter falls is for the reader to determine; though we fear that any readers brought up on a diet of detective fiction in which Father Brown or Hercule Poirot unties every knot and explains every uncertainty in the last ten pages will be sorely disappointed.

The story so far

Chapter 1 focused mainly on two themes: the creation of a new nexus of State control, and the expansion of the control which the nexus both represented and sustained. But, as an overture to the book as a whole, the chapter also adumbrated certain other themes which were to emerge in more developed form later: the increasing centrality of the experts; the complementary trends of a blurring of boundaries *between* systems and a development of more boundaries *within* systems, principally by the process of classification and other strategies of individualization; the expansionist logic of both failure and kindness.

We also characterized the Children and Young Persons Act, 1969, as representing not so much a revolution in juvenile justice as a comprehensible extension of already discernible trends. But the instability of its neo-classicism combined with its technical deficiencies to create a huge void manoeuvrable by courts and experts alike. This void, which was to re-emerge in Chapter 3 as 'the social', permitted an enormous array of actions to both courts and experts with almost any of them being able to be justified according to some precept or other, and the selection from among the possible strategies being based upon a knowledge which was anything but scientific or verifiable.

Chapter 2 examined the two sets of experts – probation officers and social workers – in greater detail, and we demonstrated historically certain differences between them. The probation service, with its longstanding tradition of operating within the criminal justice system, had attained a degree of homogeneity by structuring its activities around certain successive unifying symbols – saving sinners, curing by casework, decarceration. Though we showed that within all of these, but particularly the last one, there were dissent and controversy, these were insufficient to divert the organization from what, in Chapter 4, we came to term its organizational resolve in pursuing this objective.

But for social services departments the situation was quite different. An uneasy coalition of numerous conflicting traditions from the Poor Law to child psychiatry, these departments had come into existence only in 1971. Their remit both amalgamated the existing tasks of three hitherto distinct local government departments and included certain new duties, of which the management of supervision orders for young offenders was one. This particular duty had, therefore, to be tackled *de novo*, with neither tradition nor routine on to which to fall back, a sense that probation officers' methods neither could nor should be emulated, and in a central government policy vacuum. These departments, then, far from having organizational resolve, represented the very destruction of such resolve as had existed in the former children's, health and welfare departments, and introduced an initially reluctant and shell-shocked staff to the new and unwelcome demands of court-based supervision.

Chapter 3 began the three-part macro, mezzo, and micro level analysis of welfare work which followed. It was argued that Foucault's analysis of power constituted a plausible framework within which to analyse the spread and present practice of welfare work. Power, to Foucault, is immanent in human relations, and the experts, as agents of the State, are instrumental in contributing to a disciplinary society (of which the Panopticon is the ideal type) in which the exercise of power and subjection to it are often almost indistinguishable. We developed this argument by utilizing Donzelot's notion of tutelage, the supervised freedom of the working classes, conducted within the sphere of the social. We showed how norm-distributing activities within the social help create prescriptive as well as proscriptive law, but how the social is itself subject both to interpenetration with the adjacent spheres of the civil and the political, and to an internal process of intertwining, in which many of its prescriptive activities are inextricably linked together. Hence the likelihood of a coherent, consensual, and circumscribed mandate is low.

But when we applied the framework to the practice of the workers we found quite a chasm between the theory of creeping, insidious power and the practice of low-key, often dilatory supervision, which was explained by reference to the characteristics of the social. So unclear are the knowledge and role which permeate this sphere that almost any action can be justified. Hence was uncovered a central, self-limiting paradox: that from the very processes by which the social expands the power of the State through its norm-distributing activities emerge also the disagreements and uncertainties which modulate that expansion. If those who supervise young offenders may variously be carer, controller, surrogate parent, agent of the court, therapist, educator, prosecutor, classifier, translator, and negotiator, the room for different practices among different supervisors or for one supervisor with different 'clients' is considerable. When the knowledge-base on which such decisions are made is anything but certain or agreed-upon, the likelihood of idiosyncracy and arbitrariness is greater still: 'choose your report writer with care, for one may recommend prison, another may recommend a fine', advises Philip Bean (cited in Hardiker 1977: 134) with just this kind of consideration in mind. But the overall impact of this uncertainty is to make the supervisor relatively impervious to organizational accountability or, so far as the client is concerned, to predictability. This in turn augments the power of the expert and concomitantly diminishes that of on one side the agency, and on the other the client.

Chapter 4 considered this organizational base of welfare practice further. The activities of the experts are embedded in and ultimately an inextricable aspect of, the history, tradition, culture, mandate, and procedures of the agencies. The organizations themselves, as conduits, both convey and transform the ideologies of the court. At the most central ideological level they turn into bureau-professional practice the implications of the idea of crime as an individualistic phenomenon: every client is individualized but also becomes a file on a caseload. We illustrated by reference to the Charity Organization Society the genesis and development of these procedures of information gathering and social enquiry, and showed how, then as now, rational theory typically became erratic and capricious practice. But as transformers of ideology, the organizations also deal with the practicalities of having to manage quite difficult clients by explicitly or implicitly sanctioning concealment of infractions committed by them. This is not entirely a matter of pragmatics but also reflects the conflict between the agency service and independent practice models of service delivery, behind which conflict lies the further question often asked by the experts themselves: 'Whose side are we on?' But the concealment reflects a transformation of a judicial pronouncement that a defendant *shall* obey a particular instruction and lead a certain kind of life into a bureau-professional judgement as to *how much deviance* will be allowed before disciplinary action is taken. The effect of this is in turn to create a new filter for judging the offender extra-judicially, a new suspensive element in the supervision, and the exposure of that offender to the conflicting prescriptive norms of the social as well as the predominantly proscriptive rule of law.

This relationship between models of service delivery combines with a further variable – the agency's vulnerability to external influences – to constitute a function of *organizational resolve*. The greater the system's internal harmony and consonance with external demands, the greater its organizational resolve. Probation has tended, though by no means unproblematically, to achieve such resolve around the symbol of decarceration, whereas social services departments, having no such denominator, demonstrate significantly less organizational resolve in their activities.

Chapter 5 approached its micro-level analysis of the experts at work in two ways. First it elaborated some of the implications for the experts of the vulnerabilities and uncertainties to which they were subject. These included a vulnerability to attack from without, the experience of conflicts and contradictions within the organization, the management of different and competing occupational cultures and traditions, an uncertainty of knowledge base, and a confusion of role. The co-existence of these equivocations and paradoxes in the sphere of the social creates for the experts a curious kind of freedom based on fear and uncertainty: the checks on what they did were few and inefficient, but they lacked a clarity of purpose which would offer them unambiguous professional guidelines. This problem led to a number of professional fragmentations which, while they may have created a certain consonance for individual workers as they focused their energies on some small part of the job or on some arcane method of doing it, nevertheless increased a more general sense of occupational uncertainty, confronting the experts as a whole with the question: 'what is welfare work?' This existential question, we suggested, was typically translated into a form of action we termed *routine individualization*, which involved neither strict, coherent and accountable routinization nor creative and flexible individualization, but rather an adherence to a set of assumptions and procedures which reflected simply the way things were normally done and judgements normally made in the agency. These assumptions, though clear to the experts, were less so to those outside their professional world, but typically involved the imposition of an inert power, a suspension of suspensiveness, a failure to act decisively or according to clearly articulated principles.

Then in the second part of the chapter we sought to see some of these processes at work. In a brief empirical report, we considered first the supervised population and then the process of supervision itself. The supervisees transpired to be a remarkably ordinary set of working-class youths, neither presenting great needs nor posing great risk. Many of them were poor, and they were almost twice as likely as the population as a whole to come from a one-parent family. It was almost as though the supervision order sought to 'complete' a fractured family unit by buttressing the unsuccessful attempts of (almost always) the mother to control her errant son.

Yet theory and practice diverged somewhat and as far as our essentially quantitative methodology enables us to see, the latter was far more likely to reflect agency norms and cultures than client need or risk: differences in practice within the two agencies were significantly fewer than those which occurred between them. Routine individualization therefore reflected the failure of the workers from the two agencies *either* to agree together (and, doubtless, with the courts) what ought to be done in a supervision order (a routinization model) *or* to use their freedom in a truly creative and individualistic way, their agencies bolstering the innovative aspects of professionalism, so that the order became needs-based (an individualization model). Routine individualization, though in one sense yoking these conflicting models of practice, was neither fish nor fowl, an example of professional uncertainty rather than an elegant and accountable synthesis of care and control.

In Chapter 6 we examined the supervision of girls as a case study in tutelage. The juvenile court socializes children and young people into acceptable behaviour generally, but girls, we argued, experience a second and additional set of demands that they shall behave in a way appropriate *not only* to children, but also to girls. Although the same dual process obviously applies to boys, its impact on them is less, principally because greater latitude is conventionally afforded them.

Nevertheless, we were critical of the assumption that female delinquency is perceived by those involved with it as almost exclusively pathological, and we were also anxious to avoid suggesting that girls were *in some simple way* more liable to experience tutelage. In the first instance we suggested that the feminist criminologists had been too easily seduced by the theoretical hegemony of the psychiatrists, and had failed to address the confusions embedded both in lay opinion and in the day-to-day practices of courts and experts. Consideration of these would have located the treatment of girls within the same neoclassical tradition as that of boys, though undoubtedly with a different inflexion. In the second instance we stressed that an analysis of criminal statistics makes plain that there is no simple binary divide between the treatment by juvenile courts of boys and girls: girls are more likely to be sentenced not only to the tutelary disposals of care and supervision, but also to the non-tutelary discharge. They are also very much more likely to be diverted from court by a caution, and significantly less likely to be committed to custody. The explanations of these differences, however, lie not only in gender expectations but also, and especially, in legal or non-gender-biased extra-legal variables, and there is no reason from our analysis to believe girls to be subject to some systematic discrimination.

Nevertheless, in our own study of supervision orders, girls were even more marginal offenders than the very ordinary boys in the sample. In particular, an expert's recommendation for supervision was less likely to be defended than was the case with boys when made in the case of a trivial first offender. This suggested to us that the supervision order was not being seen as a high tariff disposal to be argued for strongly in such an ostensibly unsuitable case, but rather as a fairly 'natural' sentence for a girl whose report doubtless itemized certain needs and problems. From this we developed a concept of the *need–push supervision order* which considered problems outside of the context of possible solutions to them, hence justifying precisely the kind of almost boundless intervention we had been discussing earlier in the book: the more one looks the more one finds, but the less one is sometimes able to do about it. The logic of such a situation is clearly more of the same, and supervisor and client find themselves almost by default engaged in a 'game without end', that process which 'cannot generate from within itself the conditions for its own change; it cannot produce the rules for the change of its own rules' (Watzlawick, Weakland, and Fisch 1974: 22).

This, then, is the argument so far. Though the structure by which we have expressed and defended it is somewhat elaborate, in essence the case itself is simple. We have analysed, both historically and conceptually, certain trends which are emerging within the juvenile justice system. We now project certain of these trends into the future, not as a prediction exactly, for predictions are vulnerable to contingencies which are themselves literally unpredictable, but rather as a logical development of current trends, should they continue in their present general direction.

Towards the future: five trends in welfare work

The path we are about to take is already well trodden, not merely by political and science fiction novelists and by such futurologists as Alvin Toffler (see, for example, Toffler 1970, 1974), but, more usefully because more conceptually and less predictively, by philosophers of science including Gregory Bateson (Bateson 1972, 1980), Fritjof Capra (Capra 1975, 1982), and Ilya Prigogine (Prigogine and Stengers 1985), as well as by other social control theorists, notably Stanley Cohen (Cohen 1985).

In this section we extract from the argument thus far five trends which have surfaced in it, and which seem likely to exert a decisive influence on the future direction of social control. They are: *diversification of penality; an increasing reliance on the experts; humanitarianism; netwidening;* and *boundary-blurring*. In the amorphous world of the social, they are not always distinguishable clearly from each other, nor do they apply only to juveniles. But we do use these trends as a base from which to extrapolate two possible scenarios for the social control of the future; and we end the book by mapping out in general terms certain issues which might usefully be addressed by other researchers and theoreticians, as well as by policy-makers.

Diversification of penality: we have demonstrated clearly that the matters under discussion have been associated with a considerable increase in the sentencing options available to courts. In a superficial sense the spread of ever more imaginative and inclusive community corrections might seem almost to be a return to that pre-industrialized penal system which, though characterized by Foucault as dominated by torture, is more accurately seen as embracing a wide range of both bodily and social punishments. But the diversifications of the late twentieth century are by no means reversions to these arrangements: they are not simply better ways of inflicting pain and shame, but rather a set of technologies designed to address and control the apparently criminogenic aspects of mind, body, and social situation.

In this sense we see in twentieth-century correctionalism not a reversion to a pre-penitentiary era, but a refinement of the purposes and technologies of the penitentiary itself, a restructuring of the institution by the creation and development of a set of middle-range correctional strategies designed precisely to break down the divide between community and institution, to put additional rungs in the ladder from one to the other and hence, curiously, to make the institution seem more immediate, more attainable. T.S. Eliot, in the essay we cited earlier, remarked:

> 'Someone said: "The dead writers are remote from us because we *know* so much more than they did". Precisely, and they are that which we know.' (Eliot 1951: 16)

What *we* know today is Victorian penal theory: its lessons have been learned all too clearly, its failures have facilitated the development of more intrusive and extensive technologies, more varied strategies of power. Hence we have:

> '*disciplinary* modes and techniques (that is, practices of physical *dressage*) . . . various techniques of *normalisation* utilised in probation work . . . *financial control* (particularly through the fine, compensation orders, restitution, etc.) which operate by quite different means to produce a form of self-discipline and internalised control in an "automatic" manner, without the requirement of personal intervention by a penal agent . . . *incentive schemes* that reward the "good behaviour" of inmates with minor privileges.'
> (Garland and Young 1983: 19–20)

As part of these strategies we see also a significant trend in the direction of combining their characteristics in single sentences. *Pace* Garland and Young, 'normalization' is not the main attribute of probation supervision, especially (though not exclusively) when it is an aspect of the implementation of some other sentence such as a fine (in a money payment supervision order) or community service. But an especially clear aspect of penality to emerge has been the blending into a single sentence of the substantive and the suspensive. Sentences become neither the thunderbolt of Zeus nor the sword of Damocles (such as the activated and the suspended prison sentence respectively), but the means whereby a sentence is both carried out *and* suspended. We have, of course, the partly suspended sentence; but we have also the deferred sentence, in which judgement on an offence is passed in the future on the basis of an aggregation of the gravity of the offence already committed and an evaluation of the conduct of the offender during the period of deferment. This hybrid sentence seeks to address the concerns of both retributivists and deterrent theorists by punishing the past and controlling the future in the self-same process.

But this hybridity also exists in a slightly different but more extensive way in the tutelary sentences managed by the experts. Supervision, care, community service orders, and the various forms of community corrections which can be attached to probation orders all combine substantiveness of sentence and suspensiveness. In all of these cases the sentence exists not only in its own right; it serves, too, as a test of character, a vehicle for the evaluation of its object in relation to both the demands of this particular sentence and the nature of any future sentence which may be imposed should further infractions occur. So offenders who perform conscientiously and in a trustworthy manner some unpleasant task within a community service order are more than likely to be 'promoted' to a more interesting activity by means of which they can achieve the greater satisfaction of meeting and serving selected deserving groups and individuals within the community; they are also likely to be reported on favourably if they re-offend. Compliance with the expectations of the experts – expectations which go far beyond the simple demands of the conditions of the order – leads to rewards of numerous kinds expressed in either material or psychological ways. Hence the apparent contradictions within, say, community service orders (that the same order may involve some unpleasant form of chain gang labour and the intrinsically satisfying use of a particular skill or piece of knowledge) are central to their power as well as to their widespread popularity. Readers who have heard the same proponent of community service giving different, and ostensibly contradictory talks to, respectively, local magistrates and trainee probation officers will readily appreciate this point.

Reliance on the experts: this flexibility which so enhances the power of the experts is also essential for the expansion of the power of the courts. The experts and their organizations simultaneously transmit and transform the edicts of the courts, and therein lies the paradoxical nature of professionalism: the experts are not simple agents of State power, but contain within their own functions and ideologies certain contradictory aims designed to have positive and indeed liberating outcomes for their clients. The courts need the flexibility enshrined in professional judgements for their power to be extended beyond their jurisdiction, for the parents to be resocialized or remoralized, the child to be steered away from unsuitable friendships, the school to be encouraged to treat the child differently. But the transformational nature of the experts' ideologies means that the flexibility which expands the courts' power simultaneously constrains it: the experts both sustain and subvert the system.

The ideology of decarceration (of which more later) is an example of this process. At one level, when manifested, say, in recommendations in social enquiry reports, it has a transformational impact and constitutes a source of friction between expert and court with welfare workers being, perhaps, accused of unrealistic leniency. But at the same time, the ideology is a necessary feature of that development of community corrections which has so increased the sentencing options available to courts, and which they have seized to such effect that the power they exercise over quite marginal offenders has increased considerably. It is also just possible – though this is speculative – that community corrections, in that they constitute not just 'opportunities' for offenders but also 'hurdles', may in some circumstances provoke further infractions (in relation, say, to matters of discipline) which, once committed, come to legitimize the accelerated use of custodial sanctions.

Humanitarianism: these additional penalties, then, are infected by the creed of humanitarianism and tend to be both advocated and administered on this basis: they are 'more humane', that is to say, than prison. What this means is not, however, precisely clear: it may be that the punishment itself is deemed in some way dignity-enhancing (reparative penalties have on occasion been promoted thus), or that the punishment, though intrinsically stigmatizing and demeaning, is less so if proceeded with in a friendly and courteous manner. But whichever of these interpretations is correct (and doubtless the experts themselves will tell us that there is something in both of them), welfare workers encounter a serious problem as a result of their humanitarianism, for it renders community corrections actually unsuitable as an alternative to custody:

> 'prisoners are not clients, and pain, privation and suffering are seen by many as their just deserts. But because they "choose" to offend, retribution is in order. The "humanity" of community corrections is thus its Achilles' heel, precisely the feature most likely to alienate (fiscal) conservatives and indeed the public at large, who might otherwise be attracted by the idea . . . if prisons are unpleasant places, that is precisely what they should be.'
> (Scull 1983: 158)

To the reply that the sentence of prison not its experience is the intended penalty, we can only, in suggesting that the speaker visits almost any British or American prison, observe that, in the social world at least, actions speak louder than words. The humanitarianism of community corrections not only justifies but also makes inevitable its use for non-serious offenders.

Widening the net: humanitarian ideologies are not alone in making the net-widening process inevitable. There are, it is true, certain recorded instances of well-planned diversion or correctional schemes where this effect seems to have been largely avoided (see in particular Clear and O'Leary 1983; Esbensen 1984). These instances entail not only a multilevel systemic approach to a local juvenile justice system but also the propitious circumstances of broad system consensus with the aims of the programme itself, including (at worst) passive acquiescence from police, the experts, court officials and administrators, sentencers and key community figures. Where this support is not present, or is withdrawn, either the programme folds through lack of use, or it sustains itself by the absorption of the kind of marginal delinquent whom it had previously been anxious to exclude. There are a number of reasons for this, quite apart from the vulnerability of other points in the system (in the face, say, of rising crime or of some particular and reprehensible offence) to community pressure to elevate protective sentencing aims above rehabilitative ones. The first is that such programmes depend for their success on a degree of active co-operation from their consumers; the second that, because of their community location, they require a track record of positive user conduct to avoid being subjected to political lobbying for their closure – by parent groups, for example, or discontented neighbours; and thirdly, such schemes are typically dependent on measurable 'success' (preferably in apparently lowering recidivism rates, but at the very least in limiting misbehaviour) for continued funding. All these objectives are most easily achieved if the schemes contain, if not a preponderance then at least a liberal smattering, of what Cohen refers to as 'cream puff cases' (Cohen 1985). Hence referring experts are not uncommonly told by such schemes that their client, though in principle acceptable, is in some way too risky or difficult to be taken because there are so many other problems at that moment: what is needed are some 'easy' cases to achieve a manageable set of working relations.

The point of all this is not at all to be simplistically critical of the managers of these schemes: indeed we are full of admiration for the way in which many of them have struggled with so many hopelessly disagreeable cases, experiencing verbal and physical abuse, drunken brawls, and outbursts of quite outrageous behaviour in the course of their duty. The point is rather that both the nature of the schemes themselves and their location within the juvenile justice system make it almost inevitable that this net-widening effect will occur. It is simply outside the hands of those ostensibly managing the schemes to prevent it: the only way they can contain hordes of serious and sophisticated offenders is by assuming many of the attributes of the coercive institution they seek to replace.

Blurring the boundaries: the developing role of the experts has involved a blurring of certain boundaries and a reconstruction of those boundaries elsewhere, on the basis of 'professional' forms of assessment and classification rather than of common-sense attributions. Hence the juvenile justice and child care systems, and the institution and community, have become *less* clearly differentiated, but *within* the new larger systems which have emerged from this blurring, new evaluations have been made and distinctions drawn on the basis of judgements about need, risk and response. That these judgements are not of a qualitatively different order from those which they have replaced will be obvious: the knowledge upon which they are based is insecure, and the location within which the judgements are made is by no means insulated from the wider world of common-sense opinion. The logic of this is that an inevitable augmentation of control occurs with the superimposition of a new layer of judgement but not the elimination of the pre-existing one. So community corrections typically develop alongside, not instead of, institutions, and this twin growth is one of the hallmarks of late-twentieth-century penal policy: 'The dream of criminal justice reform come true can readily become the nightmare of the benevolent state gone mad' (Doleschal 1982: 138). Even when numbers of offenders *are* diverted from court, many petty delinquents are still processed:

> 'Perhaps in the absence of serious crime it is "necessary" for the court to maintain a certain level of "business" in order to continue to perpetuate its social control role.'
> (Bynum and Greene 1984: 142)

Two responses to the five trends

Academics and policy-makers have by no means been blind to the expansionist logic embedded in these trends. In relation to juvenile justice the tendency has been for the problems to be perceived as emerging from the 'contradictions' between justice and welfare, and for proponents of each to argue that this enveloping control could be contained if their own favoured concept were to predominate over the other. So we have, both in Britain and the USA, a 'justice' movement which argues for minimalist principles in juvenile justice, and a 'welfare' movement which, like its predecessors in the 1960s, argues for the State to surrender its powers to punish young offenders and to be concerned instead principally with their welfare. By this means it is said, we shall see, respectively, greater protection of the 'rights' of offenders by the judicial system, and greater concern for their needs existing in a form unadulterated by the residual punitive powers of the juvenile court.

In the USA the justice movement emerged as early as the 1950s (Binder 1979), having its roots in constitutional law, and developing under the influence of the Civil Rights movement and the Vietnam draft dodgers who were imprisoned in the 1960s (American Friends Service Committee 1971). Supreme Court judgements in *Kent* and *Gault* in the 1960s were in the direction of constitutional safeguard and due process, and *Gault* in particular became a *cause célèbre*:

> 'A fifteen year old was adjudicated delinquent and sent to a state reform school for a six-year period on the basis of hearsay, no statement of charges, no transcript of trial proceedings, no opportunity for appeal, no right to counsel, no right to confront and cross-examine witnesses, and no privilege against self-incrimination. And the offense was one that carried a maximum penalty of two months' imprisonment if committed by an adult! The opinion carries the following succinct appraisal of Gault's hearing: "Under our Constitution, the condition of being a boy does not justify a kangaroo court".'
> (Binder 1979: 641)

The support of liberals and radicals for the idea of 'justice' in the USA led, however, not to the intended leniency towards young delinquents but to a displacement of discretion within the system and to longer institutional sentences (Cullen and Gilbert 1982). Mitigation based on social disadvantage or personal misery came logically to lose its force:

> 'If I lose my job because the economy is in a state of contraction and then steal to support myself and my family – or if I am a juvenile and steal because the state has passed child labor legislation – or if I strike out in rage because the color of my skin subjects me to discrimination that reduces my opportunities – the just deserts model simply indicates that I should be punished for my wrongful act . . . other topics are pushed to the periphery.
> (Greenberg and Humphries 1980: 215–16)

These problems need not unduly surprise us, for the logic of 'justice' is flawed in at least two ways. First, it assumes that a shift in rhetoric accompanied by certain administrative and legislative modifications will lead to a change in practice at all the levels of the system where such changes are necessary for radically different outcomes to occur; and secondly, it takes as unproblematic the notion that 'like cases should be treated alike', that principle apparently so flagrantly breached by welfare sentencing. We say something about these two fallacies in turn.

First, the central lesson for the analyst of juvenile justice is to be guided not by what the various participants in the drama claim to be doing, but by what actually happens. Approaching the matter thus, we are forced to conclude that to regard the expansion of State control as a side-effect of welfarism is an analytic error: it is the control which is the central purpose and the welfarism the side-effect, the means and consequence of the control but not its cause. The altruism embedded in welfare is part of the experts' brief but not its core, and to remove the welfare is accordingly not to remove the control. Historically welfare has emerged to fill a vacuum which is itself the product of a series of conflicts, confusions, compromises; it is a strategy of power, a means of investigating families, of controlling non-delinquent children, an acceptable means of expanding the power of the State. In what ways such an extension is desirable is, therefore, a question of political philosophy, and to assume that this 'bio-politics of the population' (Foucault 1977) will disappear on the basis of modest amendments to the powers of the juvenile court is patently absurd. We should expect the new powers to be regrouped and implemented in such a way as to achieve what controlling objectives are at that time sought. Police intake decisions, plea bargaining outcomes (which British readers should in no way take to be an exclusively American phenomenon), sentencing dispositions and post-sentence allocations are all decisive *practical* decision-points which will exercise greater influence on the fate of young offenders than will the changing of some governing abstraction.

Secondly, the idea of 'justice' is vague and ambiguous. This, of course, is the essence of its attractiveness, for one can no more oppose it than one can any other intrinsic good (Harris 1985). But of itself, 'justice' means very little.

> 'The notion basic to justice is that distinctions should be made if there are relevant differences and that they should not be made if there are no relevant differences or on the basis of irrelevant differences.' (Peters 1970: 123)

It is by no means an immutable truth that only offence variables are relevant differences, and that the offender variables introduced by welfare theorists are demonstrably irrelevant. There is a politicality in the concept 'relevant difference' which cannot be resolved merely by discarding welfare, and to reject those factors which concern the proponents of welfare is not to revert to a state of apolitical equality before the law, but to embrace a particular conservative political ideology. It follows inevitably that these differences will be reflected in the sentencing behaviour of the judges and magistrates, who are by no means agreed on these matters among themselves (Ashworth 1983), and accordingly that operationally, considerable differences will continue to occur, and numerous hobby-horses to be ridden.

Similar points can, of course, be made in relation to the opposite expedient of abolishing the court's powers to punish and handing the offenders over to the experts (McCabe and Treitel 1983; Jillings 1985). Part of the lesson of the 1960s, it is true, is that technical inefficiencies created unintended consequences; but part of it too is that welfare, when projected towards the centre of the stage, overtly took on the aspect of control: in short, it once again filled a vacuum, this time one which was created largely by the abolition of the approved schools; and its agents found themselves increasingly making custodial recommendations in respect of those of their clients who flouted their best efforts (D.H. Thorpe *et al.* 1980). When the undesirability of this was brought to the experts' attention and many of them desisted from making such recommendations, no fall in the use of custody occurred, and in fact there continued a gradual upward trend (Burney 1985). Should the possibility of committal to custody be removed, it is not sufficient to *assume* that the decarcerated offenders would quietly go away: they would in fact tax the tolerance not only of the experts but also of others to quite a considerable degree, and we could confidently expect pressure quickly to mount, demanding that such a growing menace should be dealt with. Neither police nor magistrates (both of whom, in England and Wales, constitute a powerful political lobby) could be expected to witness such an eventuality impassively, and nor should it be assumed that the experts themselves would do so. Already there are indications, for example, that the heavily unionized and radical experts in certain local authorities are responding to the decarcerative policies being developed by their equally radical employers by demanding punitive action against violent children: that residential staff have been known to walk out of a community home, downing tools in protest against the retention in open conditions of a violent child is a clear reminder that agencies are not simply bearers of a charter in relation to the welfare of their clients but that they can be called upon also to discharge certain protective duties as employers, in relation to their staff. The world of the social is indeed a complicated one.

The future: two scenarios

The perceptions of community corrections held by experts and sentencers differ markedly. To the one, they represent a decarcerative strategy, to the other, an additional set of sentencing options. From the point of view of the experts, part of the very driving force behind the creation of such systems is their dislike of prison, and it is sometimes difficult to disentangle the reformative or classificatory aspects of community corrections from their purpose as a defensive manoeuvre against custody, as though the punitive logic of one part of the system creates and itself generates a conflicting, liberal logic elsewhere: a system fighting itself, producing sentences which simultaneously conflict with, and perfectly complement each other. There can, after all, be no 'alternatives to custody' without custody itself being at the very heart of the matter. To the sentencers, to have any credibility community corrections must not be an easy option; but if they are not easy their very difficulty will lead to the failure of some of their consumers; and if the consumers fail, what can the weary sentencer do other than give a shrug of the shoulders and commit the recalcitrant to prison? Perhaps in some circumstances, the directly *in*carcerative impact of community correction is, like that of the suspended sentence (Bottoms 1980) greater than its decarcerative potential.

Thoughts such as these suggest that the organizational resolve within the probation service, based as it is on decarceration, may in the future prove unstable; that the best way of achieving decarceration may be to withdraw the options rather than increase them. In spite of the individual triumphs to which the experts can justly point, and with which they regale Rotary Clubs and Women's Institutes when invited to address them, the proliferation of community corrections has accompanied rather than replaced an expansion in custodial provision. This may be because there are insufficient options; equally plausibly it may be that there are too many, that the pathway to custody created by the line of such schemes is in fact too easy a one to take.

There are also other, professional 'ethical' questions which community corrections raise for the experts. 'Does it matter', asks Peter Raynor, 'if clients dig ditches all day so long as they are not in prison?' (Raynor 1985: 67). A firm decarcerative strategy might incline the expert to reply 'probably not', but once this ideology becomes infected with the disturbing thought that community corrections are not so much (or at best not only) a simple 'alternative to custody' but the very child of the carceral, occupying it is true a different set of places on a continuum of control, but being on the continuum notwithstanding, the question becomes more complex. It surfaced precisely in relation to the Younger Report in the 1970s, as we saw in Chapter 2, and it re-emerges as a central issue in the light of the present analysis: could it be that the very availability of the ditch-digging option means that some wielders of the fork and spade might otherwise have been not in prison, but paying off a fine, or sitting in the relative comfort of their local probation office? Such questions are central ones for the experts and are likely to become more so. There are few indications that they are presently being addressed by them coherently; it seems rather that the experts are all too often being carried along on the tide of an evangelical objection to the use of custody, and are failing to be equally critical of the nature and implications of their own actions.

In our first scenario of the future this particular chicken comes home to roost. The conceptual distinction the experts draw between custody and non-custody collapses, as it becomes quite clear that community corrections constitute not the polar opposite of the prison, but part of a penal continuum involving no less harshness at its extremes, but considerably greater diversity. Community corrections, far from being part of a humane and liberal assault on the prison, prove themselves rather to be a necessary aspect of an emergent penality which involves also continuing increases in prison places, a strengthening of the police force, and the creation within that force of more specialist units targeted at specified forms of dissent.

Such strategies will draw their legitimation from the belief that, if we may put it crudely, community corrections will empty the prisons in order for them to be filled by the hordes of really serious offenders (child killers and rapists have especially few friends amongst even liberal opinion-formers, for example) who will be increasingly detected and incarcerated. But the real impact of increased policing and penal provision is in fact always likely to be on middle- to low-range offenders, who will be slightly more likely to be detected and, once detected, will have to be classified and processed by other elements within the penal system: the streets will be no safer for women and children, nor will more than a small minority (though a marginally higher minority than at present) of burglars and thieves be caught, but society will become more disciplinary, and in this growth of discipline the experts will play a central role. Routine individualization will become ever more necessary as more offenders are classified and their responses to one form of penality monitored as a means of assessing their suitability for another. Everyone and no one is individualized.

But in the second scenario, decarceration actually occurs: it is not beyond the scope of the imagination to conceive of this in particular political circumstances. In this scenario the present prison building programme represents the death throes of a moribund and redundant system. But why might such a situation come about?

Not, surely, through the accumulated wisdom and humanitarianism of the judges, persuaded at last by the liberal reform lobby that they have been in error all these years, that they have been sentencing people to an inhumane and ineffective regime in the mistaken belief that it would deter them and others in the future. Reforms do not on the whole occur for such reasons, not least because there tends to be a permanent assumption amongst the powerful that they are already being quite lenient, possibly too much so, in the face of deteriorating standards of social behaviour compared, say, with thirty years ago (Pearson 1983). Such decarceration, if it occurs, may do so for economic reasons (Scull 1977); equally it may reflect *political exigencies* or *technological opportunities*.

Politically such a strategy could be an attacking or a defensive manoeuvre. It is certainly conceivable that a set of circumstances could emerge in which it became expedient for government to attack certain of the vested interests of the criminal justice and penal systems: the judges might, perhaps, be called into line by a socialist government, or the prison officers – whose industrial action in 1986, leading as it did to prison riots, might be just the kind of muscle to which government does not wish to be exposed too often – by a conservative one. Decarceration could, therefore, constitute part of an attack on either professional autonomy or a powerful trade union, and in such a context is a perfectly plausible strategy.

More defensively, it is widely assumed by those within the penal system that further riots are inevitable (Fitzgerald 1977). Such riots could conceivably constitute a more severe political embarrassment than decarceration itself, with the result that decarceration might emerge as a damage limitation strategy. Or again the government's hand could be forced by a series of adverse judgements in the European Court of Human Rights, either in relation to the holding of particular categories of prisoner (most probably unconvicted and Immigration Act prisoners, though quite possibly fine defaulters or the mentally disordered) or to prison conditions generally. In the USA limited decarceration has already occurred in some states in the wake of Supreme Court judgements that overcrowding is unconstitutional.

Technologically, advances in computer and video technology, combined with the remarkable increase in public acceptance of their utilization in a wide variety of contexts may actually render the prison redundant except for the long-term containment of the dangerous and as an aspect of a flexible disciplinary system. Developments such as the Spiderman solution of the New Mexico judge in our lead citation may conceivably mean that historically the prison will come to be seen as a clumsy and outmoded phase of penal history, and that it will come to be replaced by increasingly finely tuned community disposals from the marginally to the intensively intrusive, with offenders and other deviants subjected to flexible levels of control on the basis less of their offence than of their subsequent conformability. In such a continuum prison might feasibly become the extreme of some kind of flexible 'control order', to be used only to the extent that it is necessary to ensure conformity to the demands of lesser disposals. Such an order would perfectly deal with the economic arguments against prison, for the levels of imprisonment could be minutely adjusted upwards or downwards according to the ever shifting relationship between supply and demand: if the prisons are full, either nobody goes in or somebody comes out: such matters are eminently determinable by computer, and any notion of desert becomes subordinated to considerations of conformability. Doubtless community control would entail a range of hostels (quarter-way, half-way, and three-quarter-way houses), day centres, work programmes, attendance centres, restitution centres, rehabilitation centres, and the like, and one might expect the development of computer applications to these centres to begin to eliminate at least some of those subversions of the experts themselves which part of this book has been devoted to describing. Not only would the net widen, but also its mesh would become finer.

The irony of such a scenario, of course, is that it would precisely replicate the city of Panopticon, that Benthamite institution which the government, in the early nineteenth century, and to Bentham's disgust, failed to build. But in this new model, the walls of the prison would be no longer needed: the prison would move instead into the home, the school, the place of work. The disciplinary society of the Panopticon would become technically possible and economically realistic as well as ideologically acceptable both to the fiscal conservative and to the liberal: it would after all be both cheap and humane. In relation to the latter it could be defended in the same way as Bentham defended his Panopticon; in relation to the former it would be vastly superior.

Now we are aware that these are flights of fancy; that the experience of living through 1984 reminded us all that the Orwellian nightmare had not really arrived. These are not confident predictions, though if the theoretical framework we have developed in this book is even partly correct, either of these scenarios is possible; and it is also possible that the first will be a stepping stone to the second. Diversification, classification, humanitarianism, wider social control, the blurring of boundaries – all these things *have* developed remarkably over the last century to the extent that a citizen of a hundred years ago would stare in disbelief at the intrusiveness yet the inefficacy of our present arrangements. So it is not surprising if we are equally wide-eyed about the possibilities for the twenty-first century. But if the intrusiveness continues but the inefficiency is reduced, community corrections will take on an altogether different visage.

It is, of course, possible that we are quite wrong, that there will be a retraction of State involvement in correction of the kind advocated by the British and American justice movements. We should be surprised, but prediction is, as we have said, a risky business. But what does not seem plausible is that a growth in community corrections will *accompany* such a retraction elsewhere in the system: *pace* some writers (Jones 1983, for example) welfare workers cannot really stand outside of these policy issues as free-floating altruists; nor does the spread of welfare seem likely to allow the police force and prison service to pack their collective bags and go home. The experts and these other controllers are closely linked to each other in their role and function: an increase in the numbers or powers of any one of them is liable to have expansionary consequences for the others too. This process typically occurs whether or not a new correctional facility, say, is 'successful', though in slightly different ways and to a different degree.

If the project fails, it is possible that it will simply wither away, though if its target is a serious one, and if the organization is in some way committed to hitting it, the failure is more likely to lead either to the replacement of the unsuccessful programme with a different programme targeted at the same consumers but with a different methodology, or to the buttressing of the unsuccessful programme with additional resources in order to help it succeed. This latter consequence is, of course, a modified version of the expansionist logic of failure which we discussed in Chapter 3: more resources are ploughed into the programme in training budgets, supervision, consultation, improved facilities, and the like in order to counter whatever identified problem has emerged which is preventing the programme from succeeding.

But supposing the programme is a success? Supposing that it hits its target, whether that is to reduce recidivism rates or to occupy fairly serious offenders in innocent activities? Does this mean that one has found the answer, that the prison can be closed and the police force weakened? Quite the reverse; so much so indeed that we might, in flippant vein, coin the Harris and Webb Law: that in the correctional sphere, the more successful a new facility is, the more all the other facilities will expand. The reasons for this are threefold: *first*, the character of the social is such that a facility which controls the *supply* of some problem population by dint of doing so stimulates *demand* either for more extensive provisions for processing different but related problem populations or for more intensive provisions to deal more thoroughly with the original problem population. Perhaps preventive work is required, or a new need surfaces among the population whose characteristics have come to be known so well: perhaps one should fund, for example, a problem population wives' group or a problem population children's centre to help counteract the disadvantages experienced by these people. *Secondly*, the new programme does not exist in a vacuum, but transacts daily with other elements in the system which it wishes to influence or which wish to influence it in the direction of their own policy preferences. It will require good working relationships with police and courts, for the former will have on occasion to be persuaded to exercise their discretion in favour of the problem population and the latter will have to be persuaded of the project's suitability for the same population, since they will be controllers of its intake. So a steering group will be formed, visits arranged, and tea parties and charitable events will take place. If the project does indeed meet a need the police will wish to be associated with it, and doubtless in doing so will show their human face to the project staff and prove not to be so bad after all. Friendships will be formed, informal referrals taken directly from concerned policemen, talks given about the dangers of drug abuse, and before long the system as a whole will have adjusted to incorporate the new project and the agencies will find resources both to support it and to influence its progress. *Thirdly*, out of this success will emerge a subtle but definite shift in power in the direction of the new arrangement. There will be a sellers' market, with more offenders referred to the programme than can be dealt with. So new criteria for acceptability will be drawn up, and once those applicants deemed unsuitable have been rejected they too will be found to have unmet needs: further meetings, funding applications, and consultations will then take place. Success has met a need, but in doing so has, in a process which is, literally, endless, stimulated demand. But the prison will be largely unaffected: serious offenders will continue to be committed there, numerous past users of the new correctional project who have ungratefully failed to lead conformist lives on the basis of their contact with it will be punished for their recalcitrance in the face of such an excellent opportunity. In the world of corrections, the unsuccessful scheme may have unpredictable consequences, but the successful scheme really does stimulate the most frenetic activity.

A concluding note

Our journey is done, and we have kept our promise of telling a long story in a fairly short book. For some readers our analysis will be despiriting in its focus on the seeming powerlessness of individuals to control the system of which they are a part, to avoid the unintended consequences of their own best efforts; but for others we hope it will be liberating, the start of a process of clarifying just what influence can be exerted, what changes introduced, and how the unexpected, the chance knock-on effects of those modifications, can best be dealt with.

Our analysis is, of course, incomplete, and is best seen as having cleared away some of the undergrowth in order that more work may be done. We have analysed the spread of power and its subversion, we have shown how things go wrong, and emphasized the extent to which the 'free' actions of those within the systems are constrained by both history and function, as well as by the impetus generated from within the systems themselves. But we have offered no ethnographic data, no appreciative account of the work of the experts, no comparative study of juvenile justice – between England/Wales and Scotland, for example, or between Maine and California; nor have we engaged in an *evaluative* study of power and control: the moral question of the right and wrong uses of these in juvenile justice must be the subject of another book.

We have, however, argued that those welfare workers who perceive themselves as operating somehow 'outside' the system of juvenile justice misunderstand both the system itself and their own role in it. They are not on the fringe of some homogeneously punitive system, trying to influence it for good or, if that fails, to sabotage it. Rather they are firmly within the system, their activities and influence crucial for its development: as we have repeatedly remarked, the action which subverts also sustains. Hence for the experts to seek *more* power and influence as a means of providing more care is to base an action on an analytic error, and though this book is not one which includes clear policy proposals it implicitly puts back on the agenda the merits in some circumstances of doing less, of being more marginal.

So to create community corrections is both to expand power directly and to set in motion a process whereby power will continue to be further expanded in quite unintended ways; likewise, to make of the social enquiry report a quasi-sentencing document is to take on board the controlling functions of the sentencers and so to be subjected to the charge of being unrealistic when the attempt is made to avoid these functions. Something very curious is going on: the more the experts seek to decarcerate individuals by strategic recommendations, the more the national custody figures increase; the more central the experts have become in juvenile justice, the more this escalation has occurred. Our analysis suggests that for the experts to console themselves with the thought that had they not been there things might have been even worse is probably unjustified. The experts might usefully reflect that their interventions have unintended as well as intended consequences, negative as well as positive outcomes, and that for an intervention to be justified they should consider carefully which of those kinds of outcome is likely to predominate. Perhaps if courts were to make *less* use of social enquiry reports, if six-month supervision orders (instead of two-year orders) were to become the norm, the world would not entirely cave in. Perhaps if the experts did not incline quite so much as they now do to assuming that they can make a contribution to any social problem – unemployment, poverty, glue-sniffing – by setting up a group or a day centre for the populations concerned the incidences of those unfortunate eventualities would be no greater, the experience of them no more distressing: after all, most people are really quite good at finding or creating their own resources. But where expansionary activities *are* undertaken the experts could certainly usefully ensure that they are carefully planned, monitored, and independently evaluated; the analysis which we can offer in this book has been badly hamstrung by the absence, in all too many situations, of just such an evaluation; it would be useful to know at what activities the experts are actually and unequivocally successful.

So we do not end with a rallying call for destructuring, for radical non-intervention, and our suggestions are deliberately modest in the extreme. To call for radical change would be not only undesirable but would also fly in the face of our argument that such change simply cannot happen; and to those critics who accuse us of over-determinism we reply that history is rather on our side, that while modest destructurings can occur – and middle- to low-level shifts in power and technique clearly happen daily – the consequence of some magical destructuring of the State's controlling apparatus would merely be the creation of a new vacuum to be filled in turn by another, equally if not more capricious, form of power.

Our intention in this book has been no more than to alert the reader to certain dangers, paradoxes, and arrogances which repeatedly surface in the study of juvenile justice and which, if nothing else, certainly ensure that the system seldom fails to surprise us. Crime and human unpleasantness are very likely as incurable as they are ubiquitous; doubtless they flourish when they go unchecked, but the price of certain apprehension, even if such were possible, would be one which few of us would wish to pay. There are no simple solutions to these matters; sometimes indeed there are no solutions at all, though such a consideration only infrequently dissuades us from seeking one with ever increasing intensity.

So much more thinking needs to be done that this last page is as much a beginning as an ending. But end we must, and we do so just as we started, with *The Grim Smile of The Five Towns*, and its timely reminder that if it is human wickedness which we seek to control, the scope for our attempts to do so is rather greater than the likelihood of our ultimate success:

> 'Supposing that by just taking thought, by just wishing it, an Englishman could kill a mandarin in China and make himself rich for life, without anybody knowing anything about it! How many mandarins do you suppose there would be left in China at the end of a week!' (Arnold Bennett 1907: 245)

In truth, precious few, and none the more, perhaps, for all the best efforts which the powers that be might summon up to protect the interests, and ensure the survival, of such a desperately endangered species.

Appendix A: The Criminal Justice Act, 1982

This Act is periodically referred to as representing a change in the powers of juvenile courts since the empirical research here reported was completed. This appendix specifies *very briefly* the nature of the changes, but for fuller details the reader is obviously referred to the Act itself.

Custody and detention of young persons aged under 21

The semi-determinate sentence of Borstal training was abolished and replaced by the determinate sentence of youth custody for young people aged 15 to 20 for sentences of over four months where the offence was imprisonable if committed by an adult.

The existing detention centre sentence was reduced in length to a minimum of three weeks and a maximum of four months.

Restrictions were placed on the making of custodial sentences. The thrust of the legislation was simultaneously to increase the *rights* of young persons and the *powers* of the courts in relation to them.

Supervision orders

In addition to the existing arrangement whereby a supervisee could be ordered to undertake intermediate treatment *if so directed by the supervisor*, courts were now empowered to order directly that supervised activities should be undertaken. Other possible conditions were the imposition (with consent) of a 'night restriction order' and precise details of reporting expectations. (For details of the court's powers here, see sections 20–21.)

Care orders

Courts were empowered to make a charge and control order in respect of a child in care for an offence who committed a further imprisonable offence. This empowered the court to order the child's removal from home for up to six months.

The 'care or control' test of the Children and Young Persons Act,

1969, section 1(2)(f) was extended to care orders made under section 7(7) of that Act. This had the effect of removing the serious anomaly which is described in Chapter 1.

Strict limitations were placed on the holding of children in care in secure accommodation.

Sanctions against parents and guardians

Fines ordered against juveniles would normally be levied on the parent or guardian.

Community service orders

Such orders could now be made in respect of 16-year-olds.

Appendix B: welfare work and the supervision order: a note on research methodology

1 The study examined all supervision orders made in 1978 for the first time on male and female offenders aged 14 to 16 in six counties in England and Wales (n = 971 boys; n = 241 girls). The original intention of the study was to examine the cases of boys; it was subsequently decided also to include girls: hence the girls are sometimes referred to as a subsample.
2 The areas were controlled for high delinquency and authorities affected by the social work strikes of 1978 were omitted from the study.
3 One social services department declined to co-operate with the research; we were able, however, to determine from court records that this agency held only nineteen cases, so it could safely be omitted.
4 The research sought to *explain* vast discrepancies among courts in the making of supervision orders, and to *describe* the pattern of contact between supervisor and supervisee. The first of these aims involved an analysis of present and previous criminal record of the supervisee, and a content analysis of the social enquiry report and school report. No significant differences emerged among the six areas, of which two made a high, two a medium, and two a low usage of supervision. The second aim involved detailed study of the supervisory records of all these 1,212 offenders, including patterns of contact, place of contact, use of intermediate treatment, and so on. These details were coded on to a lengthy schedule.
5 The schedule was piloted through twelve trial versions where ambiguities were removed and inter-coder reliability among the three researchers ratified. Coding procedures for allocating the raw data to categories were thereby established, which meant that instructions for coding emerged from the exigencies of having to summarize the rich content of the records.
6 In piloting the schedule we aimed for complete unanimity among the researchers while coding a 'bank' of six case files. 'Random' discrepancies in coding – that is, departures not attributable to any one coder – were admitted only so long as this occurred no more than three out of the eighteen occasions the item was piloted.

7 Offences were categorized 'trivial', 'medium', and 'high' as follows:

Trivial
i Property offence up to £10 value in total
ii Common assault
iii Minor public order offence (causing an affray, for example)

Medium
i Property offence (including criminal damage) (£10–£100)
ii Assault occasioning actual bodily harm
iii Indecent assault
iv TDA/Allow to be carried

High
i Property offence over £100
ii Grevious bodily harm/malicious wounding (section 18/20)
iii Rape or serious act of indecency
iv Robbery (even where sum involved is trivial)
v 'Obvious' serious offences – conspiracy, unlawful killing, and so on

If more than one offence
i Up to five trivial	Trivial
ii Six trivial and over	Medium
iii Up to three medium	Medium
iv Four medium and over	High
v Up to five (trivial and medium) (except where four medium and one trivial	Medium
vi Over five (trivial and medium)	High
vii One high plus any other	High

8 We were unable, for administrative reasons, to include police cautioning data in our study. Variations in practice here are considerable, and this unavoidable absence may reduce the reliability of certain parts of our data and hence the conclusions drawn from it. Overall, however, this is unlikely to prove substantial.

9 Fieldwork for the project was undertaken between 1980 and 1982 (the last of the three-year orders having expired in December 1981). Initial details of supervisees were obtained from all court registers in the six counties. (One court clerk refused to participate but it is almost certain that negligible numbers of orders had been made at that court; certain of them were collected via the probation

and social services offices.) A researcher then visited all area offices in the six counties and undertook the data collection. The large majority of fieldwork was undertaken by a single research assistant, Gillian Bevis, with modest help from the two project directors who have jointly authored this book.

Bibliography

Acts of Parliament

Justices of the Peace Act, 1361
Vagrancy Act, 1597
Acte for the Releife of the Poore, 1598
Larceny Act, 1847
Youthful Offenders Act, 1854
Industrial Schools Act, 1857
Prisons Act, 1865
Industrial Schools Act, 1866
Summary Jurisdiction Act, 1879
First Offenders Act, 1887
Prison Act, 1898
Reformatory Schools Amendment Act, 1899
Probation of Offenders Act, 1907
Prevention of Crime Act, 1908
Children Act, 1908
Criminal Justice Administration Act, 1914
Criminal Justice Act, 1925
Children and Young Persons Act, 1933
Children Act, 1948
Criminal Justice Act, 1948
Children and Young Persons (Amendment) Act, 1952
Children and Young Persons Act, 1963
Social Work (Scotland) Act, 1968
Children and Young Persons Act, 1969
Local Authority Social Services Act, 1970
Race Relations Act, 1976
Criminal Law Act, 1977
Criminal Justice Act, 1982

Official reports and publications (Command papers)

Report of the Select Committee on Police (1817).
Report from the Departmental Committee on Prisons (1895) C. 7702. (Gladstone Report).

Report of the Departmental Committee on the Treatment of Young Offenders (1927) Cmd 2831.
Report of the Care of Children Committee (1946) Cmd 6922 (Curtis Report).
Report of the Committee on Children and Young Persons (1960) Cmnd 1191 (Ingleby Report).
Report of the Inter-Departmental Committee on the Business of the Criminal Courts (1961) Cmnd 1289 (Streatfeild Report).
The Child, the Family and the Young Offender (1965) Cmnd 2742.
Children in Trouble (1968) Cmnd 3601.
Report of the Committee on Local Authority and Allied Personal Social Services (1968) Cmnd 3703 (Seebohm Report).
Report on the Butterworth Inquiry into the Work and Pay of Probation Officers and Social Workers (1972) Cmnd 5076.
Report on the Work of the Probation and After-Care Department 1972–75 (1976) Cmnd 6590.
Criminal Statistics: England and Wales, 1984 (1985) Cmnd 9621.

Book and article references

Ackland, J.W. (1982) *Girls in Care*. Aldershot: Gower.
Adams, R., Allard, S., Baldwin, J., and Thomas, J. (1981) *A Measure of Diversion?* Leicester: National Youth Bureau.
Adler, M. and Asquith, S. (eds) (1981) *Discretion and Welfare*. London: Heinemann Educational.
Albanese, J.S. (1984) *Justice, Privacy and Crime Control*. Lanham, Md: University Press of America.
Albrecht, G. and Albrecht, M. (1977) A Critical Assessment of Labeling in the Juvenile Justice System. *Justice System Journal* 4.
American Friends Service Committee (1971) *Struggle for Justice*. New York: Hill & Wang.
Anderson, R. (1978) *Representation in the Juvenile Court*. London: Routledge & Kegan Paul.
Ashworth, A. (1983) *Sentencing and Penal Policy*. London: Weidenfeld & Nicolson.
Bailey, R. and Brake, M. (eds) (1975) *Radical Social Work*. London: Edward Arnold.
Baker, R. (1983) Is there a Future for Integrated Practice? Obstacles to its Development in Practice and Education. *Issues in Social Work Education* 3.
Barclay, P. (chairman) (1982) *Social Workers: Their Role and Tasks* (Barclay Report). London: Bedford Square Press.
Barton, W.R. (1959) *Institutional Neurosis*. Bristol: John Wright.

Bateson, G. (1972) *Steps to an Ecology of Mind*. New York: Ballantine.
——— (1979) *Mind and Nature: A Necessary Unity*. London: Wildwood House.
Bean, P. (1976) *Rehabilitation and Deviance*. London: Routledge & Kegan Paul.
Belson, W.A. (1975) *Juvenile Theft: The Causal Factors*. London: Harper & Row.
Bendix, R. (1966) *Max Weber: An Intellectual Portrait*. 2nd ed. London: Methuen.
Bennett, A. (1907) *The Grim Smile of the Five Towns*. London: Chapman & Hall.
——— (1908) *The Human Machine*. London: New Age Press.
Bennett, T. (1979) The Social Distribution of Criminal Labels. *British Journal of Criminology* 19.
Bentham, J. (1791) *Panopticon; or, the Inspection House*. Reprinted in *The Works of Jeremy Bentham* (1962) Vol. 4. New York: Russell & Russell.
Berlins, M. and Wansell, G. (1974) *Caught in the Act*. Harmondsworth: Penguin.
Bibby, P. (1976) Can Colleges Educate and Train Social Workers? *Probation Journal* 23.
Billis, D. (1984) *Welfare Bureaucracies*. London: Heinemann Educational.
Binder, A. (1979) The Juvenile Justice System: Where Pretense and Reality Clash. *American Behavioral Scientist* 22.
Black, D.J. (1976) *The Behaviour of Law*. London: Academic Press.
Blau, P.N. and Scott, W.R. (1963) *Formal Organizations: A Comparative Approach*. London: Routledge & Kegan Paul.
Blom-Cooper, L. (ed.) (1974) *Progress in Penal Reform*. Oxford: Clarendon Press.
——— (chairman) (1985) *A Child in Trust: The Report of the Panel of Inquiry into the Circumstances Surrounding the Death of Jasmine Beckford*. London: London Borough of Brent.
Blos, P. (1962) *On Adolescence: A Psychoanalytic Interpretation*. New York: Free Press.
Bochel, D. (1976) *Probation and After-Care: Its Development in England and Wales*. Edinburgh: Scottish Academic Press.
Boli-Bennett, J. and Meyer, J.W. (1978) The Ideology of Childhood and the State Rules Distinguishing Children in National Constitutions, 1870–1970. *American Sociological Review* 43.
Booth, C. (1889) *Life and Labour of the People in London*. Vol. I. London: Williams & Norgate.
——— (1891) *Life and Labour of the People in London*. Vol. II. London: Williams & Norgate.

Booth, W. (1980) *In Darkest England and the Way Out*. London: Salvation Army.

Boss, P. (1971) *Exploration into Child Care*. London: Routledge & Kegan Paul.

Boswell, G. (1985) *Care, Control and Accountability in the Probation Service*. (Social Work Monographs) Norwich: University of East Anglia.

Bottoms, A.E. (1974) On the Discriminalisation of English Juvenile Courts. In R. Hood (ed.) *Crime, Criminology and Public Policy: Essays in Honour of Sir Leon Radzinowicz*. London: Heinemann.

────── (1980) *The Suspended Sentence after Ten Years*. Leeds: University of Leeds Centre for Social Work and Applied Studies.

────── (1983) Neglected Features of Contemporary Penal Systems. In D. Garland and P. Young (eds) *The Power to Punish*. London: Heinemann Educational.

Bottoms, A.E. and McWilliams, W. (1979). A Non-Treatment Paradigm for Probation Practice. *British Journal of Social Work* 9.

Bowlby, J. (1944) Forty-Four Juvenile Thieves: Their Character and Home Life. *International Journal of Psychoanalysis* 25.

────── (1951) *Maternal Care and Mental Health*. (Geneva: World Health Organisation) London: HMSO.

Box, S. and Hale, C. (1983) Liberation and Female Criminality in England and Wales Revisited. *British Journal of Criminology* 23.

Box, S. and Hale, C. (1984) Liberation/Emancipation, Economic Marginalization, or Less Chivalry. *Criminology* 22.

Brager, G. and Holloway, S. (1978) *Changing Human Service Organizations: Politics and Practise*. New York: Free Press.

Brewer, C. and Lait, J. (1980) *Can Social Work Survive?* London: Temple Smith.

British Association of Social Workers (1978) *Children and Young Persons Act 1969: Some Implications for Practice*. Birmingham: British Association of Social Workers.

Brockway, A.F. (1928) *A New Way with Crime*. London: Williams & Norgate.

Bruce, M. (1961) *The Coming of the Welfare State*. London: B.T. Batsford.

Brundage, A. (1978) *The Making of the New Poor Law: The Politics of Inquiry, Enactment and Implementation, 1832–39*. London: Hutchinson.

Brunel Institute of Organization and Social Studies (1974) *Social Services Departments*. London: Heinemann Educational.

Burney, E. (1979) *J.P., Magistrate, Court and Community*. London: Hutchinson.

────── (1985) *Sentencing Young People: What Went Wrong with the Criminal Justice Act 1982*. Aldershot: Gower.

Bynum, T.S. and Greene, J.R. (1984) How Wide the Net? Probing the Boundaries of the Juvenile Court. In S.H. Decker (ed.) *Juvenile Justice Policy: Analyzing Trends and Outcomes.* Beverly Hills, Calif: Sage.

Camp, J. (1974) *Holloway Prison: The Place and the People.* Newton Abbott: David & Charles.

Campbell, A. (1981) *Girl Delinquents.* Oxford: Blackwell.

Capra, F. (1975) *The Tao of Physics.* London: Wildwood House.

—— (1982) *The Turning Point: Science, Society and the Rising Culture.* London: Wildwood House.

Carlebach, J. (1970) *Caring for Children in Trouble.* London: Routledge & Kegan Paul.

Carlen, P. (1983) *Women's Imprisonment: A Study in Social Control.* London: Routledge & Kegan Paul.

Carlen, P. and Powell, M. (1979) Professionals in the Magistrates' Courts: The Courtroom Lore of Probation Officers and Social Workers. In H. Parker (ed.) *Social Work and the Courts.* London: Edward Arnold.

Carpenter, M. (1851) *Reformatory Schools for the Children of the Perishing and Dangerous Classes, and for Juvenile Offenders.* London: C. Gilpin.

Casburn, M. (1979) *Girls will be Girls.* London: Women's Research and Resources Centre.

Cawson, P. and Martell, M. (1979) *Children Referred to Closed Units.* DHSS Statistics and Research Division: Research Report no. 5. London: HMSO.

Central Statistical Office (1980) *Social Trends 1980.* London: HMSO.

Chute, C.L. and Bell, M. (1956) *Crime, Courts and Probation.* New York: Macmillan.

Clarke Hall, W. (1926) *Children's Courts.* London: C. Gilpin.

Clear, T.R. and O'Leary, C. (1983) *Controlling the Offender in the Community: Reforming the Community-Supervision Function.* Lexington, Mass: Lexington Books.

Cohen, S. (1972) *Folk Devils and Moral Panics.* London: MacGibbon & Key.

—— (1979) How Can We Balance Justice, Guilt and Tolerance? *New Society* March.

—— (1985) *Visions of Social Control.* Cambridge: Polity Press.

Cohn, Y. (1970) Criteria for the Probation Officer's Recommendation to the Juvenile Court Judge. In P. Garabedian and D. Gibbons (eds) *Becoming Delinquent.* Chicago, Ill: Aldine.

Collins, P. (1962) *Dickens and Crime.* Cambridge Studies in Criminology, Vol. XVII. London: Macmillan.

Conrad, J. (1984) The Redefinition of Probation: Drastic Proposals to Solve an Urgent Problem. In P. McAnany, D. Thomson, and D. Fogel (eds) *Probation and Justice*. Cambridge, Mass: Oelgelschlager, Gunn & Hain.

Compton, B. and Galaway, B. (eds) (1975) *Social Work Processes*. Homewood, Ill: Dorsey Press.

Cooks, R.A.F. (1958) *Keep them Out of Prison*. London: Jarrolds.

Cordon, J. (1980) Contrasts in Social Work Practice. *British Journal of Social Work* 10.

Cullen, F.T. and Gilbert, K.E. *Reaffirming Rehabilitation*. Cincinatti, Ohio: Anderson.

Davies, M. (1969) *Probationers in their Social Environment*. Home Office Research Study no. 2. London: HMSO.

——— (1985) *The Essential Social Worker*. 2nd edn. Aldershot: Gower.

Davis, K.C. (1971) *Discretionary Justice: A Preliminary Inquiry*. Urbana, Ill: University of Illinois Press.

Day, S. (1858) *Juvenile Crime, its Causes, Character and Cure*. London: J.F. Hope.

Decker, S.H. (ed.) (1984) *Juvenile Justice Policy: Analyzing Trends and Outcomes*. Beverly Hills, Calif: Sage.

Dell, S. (1971) *Silent in Court: The Legal Representation of Women who Went to Prison*. London: Bell.

Department of Health and Social Security (1972) *Intermediate Treatment: A Guide for the Regional Planning of New Forms of Treatment for Children in Trouble*. London: HMSO.

——— (1978) *Social Service Teams: The Practitioner's View*. London: HMSO.

——— (1981) *Offending by Young People: A Survey of Trends*. London: HMSO.

Dingwall, R., Eekelaar, J., and Murray, T. (1983) *The Protection of Children: State Intervention and Family Life*. Oxford: Blackwell.

Ditchfield, J.A. (1976) *Police Cautioning in England and Wales*. Home Office Research Study no. 37. London: HMSO.

Dobash, R.P. (1983) Labour and Discipline in Scottish and English Prisons: Moral Correction, Punishment and Useful Toil. *Sociology* 17.

Dobash, R.P., Dobash, R.E., and Gutteridge, S. (1986) *The Imprisonment of Women*. Oxford: Blackwell.

Doleschal, E. (1982) The Dangers of Criminal Justice Reform. *Criminal Justice Abstracts* 14.

Donnelly, M. (1983) *Managing the Mind: A Study of Medical Psychology in Early Nineteenth Century Britain*. London: Tavistock.

Donzelot, J. (1980) *The Policing of Families: Welfare Versus the State*. London: Hutchinson.

—— (1984) *L'Invention du Social*. Paris: Fayard.
Downes, D. and Rock, P. (eds) (1979) *Deviant Interpretations*. Oxford: Robertson.
Downie, R.S. and Telfer, E. (1980) *Caring and Curing: A Philosophy of Medicine and Social Work*. London: Methuen.
Dreyfus, H.L. and Rabinow, P. (1982) *Michel Foucault: Beyond Structuralism and Hermeneutics*. Chicago, Ill: University of Chicago Press.
Dunlop, A.B. and McCabe, S. (1965) *Young Men in Detention Centres*. London: Routledge & Kegan Paul.
Eekelaar, J., Dingwall, R., and Murray, T. (1982) Victims or Threats? Children in Care Proceedings. *Journal of Social Welfare Law* March.
Ehrenreich, B. and English, D. (1979) *For Her Own Good: 150 Years of the Experts' Advice to Women*. London: Pluto Press.
Eliot, T.S. (1951) Tradition and the Original Talent. In *Selected Essays*. 3rd edn. London: Faber & Faber.
Elkin, W. (1938) *English Juvenile Courts*. London: Kegan Paul, Trench, Tubner.
—— (1957) *The English Penal System*. Harmondsworth: Penguin.
Esbensen, F.-A. (1984) Net Widening? Yes and No: Diversion Impact Assessed through a Systems Processing Rates Analysis. In S.H. Decker (ed.) *Juvenile Justice Policy: Analyzing Trends and Outcomes*. Beverly Hills, Calif: Sage.
Farrar, F.W. (1858) *Eric, or Little by Little*. London: Adam & Charles Black.
Farrington, D. and Morris, A. (1983) Sex, Sentencing and Reconviction. *British Journal of Criminology* 23.
Festinger, L. (1957) *A Theory of Cognitive Dissonance*. Evanston, Ill: Row, Peterson.
Fielding, N. (1984) *Probation Practice*. Aldershot: Gower.
Fitzgerald, M. (1972) *Prisoners in Revolt*. Harmondsworth: Penguin.
Fogel, D. (1984) The Emergence of Probation as a Profession in the Service of Public Safety: The Next Ten Years. In P. McAnany, D. Thomson, and D. Fogel (eds) *Probation and Justice*. Cambridge, Mass: Oelgelschlager, Gunn & Hain.
Foucault, M. (1967) *Madness and Civilization*. London: Tavistock.
—— (1977) *Discipline and Punish*. Harmondsworth: Allen Lane.
—— (1979) *The History of Sexuality, Vol. I: An Introduction*. London: Allen Lane.
Friedlander, K. (1947) *The Psychoanalytical Approach to Juvenile Delinquency*. London: Kegan Paul, Trench, Tubner.
Garabedian, P. and Gibbons, D. (eds) (1970) *Becoming Delinquent*.

Chicago, Ill: Aldine.

Garland, D. (1985) *Punishment and Welfare*. Aldershot: Gower.

Garland, D. and Young, P. (eds) (1983) *The Power to Punish*. London: Heinemann Educational.

Garofalo, R. (1914) *Criminology*. Boston, Mass: Little, Brown.

Giller, H. and Morris, A. (1981) *Care and Discretion: Social Workers' Decisions with Delinquents*. London: Burnett Books.

Glastonbury, B. (1982) *Social Work in Conflict: The Practitioner and the Bureaucrat*. Birmingham: British Association of Social Workers.

Glover, E. (1949) *Probation and Re-Education*. London: Routledge & Kegan Paul.

Goffman, E. (1961) *Asylums: Essays on the Situation of Mental Patients and Other Inmates*. New York: Anchor.

Greenberg, D.F. and Humphries, D. (1980) The Cooptation of Fixed Sentencing Reform. *Crime and Delinquency* 26.

Griffith, J.A.G. (1985) *The Politics of the Judiciary*. 3rd edn. London: Fontana.

Griffiths, W. (1982) Supervision in the Community. *Justice of the Peace* August.

Grunhut, M. (1956) *Juvenile Offenders Before the Courts*. Oxford: Oxford University Press.

Hackler, J.C. (1984) Implications of Variability in Juvenile Justice. In M. Klein (ed.) *Western Systems of Juvenile Justice*. Beverly Hills, Calif: Sage.

Hadley, R. and Hatch, S. (1981) *Social Welfare and the Failure of the State: Centralised Social Services and Participatory Alternatives*. London: Allen & Unwin.

Hall, A. (1974) *The Point of Entry: A Study of Client Reception in the Social Services*. London: Allen & Unwin.

Hall, P. (1976) *Reforming the Welfare*. London: Heinemann.

Halmos, P. (1965) *The Faith of the Counsellors*. London: Constable.

Handler, J. (1973) *The Coercive Social Worker*. Chicago, Ill: Rand McNally.

Hardiker, P. (1977) Social Work Ideologies in the Probation Service. *British Journal of Social Work* 7.

Hardiker, P. and Barker, M. (eds) (1981) *Theories of Practice in Social Work*. London: Academic Press.

Hardiker, P. and Webb, D. (1979) Explaining Deviant Behaviour: The Social Context of 'Action' and 'Infraction' Accounts in the Probation Service. *Sociology* 13.

Harding, G. (1953) *Along My Line*. London: Putnam.

Harris, R. (1977) The Probation Officer as Social Worker. *British Journal of Social Work* 7.

―――― (1980) A Changing Service: The Case for Separating 'Care' and 'Control' in Probation Practice. *British Journal of Social Work* 10.

―――― (1982) Institutionalized Ambivalence: Social Work and the Children and Young Persons Act, 1969. *British Journal of Social Work* 12.

―――― (1985) Towards Just Welfare: A Consideration of a Current Controversy in the Theory of Juvenile Justice. *British Journal of Criminology* 25.

Harris, R. and Webb, D. (1983) Social Work and the Supervision Order. *Research Bulletin* (Home Office Research and Planning Unit) 16.

Hasenfeld, Y. and English, R. (eds) (1974) *Human Service Organizations*. Ann Arbor, Mich: University of Michigan Press.

Haxby, D. (1978) *Probation – A Changing Service*. London: Constable.

Healy, W. and Bronner, A.F. (1936) *New Light on Delinquency and its Treatment*. New Haven, Conn: Yale University Press.

Heidensohn, F. (1985) *Women and Crime*. London: Macmillan.

Henriques, B.L.Q. (1950) *The Indiscretions of a Magistrate*. London: Harrap.

Hepburn, J.R. (1977) The Impact of Police Intervention upon Juvenile Delinquents. *Criminology* 15, 2, August.

Hibbert, C. (1963) *The Roots of Evil*. London: Weidenfeld & Nicolson.

Hiller, A. and Hancock, L. (1981) The Processing of Juveniles in Victoria. In S. Mukherjee and J. Scott (eds) *Women and Crime*. Sydney: Allen & Unwin.

Home Office (1968) *Detention of Girls in a Detention Centre: Report of the Advisory Council on the Penal System*. London: HMSO.

―――― (1970) *Detention Centres: Report of the Advisory Council on the Penal System*. London: HMSO.

―――― (1974) *Young Adult Offenders: Report of the Advisory Council on the Penal System*. London: HMSO.

―――― (1984) *Probation Service in England and Wales: Statement of National Objectives and Priorities*. Mimeograph.

―――― (1985) *Prison Statistics: England and Wales, 1984*. London: HMSO.

Hood, R. (ed.) (1974) *Crime, Criminology and Public Policy: Essays in Honour of Sir Leon Radzinowicz*. London: Heinemann.

House of Commons Expenditure Committee (1975) *Eleventh Report from the Expenditure Committee: The Children and Young Persons Act, 1969*. London: HMSO.

Howe, D. (1980) Inflated States and Empty Theories in Social Work. *British Journal of Social Work* 10.

―――― (1986) *Social Workers and their Practice in Welfare Bureaucracies*.

Aldershot: Gower.
Hoyles, J.A. (1952) *The Treatment of the Young Delinquent*. London: Epworth Press.
Hudson, A. (1983) The Welfare State and Adolescent Femininity. *Youth and Policy* 2.
Hutter, B. and Williams, G. (1981) *Controlling Women: The Normal and the Deviant*. London: Croom Helm.
Ignatieff, M. (1978) *A Just Measure of Pain*. London: Macmillan.
—— (1981) State, Civil Society, and Total Institutions: A Critique of Recent Social Histories of Punishment. In M. Tonry and N. Morris (eds) *Crime and Justice*. Vol. 3. Chicago, Ill: University of Chicago Press.
Jarvis, F.V. (1974) *Probation Officers' Manual*. 2nd edn. London: Butterworths.
Jillings, J. (chairman) (1985) *Children Still in Trouble: The Report of a Study Group on Juvenile Justice*. Taunton: Association of Directors of Social Services.
Johnson, S. (1779) Abraham Cowley. In *Lives of the English Poets*. Reprinted in *The Works of Samuel Johnson, LL.D.* Vol IX. 1816. Printed for Nichols & Sons and others.
Jones, A.E. (1945) *Juvenile Delinquency and the Law*. Harmondsworth: Penguin.
Jones, C. (1983) *State Social Work and the Working Class*. London: Macmillan.
Jones, H. (1962) *Crime and the Penal System*. 2nd edn. London: University Tutorial Press.
—— (1981) A Case for Correction. *British Journal of Social Work* 11.
Jones, K. and Fowles, A.J. (1984) *Ideas on Institutions*. London: Routledge & Kegan Paul.
Jordan, B. (1974) *Poor Parents: Social Policy and the 'Cycle of Deprivation'*. London: Routledge & Kegan Paul.
Jordan, B. and Parton, N. (eds) (1983) *The Political Dimensions of Social Work*. Oxford: Blackwell.
Kakabadse, A. (1982) *Culture of the Social Services*. Aldershot: Gower.
Keve, P.W. (1960) *The Probation Officer Investigates*. Minneapolis, Minn: University of Minnesota Press.
King, J.F.S. (ed.) (1979) *Pressures and Change in the Probation Service*. Cambridge: University of Cambridge Institute of Criminology.
Klein, M. (1979) Deinstitutionalization and Diversion of Juvenile Offenders: A Litany of Impediments. In N. Morris and M. Tonry (eds) *Crime and Justice: An Annual Review of Research*. Vol. I. Chicago, Ill: University of Chicago Press.
—— (ed.) (1984) *Western Systems of Juvenile Justice*. Beverly Hills,

Calif: Sage.

Knell, B.E.F. (1965) Capital Punishment: Its Administration in Relation to Juvenile Offenders in the Nineteenth Century and its Possible Administration in the Eighteenth. *British Journal of Delinquency* 5.

Kogan, M. and Terry, J. (1971) *The Organisation of a Social Services Department: A Blueprint.* London: Bookstall Publications.

Kuhn, A. and Wolpe, A. (eds) (1978) *Feminism and Materialism: Women and Modes of Production.* London: Routledge & Kegan Paul.

Labour Party (1964) *Crime – A Challenge to Us All.* (Longford Report) London: Labour Party.

Landau, S. (1981) Juveniles and the Police: Who is Charged Immediately and Who is Referred to the Juvenile Bureau? *British Journal of Criminology* 21.

Landau, S. and Nathan, G. (1983) Rethinking Juvenile Justice. *Crime and Delinquency* 29.

Lawson, C.W. and Lockhart, D. (1985) The Sex Distribution of Children in Care. *Journal of Adolescence* 8.

Lea, J. and Young, J. (1984) *What is to be Done about Law and Order?* Harmondsworth: Penguin.

Lees, R. (1971) Social Work, 1925–1950: The Case for a Reappraisal. *British Journal of Social Work* 1.

Leighton, N., Stalley, R., and Watson, D. (1982) *Rights and Responsibilities. Discussion of Moral Dimensions in Social Work.* London: Heinemann Educational.

Le Mesurier, L. (1931) *Boys in Trouble.* London: John Murray.

——— (1935) *A Handbook of Probation and Social Work of the Courts.* London: National Association of Probation Officers.

Lombroso, C. and Ferrero, W. (1895) *The Female Offender.* London: Fisher Unwin.

Longford, Lord (1958) *Causes of Crime.* London: Weidenfeld & Nicolson.

——— (1961) *The Idea of Punishment.* London: Geoffrey Chapman.

Los, M. (1982) The Concept of Justice and Welfare Rights. *Journal of Social Welfare Law* January.

Lytton, C. (1914) *Prisons and Prisoners: Some Personal Experiences.* London: Heinemann.

McAnany, P., Thomson, D., and Fogel, D. (eds) (1984) *Probation and Justice.* Cambridge, Mass: Oelgelschlager, Gunn & Hain.

McCabe, S. and Treitel, P. (1983) *Juvenile Justice in the United Kingdom: Comparisons and Suggestions for Change.* London: New Approaches to Juvenile Crime.

McDonald, L. (1969) *Social Class and Delinquency.* London: Faber &

Faber.
McIntosh, M. (1978) The State and the Oppression of Women. In A. Kuhn and A.M. Wolpe (eds) *Feminism and Materialism*. London: Routledge & Kegan Paul.
McWilliams, W. (1985) The Mission Transformed: Professionalisation of Probation between the Wars. *Howard Journal* 24, 4, November.
Marris, P. (1974) *Loss and Change*. London: Routledge & Kegan Paul.
Martin, F.M., Fox, S., and Murray, K. (1981) *Children Out of Court*. Edinburgh: Scottish Academic Press.
Martinson, R. (1974) What Works? Questions and Answers about Prison Reform. *The Public Interest* Spring.
Matza, D. (1964) *Delinquency and Drift*. New York: Wiley.
May, D. (1977) Delinquent Girls before the Courts. *Medicine, Science and the Law* 17.
Mayer, J.E. and Timms, N. (1970) *The Client Speaks: Working Class Impressions of Casework*. London: Routledge & Kegan Paul.
Mayhew, H. (1861) *London Life and the London People*. Vols I–IV. London: Griffin, Bohn.
Melossi, D. and Pavarini, M. (1981) *The Prison and the Factory*. London: Macmillan.
Meyer, H.J., Borgatta, E.F., and Jones, W.C. (1965) *Girls at Vocational High: An Experiment in Social Work Intervention*. New York: Russell Sage Foundation.
Mill, J.S. (1861) *Utilitarianism*. Reprinted (1912) London: J.M. Dent.
Millard, D. (1979) Broader Approaches to Probation Practice. In J.F.S. King (ed.) *Pressures and Change in the Probation Service*. Cambridge: University of Cambridge Institute of Criminology.
Miller, E.J. and Rice, A.K. (1967) *Systems of Organization: The Control of Task and Sentient Boundaries*. London: Tavistock.
Milton, F. (1959) *In Some Authority: The English Magistracy*. London: Pall Mall Press.
Milton, J. (1667) *Paradise Lost*. Reprinted in Milton's Poetical Works: with Life, Critical Dissertation, and Explanatory Notes, by the Rev. George Gilfillan (1853). Edinburgh: James Nichol.
Morris, A. and Gelsthorpe, L. (eds) (1981) *Women and Crime*. Cambridge: Cambridge University Institute of Criminology.
Morris, A. and Giller, H. (1977) The Juvenile Court – The Client's Perspective. *Criminal Law Review*: 198–205.
────── (eds) (1983) *Providing Criminal Justice for Children*. London: Edward Arnold.
Morris, A. and McIsaac, M. (1978) *Juvenile Justice?* London: Heinemann.

Morris, A., Giller, H., Szwed, E., and Geach, H. (1980) *Justice for Children*. London: Macmillan.

Morris, N. and Tonry, M. (eds) (1979) *Crime and Justice: An Annual Review of Research*. Chicago, Ill: University of Chicago Press.

Morrison, A.C.L. and Hughes, E. (1952) *The Criminal Justice Act, 1948*. 2nd edn. London: Butterworth.

Mott, J. (1985) *Adult Prisons and Prisoners in England and Wales: A Review of the Findings of Social Research*. Home Office Research Study no. 84. London: HMSO.

Mount, F. (1982) *The Subversive Family*. London: Jonathan Cape.

Mukherjee, S. and Scott, J. (eds) (1981) *Women and Crime*. Sydney: Allen & Unwin.

Mullins, C. (1957) *The Sentence on the Guilty*. Chichester: Justice of the Peace Ltd.

Munday, B. (1972) What is Happening to Social Work Students? *Social Work Today* 3.

Nagel, I. (1981) Sex Differences in the Processing of Criminal Defendants. In A. Morris and L. Gelsthorpe (eds) *Women and Crime*. Cambridge: University of Cambridge Institute of Criminology.

Nevill, W.B. ('W.B.N.') (1903) *Penal Servitude*. London: Heinemann.

Nietzsche, F. (1886) *Beyond Good and Evil: Prelude to a Philosophy of the Future*. Trans. H. Zimmern (1909). Edinburgh: Foulis.

O'Connor, D.J. (1972) *Free Will*. London: Macmillan.

Oliver, I. (1978) *The Metropolitan Police Approach to the Prosecution of Juvenile Offenders*. London: Peel Press.

Packman, J. (1981) *The Child's Generation*. 2nd edn. Oxford: Blackwell & Robertson.

Page, L. (1936) *Justice of the Peace*. London: Faber & Faber.

Page, R. (1984) *Stigma*. London: Routledge & Kegan Paul.

Parker, H. (ed.) (1979) *Social Work and the Courts*. London: Edward Arnold.

Parker, H., Casburn, M., and Turnbull, D. (1981) *Receiving Juvenile Justice*. Oxford: Blackwell.

Parry, N. and Parry, J. (1979) Social Work, Professionalism and the State. In N. Parry, M. Rustin, and C. Satyamurti (eds) (1979) *Social Work, Welfare and the State*. London: Edward Arnold.

Parsloe, P. (1978) *Juvenile Justice in Britain and the United States*. London: Routledge & Kegan Paul.

Pearson, G. (1975a) Making Social Workers: Bad Promises and Good Omens. In R. Bailey and M. Brake (eds) *Radical Social Work*. London: Edward Arnold.

—— (1975b) *The Deviant Imagination: Psychiatry, Social Work and Social Change*. London: Macmillan.

────── (1983) *Hooligan: A History of Respectable Fears*. London: Macmillan.
Peters, R.S. (1970) *Ethics and Education*. London: Allen & Unwin.
Petrie, C. (1986) *The Nowhere Girls*. Aldershot: Gower.
Philp, M. (1979) Notes on the Form of Knowledge in Social Work. *Sociological Review* 27.
Pinker, R. (1982) An Alternative View. In P. Barclay (chairman) *Social Workers: Their Role and Tasks* (Barclay Report). London: Bedford Square Press.
Platt, A.M. (1977) *The Child Savers: The Invention of Delinquency*. 2nd edn. Chicago, Ill: University of Chicago Press.
Playfair, G. (1971) *The Punitive Obsession*. London: Victor Gollancz.
Playfair, G. and Sington, D. (1965) *Crime, Punishment and Cure*. London: Secker & Warburg.
Plummer, K. (1979) Misunderstanding Labelling Perspectives. In D. Downes and P. Rock (eds) *Deviant Interpretations*. Oxford: Robertson.
Poster, M. (1978) *Critical Theory of the Family*. New York: Seabury Press.
Powers, E. and Witmer, H. (1951) *An Experiment in the Prevention of Delinquency: The Cambridge–Somerville Youth Study*. New York: Columbia University Press.
Prigogine, I. and Stengers, I. (1985) *Order out of Chaos: Man's New Dialogue with Nature*. London: Fontana.
Radzinowicz, L. and Cambridge Department of Criminal Science. (1958) *The Results of Probation*. London: Macmillan.
Raynor, P. (1985) *Social Work, Justice and Control*. Oxford: Blackwell.
Rees, S. (1978) *Social Work Face to Face*. London: Edward Arnold.
Rhodes, M.L. (1986) *Ethical Dilemmas in Social Work Practice*. London: Routledge & Kegan Paul.
Richardson, H. (1969) *Adolescent Girls in Approved Schools*. London: Routledge & Kegan Paul.
Richmond, M. (1917) *Social Diagnosis*. New York: Russell Sage Foundation.
Roberts, E. (1982) The Impact of Work Organisation. In University of Aberdeen Department of Social Work, *Social Work Departments as Organisations*. Research Highlights no. 4, Aberdeen: University of Aberdeen.
Roberts, G. (1981) *Essential Law for Social Workers*. 2nd edn. London: Oyez Publishing.
Rodgers, B. (1968) *The Battle Against Poverty*. Vol. 1. London: Routledge & Kegan Paul.
Rose, G. (1961) *The Struggle for Penal Reform*. London: Stevens.

Bibliography

—— (1967) *Schools for Young Offenders*. London: Tavistock.
Rothman, D. (1980) *Conscience and Convenience*. Boston: Little, Brown.
Rowntree, B.S. (1901) *Poverty: A Study of Town Life*. London: Macmillan.
Rousseau, J.-J. (1762) *The Social Contract*. In *Social Contract: Essays by Locke, Hume and Rousseau* (1947). London: Oxford University Press.
Rusche, G. and Kirchheimer, O. (1939) *Punishment and Social Structure*. New York: Columbia University Press.
Rutherford, A. (1986) *Growing Out of Crime*. Harmondsworth: Penguin.
Rutter, M. and Giller, H. (1983) *Juvenile Delinquency: Trends and Perspectives*. Harmondsworth: Penguin.
Sachs, A. (1978) The Myth of Male Protectiveness and the Subordination of Women. In C. Smart and B. Smart (eds) *Women, Sexuality and Social Control*. London: Routledge & Kegan Paul.
Salgado, G. (1977) *The Elizabethan Underworld*. London: J.M. Dent.
Satyamurti, C. (1981) *Occupational Survival*. Oxford: Blackwell.
Schofield, M. (1965) *The Sexual Behaviour of Young People*. London: Longman.
Schur, E. (1973) *Radical Non-Intervention: Rethinking the Delinquency Problem*. Englewood Cliffs, NJ: Prentice-Hall.
Scull, A. (1977) *Decarceration: Community Treatment and the Deviant – A Radical View*. Englewood Cliffs, NJ: Prentice-Hall.
—— (1983) Community Corrections: Panacea, Progress or Pretence? In D. Garland and P. Young (eds) *The Power to Punish*. London: Heinemann Educational.
Sellin, J.T. (1976) *Slavery and the Penal System*. New York: Elsevier.
Shacklady Smith, L. (1978) Sexist Assumptions and Female Delinquency. In C. Smart and B. Smart (eds) *Women, Sexuality and Social Control*. London: Routledge & Kegan Paul.
Shaw, G.B. (1946) *The Crime of Punishment*. New York: Philosophical Library.
Shaw, M. (1974) *Social Work in Prisons: An Experiment in the Use of Extended Contact with Offenders*. Home Office Research Study no. 22. London: HMSO.
Sheldon, B. (1978) Theory and Practice in Social Work: A Re-examination of a Tenuous Relationship. *British Journal of Social Work* 8.
Sheridan, A. (1980) *Michel Foucault*. London: Tavistock.
Smart, B. (1983) *Foucault, Marxism and Critique*. London: Routledge & Kegan Paul.
—— (1985) *Michel Foucault*. Chichester and London: Ellis Horwood & Tavistock.

Smart, C. (1976) *Women, Crime and Criminology: A Feminist Critique*. London: Routledge & Kegan Paul.
Smart, C. and Smart, B. (1978) *Women, Sexuality and Social Control*. London: Routledge & Kegan Paul.
Smith, A.D. (1974) The Woman Offender. In L. Blom-Cooper (ed.) *Progress in Penal Reform*. Oxford: Clarendon Press.
Smith, G. (1978) The Social Work Agency. Unit 5 of *Social Work, Community Work and Society*. Milton Keynes: Open University Press.
────── (1980) *Social Need: Policy, Practice and Research*. London: Routledge & Kegan Paul.
Smith, J.C. and Hogan, B. (1973) *Criminal Law*. 3rd edn. London: Butterworth.
Specht, H. and Vickery, A. (eds) (1977) *Integrating Social Work Methods*. London: Allen & Unwin.
Spierenburg, P. (1984) *The Spectacle of Suffering*. Cambridge: Cambridge University Press.
Stalley, R.F. (1978) Non-judgemental Attitudes. In N. Timms and D. Watson (eds) *Philosophy in Social Work*. London: Routledge & Kegan Paul.
Stedman-Jones, G. (1971) *Outcast London*. Oxford: Clarendon Press.
Stevenson, O. (1981) *Specialisation in Social Service Teams*. London: Allen & Unwin.
Strachey, L. (1918) *Eminent Victorians*. London: Chatto & Windus.
Sudnow, D. (1964) Normal Crimes: Sociological Features of the Penal Code in a Public Defender Office. *Social Problems* 12.
Taylor, I. (1981) *Law and Order: Arguments for Socialism*. London: Macmillan.
Taylor, I., Walton, P., and Young, J. (1973) *The New Criminology*. London: Routledge & Kegan Paul.
Terry, R. (1970) Discrimination in the Handling of Juvenile Offenders by Social Control Agencies. In P. Garabedian and D. Gibbons (eds) *Becoming Delinquent*. Chicago, Ill: Aldine.
Thomas, J.E. (1972) *The English Prison Officer Since 1850*. London: Routledge & Kegan Paul.
Thomson, D. (1984) Prospects for Justice Model Probation. In P. McAnany, D. Thomson, and D. Fogel (eds) *Probation and Justice*. Cambridge, Mass: Oelgelschlager, Gunn & Hain.
Thorpe, D.H., Smith, D., Green, C.J., and Paley, J.H. (1980) *Out of Care: The Community Support of Juvenile Offenders*. London: Allen & Unwin.
Thorpe, J. (1979) *Social Inquiry Reports: A Survey*. Home Office Research Study no. 48. London: HMSO.
Timms, N. (1986) Value Talk in Social Work. *Issues in Social Work*

Education 6.
Timms, N. and Watson, D. (eds) (1978) *Philosophy in Social Work*. London: Routledge & Kegan Paul.
Tobias, J. (1972) *Crime and Industrial Society in the Nineteenth Century*. Harmondsworth: Penguin.
Toffler, A. (1970) *Future Shock*. London: Bodley Head.
────── (1974) *Learning for Tomorrow: The Role of the Future in Education*. New York: Random House.
Tonry, M. and Morris, N. (eds) (1981) *Crime and Justice*. Vol. 3. Chicago, Ill: University of Chicago Press.
Townsend, P. (1979) *Poverty in the United Kingdom*. Harmondsworth: Penguin.
Tulkens, H. (1979) *Some Developments in Penal Policy and Practice in Holland*. London: National Association for the Care and Resettlement of Offenders.
Tuttle, E.O. (1961) *The Crusade Against Capital Punishment in Great Britain*. London: Stevens.
Vass, A.A. (1984) *Sentenced to Labour: Close Encounters with a Prison Substitute*. St Ives: Venus Academica.
Visher, C.A. (1983) Gender, Police Arrest Decisions, and Notions of Chivalry. *Criminology* 21.
Walker, H. and Beaumont, B. (1981) *Probation Work: Critical Theory and Socialist Practice*. Oxford: Blackwell.
Watson, J. (1950) *The Child and the Magistrate*. Revised edn. London: Jonathan Cape.
Watzlawick, P., Weakland, J., and Fisch, R. (1974) *Change: Principles of Problem Formation and Problem Resolution*. New York: Norton.
Webb, D. (1981) Themes and Continuities in Radical and Traditional Social Work. *British Journal of Social Work* 11.
────── (1984) More on Gender and Justice: Girl Offenders on Supervision. *Sociology* 18.
Webb, D. and Harris, R. (1984) Social Workers and Supervision Orders: A Case of Occupational Uncertainty. *British Journal of Social Work* 14, 6.
Webb, S. and Webb, B. (1922) *English Prisons Under Local Government*. London: Frank Cass.
West, D. (1969) *Present Conduct and Future Delinquency*. London: Heinemann Educational.
West, D.J. and Farrington, D.P. (1973) *Who Becomes Delinquent?* London: Heinemann Educational.
Whitney, J. (1947) *Elizabeth Fry*. Guild Books. London: Harrap.
Wilson, T. (1972) Social Work from the Perspective of Fifty Years: A Personal History. *Smith College Studies in Social Work* XLII, 2.

Wootton, B. (1978) *Crime and Penal Policy*. London: Allen & Unwin.
Wright, M. (1982) *Making Good: Prisons, Punishment and Beyond*. London: Burnett Books.
Wright Mills, C. (1970) *The Sociological Imagination*. Harmondsworth: Penguin.
Yelloly, M. (1980) *Social Work Theory and Psychoanalysis*. London: Van Nostrand Reinhold.
Young, J. (1971) *The Drugtakers: The Social Meaning of Drug Use*. London: MacGibbon & Kee.

Name index

Ackland, J.W. 144
Adams, R. 22
Albrecht, G. 23
Anderson, R. 30, 79
Ashworth, A. 30, 168, 169

Baker, R. 124
Bateson, G. 161
Bean, P. 25, 157
Beaumont, B. 85, 109
Belson, W.A. 55, 120
Bennett, A. 1, 39, 178
Bennett, T. 75
Bentham, J. 62-3
Berlins, M. 21, 126
Binder, A. 167
Black, D.J. 154
Bochel, D. 36
Boli-Bennett, J. 55
Boss, P. 19
Boswell, G. 100
Bottoms, A.E. 23, 24, 44, 45, 73-4, 170
Box, S. 131
Brewer, C. 106
Brundage, A. 67
Burney, E. 30, 79, 83, 169
Bynum, T.S. 166

Campbell, A. 131, 134, 138, 141, 142, 152
Capra, F. 161
Carlen, P. 83, 85, 133, 153
Carpenter, M. 11, 13, 14, 70
Casburn, M. 30, 112, 142, 152
Chute, C.L. 35, 36
Clarke Hall, W. 16, 33, 36
Clear, T.R. 165
Cohen, S. 4, 13, 21, 24, 45, 46, 55, 59, 74, 135, 161, 165
Cohn, Y. 142
Conrad, J. 99
Cullen, F.T. 167

Davies, M. 22, 98, 108
Davis, K.C. 30
Day, S. 9, 10, 11, 64
Dell, S. 153
Dingwall, R. 9, 96-7, 112, 148
Ditchfield, J.A. 120
Dobash, R.P. 72, 134, 136-37
Doleschal, E. 166
Donzelot, J. 3, 6, 65, 66-8, 71, 74-7, 93, 101, 153, 157
Downie, R.S. 27
Dreyfus, H.L. 58, 59, 62, 65
Dunlop, A.B. 20

Eekelaar, J. 9, 96-7, 112, 148
Ehrenreich, B. 66
Elkin, W. 18, 20, 131, 136, 139, 142
Esbensen, F. 165

Farrington, D. 55, 117, 152
Fielding, N. 45
Fogel, D. 99
Foucault, M. 4, 14, 18, 58-66, 68-9, 70-4, 80-2, 138, 139, 156, 168

Garland, D. 12, 37, 62, 133, 162
Garofalo, R. 7, 105
Gelsthorpe, L. 132
Giller, H. 110, 112, 117, 153
Greenberg, D.F. 167

Hackler, J.C. 81

203

Halmos, P. 38, 40
Handler, J. 47, 48, 90
Hardiker, P. 41, 90, 95, 96, 114, 149, 157
Harris, R. 6, 34, 42, 44, 52, 98, 99, 105, 121, 149, 168
Haxby, D. 100
Heidensohn, F. 94, 132, 133, 134, 153
Henriques, B.L.Q. 17, 18, 140
Hepburn, J.R. 23
Hiller, A. 134, 135
Home Office 43, 44, 45, 46, 47, 73, 100, 138
Howe, D. 88, 89, 107
Hudson, A. 152, 153
Hutter, B. 132

Ignatieff, M. 10, 62, 70-3, 92

Jarvis, F.V. 42, 96
Jillings, J. 30, 169
Johnson, S. 70, 83
Jones, A.E. 40
Jones, H. 14, 56
Jones, K. 58, 60, 70, 72
Jordan, B. 47, 100

Kakabadse, A. 90, 98
Klein, M. 56, 73
Kogan, M. 89

Labour Party 23, 25
Landau, S. 75, 141, 142
Lawson, C.W. 143
Lea, J. 55
Lees, R. 37
Le Mesurier, L. 36, 37, 40, 41
Longford, Lord 25, 136

McCabe, S. 30, 169
McIntosh, M. 133
McWilliams, W. 38, 44, 45
Martin, F.M. 23
Martinson, R. 22, 56
May, D. 142
Melossi, D. 10, 62

Millard, D. 45
Miller, E.J. 96
Milton, F. 10, 80
Morris, A. 25, 30, 79, 110, 112, 132, 152, 153
Morrison, A.C.L. 20
Mott, J. 136
Mount, F. 71

Nagel, I. 133, 152

O'Connor, D.J. 25
Oliver, I. 120

Packman, J. 20-1, 23, 50
Parker, H. 30, 112, 142
Parsloe, P. 11
Pearson, G. 69, 88, 153, 172
Peters, R.S. 168
Petrie, C. 144
Platt, A.M. 36
Playfair, G. 11, 56
Plummer, K. 23, 132
Prigogine, I. 161

Radzinowicz, L. 142
Raynor, P. 44, 45, 170
Richardson, H.J. 144
Richmond, M. 38
Roberts, E. 96
Roberts, G. 96
Rodgers, B. 38
Rose, G. 16, 60, 144
Rothman, D. 36, 71, 73
Rousseau, J.-J. 61
Rusche, G. 10, 42, 62, 133
Rutherford, A. 72, 75
Rutter, M. 117

Sachs, A. 133
Satyamurti, C. 54, 128
Scull, A. 23, 42, 43, 73, 164, 172
Shacklady-Smith, L. 134
Shaw, M. 56
Sheldon, B. 107
Sheridan, A. 58, 61, 63
Smart, B. 58

Name index

Smart, C. 133, 141, 142, 143
Smiles, S. 91
Smith, A.D. 137
Smith, G. 148
Smith, J.C. 134
Stedman-Jones, G. 14, 39, 91

Taylor, I. 23, 55, 84
Terry, R. 134
Thorpe, D.H. 22, 29, 169
Thorpe, J. 85, 151
Tobias, J. 10, 14, 15

Visher, C.A. 141

Walker, H. 85, 109
Watson, J. 37, 137–138
Webb, D. 6, 30, 34, 37, 41, 52, 98, 105, 109, 114, 121, 149
Weber, M. 57
West, D.J. 55, 117
Wootton, B. 140
Wright, M. 56
Wright Mills, C. 81

Yelloly, M. 38
Young, J. 23, 55, 84, 113

Subject index

approved schools 16–18, 34

British Association of Social Workers (BASW) 53

care orders 33–4
capriciousness, as control 93, 115, 120, 153
case work 22–3; and the probation service 38, 41
Charity Organization Society 38–9; as a carrier of ideology 90–5
charter of welfare organizations 96–8, 101, 153
child care: and criminal justice 9–31 *passim*; and creation of children's departments 19, 50
Children Act, 1908 9, 11, 15
Children Act, 1948 19, 49
Children and Young Persons Act 1933 16, 17, 18
Children and Young Persons Act 1969: implementation of 26–9, 54; sentencing variation and 29; intermediate treatment 27, 53; and supervision orders 34
children's departments 19, 50
class: of offenders 116; and the criminal code 9; and censure of working-class families 75–6
community corrections 44–5, 163, 170–71; *see also* decarceration
community service orders 42, 163
computers and control 173
court reports *see* social enquiry reports

criminal justice 9, 26–27; and prescriptive legislation 69; *see also* juvenile justice
Criminal Justice Act, 1948 19, 49
Criminal Justice Act, 1982 29, 46, 179–80
criminal responsibility (age of) and implementation of 1969 Act 27–8
Curtis Report 19

decarceration 72, 164; and probation thinking 42, 45–7, 102, 171–72; *see also* community corrections
detention centres 20
discretion 5, 30, 153, 163; and the police 141
diversification (of penalty) 161–63

experts; *see* welfare workers

feminism and criminology 131–32, 138, 143

gender divisions: reproduced in welfare organizations 94; and welfare practices 14, 133; in welfare ideologies 134–37, 138–39; in police cautioning 141; in court disposals 142, 151–52; in supervision orders 146–51, 154; related to other discrimination 153–54, 160
girl delinquents: attitudes towards 134–35, 152–53; material circumstances of 144

humanitarianism 164–65

207

ideology *see* welfare workers, organizations; gender divisions
Ingleby Report 21, 50, 143
intermediate treatment 27, 53

juvenile justice: and child care lobby 23; and child welfare 16-18, 50; contradictions in 12-13, 20, 51; and Foucault 70-82 *passim*; and gender 133-34, 135, 138; historical development of, Ch 1 *passim*; and juvenile court 9, 81, 138; and 1960s debate 21-26, 166; and State control 13, 165
justice: and welfare 26-7, 30, 41, 84, 166-70; and gender 152-53; a critique of 166-68
Justices of the Peace: historical origins 80; assumptions held by 83-4; attitudes to girls 139

labelling theory, as a critique of juvenile justice 23, 24, 132-33

magistrates *see* Justices of the Peace
medical model (of crime) 25-6; and justice model 26-7, 136; and the probation service 39-40

'need-push' supervision order 150-51, 160
occupational uncertainty and social workers 52-3, 106-14

organizational resolve 98-102, 170

Panopticon 62-3, 173
prisons 72; history of 60-6
psychoanalysis and explanations of delinquency 21, 24
police cautioning 141
Poor Law 1834 67

power: defined 57-9, 63; and knowledge 4, 57, 93; Foucault's approach to 58-9, 60, 64, 71-2; tendency towards expansion 65-6, 72; operational limitations to 71; *see also* State control
probation officers *see* welfare workers, probation service
probation service: development of 35-43; and quasi-judicial functions 42; and social control 46; and organizational resolve 99-100; and supervision orders 121-28

Race Relations Act, 1976 66-7
reformatory and industrial schools 11-12, 13, 15-17
routine individualization 94, 110-11, 159

Seebohm Report 47, 50-1
sexuality and social control 138, 139-40
the social 3, 66-9, 107
social control *see* power; capriciousness; sexuality; State control
social enquiry reports 42, 119-20, 125-26, 149-50, 151, 177
social services departments 43; development of 47-51, 53-4; and organizational resolve 100-02; and supervision orders 34, 51, 121-28
Social Work (Scotland) Act 23, 51
social workers: complaints about by magistrates 52; *see also* welfare workers; social services departments; occupational uncertainty
State control 66; of children 13-15, 55, 140, 150; of welfare agencies 37, 46, 49; and the disciplinary society 62, 63, 73-4; of families 71

Subject index

supervision order 2, 27, 34; characteristics of boy offender on 116–21; characteristics of girl offender on 145–49; court reports and 119–20, 126–27, 149–50; empirical survey into 115, Appendix B; failures to conform and 126; girls and 145–54; probation and social services carrying out 121–28; as an example of tutelage 111–12, 152–53
suspensive nature of supervision 76–7, 111–12

tutelage 6, 65, 74–6, 82; as supervised freedom 75, 120; and gender 142–43, 152–53

welfare organizations Ch. 4 *passim*; charters of 96–8, 101; organizational resolve 98–102; as open systems 89, 95; as carriers of ideology 90–5; and the supervision order 127
welfare workers: as experts 8, 12–13, 22, 64, 66–7, 69, 151; in modulating state control 77, 95, 163; and the acquisition of judicial functions 82, 83–4, 163, 174; and gender typifications 134–35, 152–53; origins of COS 91–4; limitations on autonomy 97–8; and influence of family problem ideology 124; and variety of ideologies 78, 85, 95, 99, 101–02, 107–09, 114, 148
women offenders 151–52; explanations of 131–32, 134

Younger Report 43–4